PLANNING · ENVIRONMENT · CITIES

Series Editors: Yvonne Rydin and Andrew Thornley

The context in which planning operates has changed dramatically in recent years. Economic processes have become increasingly globalised and new spatial patterns of economic activity have emerged. There have been major changes in political ideology with the rise of the New Right and the collapse of communism. New debates have arisen over the relationship between the market and state intervention. A new environmental agenda following on from the Brundtland Report and the Rio Earth Summit has prioritised the goal of sustainable development and control of pollution, air and water quality.

Cities are today faced with new pressures for economic competitiveness, greater accountability and participation, improved quality of life for citizens and global environmental responsibility. These pressures are often contradictory and create difficult dilemmas for policy-makers, especially in the context of fiscal austerity. New relationships are developing between the levels of state activity and between public and private sectors as different interests respond to the new conditions.

In these changing circumstances, planners, from many backgrounds, in many different organisations, have come to re-evaluate their work. They have had to engage with actors in government, the private sector and non-governmental organisations in discussions over the role of planning in relation to the environment and cities. The intention of the *Planning, Environment, Cities* series is to explore the changing nature of planning and contribute to the debate about its future.

The series is primarily aimed at students and practitioners of planning and such related professions as estate management, housing and architecture as well as in politics, public and social administration, geography and urban studies. It will comprise both general texts and books designed to make a more particular contribution, in both cases characterised by: an international approach; extensive use of case studies; and emphasis on contemporary relevance and the application of theory to advance planning practice.

PLANNING · ENVIRONMENT · CITIES

Series Editors: Yvonne Rydin and Andrew Thornley

Published

Patsy Healey
Collaborative Planning

Yvonne Rydin
Urban and Environmental Planning in the UK

Geoff Vigar, Patsy Healey and Angela Hull with Simin Davoudi
Planning, Governance and Spatial Strategy in Britain

Forthcoming

Bob Evans and Sue Percy
Environmental Policy and Planning in Britain

Ted Kitchen
Skills for Planning Practice

Peter Newman and Andrew Thornley
Planning World Cities

Huw Thomas
Planning for Diversity

Other titles planned include

Introduction to Planning
Planning Theory
Urban Design

Planning, Environment, Cities
Series Standing Order
ISBN 0–333–71703–1 hardcover
ISBN 0–333–69346–9 paperback
(outside North America only)

You can receive future titles in this series as they are published by placing a standing order. Please contact your bookseller or, in the case of difficulty, write to us at the addre below with your name and address, the title of the series and the ISBN quoted above.

Customer Services Department, Macmillan Distribution Ltd
Houndmills, Basingstoke, Hampshire RG21 6XS, England

Collaborative Planning

Shaping Places in Fragmented Societies

Patsy Healey
Department of Town and Country Planning
University of Newcastle upon Tyne

palgrave

Published by
PALGRAVE
Houndmills, Basingstoke, Hampshire RG21 6XS and
175 Fifth Avenue, New York, N. Y. 10010
Companies and representatives throughout the world

PALGRAVE is the new global academic imprint of
St. Martin's Press LLC Scholarly and Reference Division and
Palgrave Publishers Ltd (formerly Macmillan Press Ltd).

ISBN 0–333–49573–X hardcover
ISBN 0–333–49574–8 paperback

This book is printed on paper suitable for recycling and made from fully managed and sustained forest sources.

A catalogue record for this book is available from the British Library.

10 9 8 7 6 5 4 3
09 08 07 06 05 04 03 02

Printed in China

To **Judy**, who showed me how to do it

and

To **Heather**, who produced Emma more quickly than I did this book

Contents

List of Figures

Foreword

We are delighted to launch the publication of the new *Planning, Environment, Cities* series with Patsy Healey's book *Collaborative Planning*. The aim of the series is to bring new developments in planning theory, policy and practice to a wide audience of students, academics and practitioners. As such, most of the books will be textbooks supporting courses in planning and related subjects. There is, however, also space in such a series for the innovative and polemical. Patsy Healey's work represents the cutting edge of planning theory and is certain to be one of the most influential contributions to planning thought into the twenty-first century. We hope to include other books of this calibre in the series in the future. Planning texts should not just seek to consolidate the best of current work but to stretch the horizons of thinking about planning. Patsy Healey's work encourages the reader to do just that.

YVONNE RYDIN
ANDREW THORNLEY

Preface

This book is about why urban regions are important to social, economic and environmental policy and how political communities may organise to improve the quality of their places. It has been a long time in gestation. It arises from my realisation of the need to bring together a social theory about the space and time of the dynamics of urban region change with a policy theory about the governance of those dynamics. From my experience in planning practice many years ago, and from my research on planning practice and property development processes, I have also been acutely aware of the need to have a detailed appreciation of the nature of individual action and agency, in the context of the broader forces which drive the flow of action.

I have drawn upon a wide range of areas of discussion in the search for appropriate concepts to capture this relationship as I have experienced it, through my practice as a planner, through research and through my own life experience. This includes urban political economy, phenomenology, social anthropology, institutional sociology, policy analysis and planning theory. Only in the 1980s did I begin to find in institutionalist sociology and regional economic geography the kind of social theory which seemed to be helpful, because it acknowledged both structure and agency in a relational understanding of social dynamics. In parallel, I found the communicative approach in planning theory captured the notion of planning strategies, policies and their implementation as active processes of social construction, that is, of human invention. But it has taken many more years to weave together the two strands in a way that seems to hold together. Meanwhile, in practice, much of what I have been searching for conceptually is happening in front of me in planning practices, in Britain and elsewhere. So this book is my attempt to make a statement about how I think we should understand spatial planning, a conclusion to my search. I also believe it provides a helpful integration of the dimensions which must be addressed in any attempt at the collective management of common concerns about co-existence in the shared spaces of urban regions.

This book has been written primarily for those coming into the spatial planning field who want to engage with its core debates, and those already in it who want to explore new directions in planning theory and practice. It is also of relevance to urban and regional analysts and to those exploring new forms of democratic governance in the contemporary era. I hope also it will give those outside the spatial planning field an idea of the richness of the intellectual resources to be found in the traditions of planning thought and practice, with its preoccupation with integrated conceptions of living-in-places, and with strategic and innovative ways of thinking about both the future of places and their governance.

It is almost impossible to acknowledge all those who have helped me in the development of my thinking and specifically with this book. I can only say that my intellectual life has been greatly shaped and enriched through interaction with so many other kindly critical people who have provided stimulation, challenges, critique, and support over the years. I should like to mention in particular Judith Allen, Sue Barrett, Sandra Bonfiglioli, Alessandra de Cugis, John Forester, Maarten Hajer, Jean Hillier, Margo Huxley, Judy Innes, Abdul Khakee, Ted Kitchen, Gavin Kitching, Luigi Mazza, Alain Motte, Tim Marshall, the late Brian McLoughlin, Barrie Needham, Terrtu Pakarinen, Yvonne Rydin, Huw Thomas and Urlan Wannop. I also owe a special thanks to my colleagues at Newcastle University, particularly those involved in what became our *Managing Cities* book (Healey *et al.* (eds), 1995) – Stuart Cameron, Simin Davoudi, Steven Graham, Ali Madani Pour, Ash Amin and Kevin Robins, as well as colleagues who collaborated on work which has fed into this book, especially Rose Gilroy, Angela Hull, Tim Shaw and Geoff Vigar. Many of these have commented on drafts of this book and I am very grateful for the time and editorial suggestions they provided. In particular, I must thank Yvonne Rydin, Andy Thornley, Colin Fudge and my publisher, Steven Kennedy. Their support and advice has greatly strengthened the book. The weaknesses are of course my own.

I must also thank the ESRC for support with a personal research fellowship in 1987–88, when the outline of what became this book was first sketched out; the University of Melbourne and RMIT Melbourne for giving me a base for part of this time; Curtin University, Perth for providing another base in 1994 when the first draft of the book was written, and in particular to the School of Architecture and Planning's office staff, and to Jean Hillier for her stimulation and support; and to the University of Newcastle for allowing me a sabbatical term in 1994, and my departmental colleagues for taking on some of my duties at this time. Richard Newton was a very helpful sub-editor. A big thank you also to Jill Connolly, who has been my secretary for the past few years, and who is clearly much more competent than me!

I need also to acknowledge my family members whose tolerant support of my obsessive commitments has been complete and encompassing, and in particular the women; my sisters Joan and Bridget, my niece Heather and little Emma. Finally, I also thank a friend who a few years ago said I should stop organising and just do research. Well, I more or less did and here it is.

PATSY HEALEY

Acknowledgements

The author and publishers are grateful to the following for permission to reproduce copyright material: *Journal of the American Institute of Planners* for the publication of Sherry Arnstein's ladder of citizen participation, Vol. 35(4), 1969; Butterworth-Heinemann Ltd and the authors for a figure from J. Friend and A. Hickling, *Planning under Pressure: The Strategic Choice Approach*; *Journal of Environmental Planning and Management* for a figure from A. Hull, 'New models for implementation theory', Vol. 38(3); Jessica Kingsley Publishers Ltd for a figure from U. Wannop, *The Regional Imperative*, 1995; Cambridge University Press for a figure from P. Healey, *Land Use Planning and the Mediation of Urban Change*, 1988; Jossey-Bass Inc., Publishers for a figure from J.M. Bryson and B.C. Crosby, *Leadership for the Common Good: Tacking Public Problems in a Shared-Power World*, figure 4.3 (p. 91) © copyright 1992 by Jossey-Bass Inc., Publishers. Every effort has been made to contact all the copyright-holders, but if any have been inadvertently omitted the publishers will be pleased to make the necessary arrangement at the earliest opportunity.

Part I

TOWARDS AN INSTITUTIONALIST ACCOUNT AND COMMUNICATIVE THEORY OF PLANNING

Introduction

In western societies these days, we are keenly aware of the qualities of our environments. We worry about planetary conditions and global sustainability. We empathise with the threats to peoples and species across the globe. We are concerned about changes to the local worlds in which we and our children spend our daily lives. This anxiety partly arises because we know so much about what is happening all over the place in our knowledge-rich worlds. It is reinforced by the sense that we live in worlds of multiple forces, over which we have limited control (Beck, 1992; Giddens, 1990). At the supra-national and global scale, this perception helps to mobilise the activities of global pressure groups, such as Greenpeace and the Worldwide Fund for Nature, to protect endangered species and prevent global pollution. At the level of locality – that is, the regions, settlements and neighbourhoods where we live and work and where we co-exist with each other and other species – multiple conflicts over changes to local environments are critical preoccupations of local social and political life. They form a substantial part of the agendas of local newspapers, radio and television programmes, and of daily conversation. We puzzle over how to manage our co-existence in shared spaces.

Spatial and environmental planning systems are at the heart of these local concerns. The figure of 'the planner' is both an object of blame and hostility, and the subject of our hopes for effective community regulation. Planners are attacked at different times for allowing something to happen or for stopping it; at the same time, they are loaded with responsibilities for safeguarding environmental qualities and protecting people's interests. Planning systems and practices, however much they may become routinised into unquestioned procedures, have their power and justification in the role they play in helping the political communities of places work out how to manage their collective concerns about the qualities of shared spaces and local environments. Any evaluation and critique of their role needs to engage with understanding of the social processes through which concerns about space, place and biosphere are generated, and with the political processes, or processes of governance, through which societies develop ways of managing their common affairs. The understanding and practice of planning is thus at the interlocking of the study of the dynamics of urban and regional change and the study and normative practice of governance.

The history of contemporary planning ideas and practices shows just how difficult it has been both to conceptualise this terrain and to develop organizational mechanisms to address it (Healey, McDougall and Thomas (eds), 1982; Hall, 1988; Boyer, 1983; Friedmann, 1987; Low, 1991). It comes up against powerful intellectual forces, which segment our understanding into disciplinary fields – sociology, economics, politics, geography, ecology. It challenges the organisation of government programmes into functional sectors, such as social welfare policy, economic policy, education policy or environmental protection policy. It demands a *territorial* and *spatial* perspective, through which to perceive how the different activities we engage in as we go about our daily lives or conduct our businesses 'bump up' against each other, and exploit and trample over biospheric systems.

This territorial and spatial perspective has a new salience in the contemporary world. This arises partly as a result of our environmental concerns, as will be discussed in Chapter 6. It is being given added force by the economic recognition of the role of the qualities of places in promoting economic competitiveness in trans-national and global contexts (see Chapter 5). Global considerations are promoting greater concern with the qualities of localities, of places and regions. As a result, in Europe at least, there is a new interest in the strategic role of spatial planning systems (CEC, 1994; Healey, Khakee, Motte and Needham, 1996; Motte (ed.), 1995).

However, this new interest needs to be accompanied by new understandings and practices. The planning systems in place across most western countries were designed with conceptions of integrated and self-contained local economies and societies in mind, not the open and globally-reaching relationships which characterise much of today's local economies and social life. They assumed, in Europe at least, that the state could 'take charge' and 'control' spatial organisation and the location of development, in contrast to the current interest in the combination of flexible enabling and regulatory governance which permeates much current thinking about public policy.

This sets a new challenge for the design of institutional mechanisms through which political communities can address their common problems about the management of environmental change in localities; that is, the design of planning systems and planning practices. It requires new ways of understanding with which to grasp the dynamics of urban and regional change and new ways of thinking about the institutional design of governance.

This book addresses this challenge. It develops an *institutionalist* approach to understanding urban and regional change, drawing on recent developments in regional economics and sociology. This focuses on the social relations through which daily life and business organisation are conducted, and the way social and biospheric relations interweave. It develops a *communicative* approach to the design of governance systems and practices, focusing on ways of fostering collaborative, consensus-building practices. The institutional approach emphasises the range of *stakes* which people have in local environments, and the diversity of ways we have of asserting claims for policy attention. It makes visible and explains the dimensions of that diversity and helps to reveal the way power relations enter the finegrain of practices, structuring the public policy game and inhibiting the assertion of many stakes. The communicative approach both offers a way forward in the design of governance processes for a *shared-power world* (Bryson and Crosby, 1992), and takes as a normative position an ethical commitment to enabling all stakeholders to have a voice. It offers a way of mobilising for change through collective efforts in transforming ways of thinking. It thus presents a way forward in realising the practical meaning of participatory democracy in pluralist societies. This commitment is reflected in the use of 'we' in this book, to indicate situations and dilemmas we all share, as people in our planet.

Part I of the book sets the background for these new ideas by reviewing the main lines of debate in planning thought. It introduces the institutionalist and communicative positions and some of its theoretical underpinnings and antecedents, and reviews spatial planning as a 'field' of public policy. Part II develops an institutionalist perspective on everyday life, the business world and the biosphere. Part III focuses on governance processes and the challenge of institutional design for collaborative planning. It argues for attention at two levels, the *soft infrastructure* of practices for developing and maintaining particular strategies in specific places, and the *hard infrastructure* of the rules and resources of policy systems. Throughout, the discussion proceeds by locating issues in previous approaches, as a kind of 'ground-clearing' exercise, to clear out conceptions which have little place in the new approaches, but at the same time pointing out continuities and resources in earlier ideas, upon which new approaches can build.

1 Traditions of Planning Thought

The origins of planning

Every field of endeavour has its history of ideas and practices and its traditions of debate. These act as a store of experience, of myths, metaphors and arguments, which those within the field can draw upon in developing their own contributions, either through what they do, or through reflecting on the field. This 'store' provides advice, proverbs, recipes and techniques for understanding and acting, and inspiration – ideas to play with and develop. It may also act as a foil, against which critiques are developed and new ways of thinking brought forward. Thus, such a store provides intellectual resources. But it may also act as a constraint on intellectual innovation, by locking perceptions and understandings into particular moulds which are difficult to discard. The planning tradition itself has generally been 'trapped' inside a modernist instrumental rationalism for many years, and is only now beginning to escape.

This chapter reviews the traditions of planning thought, focusing on their development in a European and American context. The objective is firstly, to identify those elements of the tradition which provide resources upon which a transformation of planning thought can build; secondly, to introduce the new communicative planning theory as a foundation for a form of collaborative planning; and thirdly, to emphasise what needs to be discarded if the transformation is to be effective.

The planning tradition is a curious one, built up through a mixture of evangelism, formal institutional practice, scientific knowledge and, increasingly, academic development. It represents a continual effort to interrelate conceptions of the qualities and social dynamics of places with notions of the social processes of 'shaping places' through the articulation and implementation of policies. As John Friedmann has repeatedly pointed out, it oscillates in its emphases between a radical, transformative intention, and a role in maintaining the way cities function and governance works (Friedmann, 1973, 1987). This leads to an ambiguous relation to the social context of planning work. Planners in Europe in the 1940s and 1950s saw themselves as being at the forefront of a transforming effort, building the welfare states which would deliver a reasonable quality of life to the majority of citizens, after the horrendous experiences of war and of the economic depression before it. They were at the vanguard of a transforming effort (Boyer, 1983; Davies, 1972; Ravetz, 1980). Their successors, in contrast, often feel themselves operating within a complex and often uncomfortable, political and economic context, within which room for transformative manoeuvre seems slight.

Cities have been planned in one way or another, in the broadest sense of the management of organisation of space, of land and property rights and the provision of urban services, for as long as they have existed. Students of planning are still sometimes taught a history of urban form, from the Greeks and Romans, through European city-states, to the present industrial and post-industrial metropolis (Mumford, 1961). This emphasizes planning as the management of a product, the physical shape and form, the morphology and spatial organisation of the urban region.

However, the culture of planning as it has evolved in the past century is rooted in a much broader philosophical and social transformation, the intellectual sea change which we now label in the history of Western thought as the 'Enlightenment' (Hall and Gieben, 1992). Towards the end of the eighteenth century, a whole body of ideas seemed to develop together, in science, philosophy and economics. This body of thought emphasised the value of scientific knowledge, empirical inquiry and acting in the world to improve it, a deliberate opposition to religious dogma and monarchial attitudes, upheld by a religious preoccupation with the inner life (Sennet, 1991). Enlightenment thinkers argued for the importance of individuals, as knowing subjects with rights and responsibilities, as against power through the 'divine right' of kings and barons. They stressed the value of an open environment for business and commerce, as opposed to the political management of the empires and city-states of Europe at the time. Contemporary western conceptions of democracy, based on the individual franchise, the rights of individuals to pursue their lives and livelihoods, and the primacy of profit-seeking, self-interested economic organisation were significantly shaped in this period (Hall and Gieben, 1992). Out of this climate of thought, and the marriage of science and individual freedom to industry and commerce, came the great surge of invention and expansion known as the Industrial Revolution. It also witnessed the rise of democratic states, displacing autocratic states across western societies, though there were intermittent periods of totalitarian regimes. It is this intellectual movement which these days we refer to as the project of *modernity* (see Chapter 2).

The complexity of the political and economic processes which resulted, with their mixture of positive advances in terms of wealth generation and the spread of benefits combined with gross social inequalities, systematic exclusions (of class, gender, ethnicity and race), environmental pollution and periodic collapse in market processes, led to a growing interest in the *management* of the social-spatial relations unfolding within states and cities. Faced by these dynamic and contradictory forces, arguments began to build up in favour of *planning* the trajectory of the future, rather than being perpetually vulnerable to the volatility of markets, or to the power of the big capitalist companies. The key resource for this project of planning was seen as scientific knowledge and instrumental rationality. Scientific knowledge could provide an objective basis for identifying present problems and predicting future possibilities. Instrumental rationality focused on relating *means* (how to do things) to *ends* (what could be achieved), in logical and systematic ways. Impartial reason could be used as the measure of just actions (Young, 1990). In this way, the irrationalities of market processes and of political dictatorships could be replaced with a new rationality, planning as the 'rational mastery of the irrational', as Karl Mannheim put it (Mannheim, 1940).

The systematic planning of economies, of cities and of neighbourhoods thus became a growing preoccupation of national and local governments faced with the burgeoning problems generated by dynamic and often volatile economic and political conditions. It offered a 'transformative mechanism' with which to change and maintain a new, more efficient and effective order to the management of urban regions and to economic management generally

Three planning traditions

The culture of spatial planning as it has arrived in our times has been woven together out of three strands of thought which have grown up in the context of this inheritance. The first is that of *economic planning*, which aims to manage the productive forces of nations and regions. It is this form of planning which Mannheim had primarily in mind, linked to social policies which together would form the framework of a 'welfare state'. The second strand is that of the management of the *physical development* of towns which promotes health, economy, convenience and beauty in urban settings (Abercrombie, 1933; Keeble, 1952; Adams, 1994). The third is the management of *public administration* and *policy analysis*, which aims to achieve both effectiveness and efficiency in meeting explicit goals set for public agencies.

Economic planning

The tradition of economic planning is a vivid expression of the materialist and rationalist conception of a planned social order. The processes of production and distribution had to be planned to ensure efficient production and continuing growth, and, for some protagonists of economic planning, a fair distribution of the benefits of growth. It was preoccupied with both the economic failures of capitalistic market processes and their social costs.

The interest in *economic planning* arose in part from a general critique of the processes of industrial capitalism. Karl Marx mounted a devastating attack on the social costs of industrial development driven by the striving of capitalist entrepreneurs to maximise profits in competitive markets by exploiting people's labour and destroying resources (Giddens, 1987; Kitching, 1988). His analysis of capitalist processes of production, distribution and exchange was immensely powerful because it combined empirical perception with intellectual coherence, and was informed by a deeply humanitarian concern with the recovery of human dignity, which he saw attacked and degraded by the production processes he observed in nineteenth-century England (Kitching, 1988). His answer, articulated as a political programme in the *Communist Manifesto*, was to replace the marketplace and the processes of production driven by capitalistic competition with a governance system which was run by the people. Initially, and in order to break the power of capitalists on governance, Marx argued that the forces representing labour should engage in 'class struggle' with the objective of taking control of the state. Ultimately, the state too should wither away, leaving economic activity and governance to be managed by local communities.

Marx's political strategy underpinned the communist political movement, which gained enormous leverage in the early part of the twentieth century as labour movements across the world struggled to improve working conditions. But where communist regimes or socialist regimes, inspired by similar ideas of class struggle, came to power, they tended to reinforce the state, and the original Marxist idea of withering away was forgotten. In the economic arena, capitalist production processes were replaced with centralised planning and programming by the state, with individual enterprises driven by centrally-established production targets rather than the drive for profitability. Economic activity was typically seen to consist of a number of production sectors, usually based on a conventional division between primary, secondary and tertiary, or service industries. Co-ordination in space was subordinated to relatively independent development programmes of the different national ministries, representing economic *sectors*. In theory, production targets were to be informed by scientific research and technical understanding. In practice, building up an adequate knowledge base at the centre proved enduringly difficult and the logic of effective and efficient production quickly got replaced by a 'politics of meeting targets'. Further, such a concentration of economic and political power at the apex of a national system not only encouraged forms of governance unresponsive to people's needs. It also provided many opportunities for corrupt practice (Bicanic, 1967). As a result, centralised 'command and control' planning was increasingly discredited, from the point of view of economic efficiency, democratic practice and social welfare. Those who criticise planning still often have this model of planning in mind.

The communist model was not the only one which proposed replacing capitalistic economic organisation. Many writers who saw problems in large scale organisation outlined proposals for 'alternative' lifestyles, characterised by forms of self-governance. These have at various times been taken up by those working within the town planning tradition (Hall, 1988). For instance, Ebenezer Howard, famous for his development of the idea of the *Garden City*, was strongly influenced by such ideas (Beevers, 1988). These ideas challenged the notion of state management and bureaucratic organisation as likely to compromise the freedom of individuals and communities to determine the conditions of their own existence. What they were searching for were ways of interacting among small groups with respect to those matters in which individuals had shared concerns. The influential planning theorist, John Friedmann (1973), describes his own intellectual odyssey from a view of planning as improving public management using the techniques of instrumental rationality, to an emphasis on collective management through interaction among small scale communities, mixing urban and rural economic and social life, a strategy of *agripolitan development*. This kind of 'bottom up' economic planning represented a challenge both to capitalist societies and communist ones, and remains an important strand of thought in planning today. It has many links to the 'new' radical environmental movements which are searching for different and more environmentally sustainable ways of organising economic life (Beatley, 1994; Goodin, 1992).

Meanwhile, the problems of economic organisation also came to pre-occupy the advocates of capitalist production processes and market societies. The problems here arose from the repeated experience of periodic *market failures*. The ideal of the marketplace is that it provides a mechanism for the continual readjustment of production in relation to consumers' preferences and ability to pay. It is efficient in that it encourages innovative production methods, to reduce costs and introduce new and better products, and it in theory maximises welfare, being driven by consumer demand. And all this happens without the need for complex bureaucracy and the politics which go with state management. However, this marketplace balancing act can get upset for all sorts of reasons (Harrison, 1977; Harvey, 1987). Sometimes markets can be dominated by the producers, in a situation of monopoly or oligopoly. Or there may be too few transactions and too little knowledge available about them. People may come to the marketplace with very different capacities to pay. Market processes will tend to exacerbate these inequalities. Consumers may decide not to purchase and producers not to invest in new equipment or expand production because there is too much uncertainty to predict future expenditure patterns. Or there may be problems in the supply and maintenance of goods and services that everyone benefits from but which are very costly for any one person to supply. Some of these problems are short term, and are 'cleared' over time. But others are more deep-seated and can lead to a general slump in economic activity. By the middle of the twentieth century, there had been several such 'depressions'. The experience of these fostered ideas which suggested that economies could be 'managed' to avoid market failure.

The most influential ideas at this time were those of John Maynard Keynes, who argued that economies slumped because of a crisis in consumer demand. If people did not have the resources to buy goods, and/or they did not have the confidence in their longer term future to be prepared to invest in purchases, then production would sag. His solution, widely adopted in western economic management in the 1950s and 1960s, was to stimulate demand (Gamble, 1988; Thornley, 1991). A key element in his solution was the maintenance of 'full employment', a term meaning unemployment levels of 2 to 4%, regarded by economists as representing necessary labor turnover, flexibility and availability. Such policies were buttressed by social welfare policies to assist people to acquire education, to maintain health, and to get housing. The welfare states established in the post-Second World War period in many European countries served to keep the costs of labour low for companies, while enabling reasonable wages. (They also provided benefits to workers, and could be viewed as a strategy to fend off the more radical demands which some workers' groups were advocating at the time.) These wages could then be ploughed back into the marketplace to stimulate production of consumer goods, and hence economic activity generally. In many countries, and notably Britain, the US and Australia, subsidies were provided to encourage people to purchase housing, generating the expansion of a residential development industry (see Ball, 1983).

Although rarely called planning, these demand promotion strategies created what came to be known as a 'mixed economy', with economic policy – planning by another name – being driven by a mixture of economic analysis of market conditions and political sensitivity to electoral consequences. As with the centrally planned economies, the 'economy' was conceptualised in terms of sectors of production. This approach provided a governance regime which seemed to have advantages for the kinds of companies and capital accumulation strategies which operated on 'Fordist' production lines (Harvey, 1989a; Boyer, 1991; Amin (ed.), 1994).

However, by the 1970s, these demand-stimulation strategies seemed to have run out of steam. An increasingly interrelated global economy enabled those countries with cheaper labour costs to undercut the high wage economies. Consumer demand, and its accompanying demand for state spending, was growing energetically, creating conditions of rising inflation. At the same time, new technology was reducing the demand for, and therefore the power of, labour. Meanwhile, as companies sought to cut costs to be more competitive, questions were raised about the scale of tax demands needed to support the various demand-stimulation strategies, and about the various regulations on working conditions which had built up over the years to protect labour. The Keynesian strategy seemed to have ground to a halt in 'stagflation' – a situation of economic slow-down combined with rising inflation. This reaction provided fertile ground for the reappearance of liberal ideas about economic organisation. By this time, state intervention itself was seen as the problem. Articulated by the neo-liberal political movements, especially in the US and Britain, new economic strategies focused on the supply side of the economy, and the reduction of constraints on adaptation and innovation (Gamble, 1988). A major objective was to reduce the role of bureaucracy and politics in the management of the economy, and to 'unfetter' business from the burdens imposed upon it by the regulatory environment built up through the welfare state. Economic planning, and spatial and environmental planning, were considered one such burden, and a particular target during the period of the neo-liberal Thatcher administration in Britain in the 1980s.

Britain under the Conservative Prime Minister, Margaret Thatcher, became the arena for the wholesale introduction of these ideas. Through strategies of privatisation and deregulation, companies and market processes generally were to be freed up, to cut costs and to innovate in the globalising marketplace (Gamble, 1988; Thornley, 1991). The role of government was restricted to the management of the money supply to squeeze inflation out of national economies and to hold exchange rates at competitive positions in the international market place. Any government programmes which created 'blockages' to supply-side activity were to be reduced or removed. This included 'bureaucratic' regulations, such as land use controls, and the concentration of the ownership of development land in public hands in cities. The adverse social and environmental consequences of such a strategy were presented as necessary costs of transition to a more soundly-based economy, which would generate the wealth to put them right in due course. Planning, or co-ordinated economic management of the economy, in this context, was seen not just as unnecessary, but as counterproductive to the project of the recovery of a growth dynamic through market processes.

This neo-liberal strategy has had enormous influence across the world at the end of this century. It offers a way to transform governance to make it more relevant to the dynamics of contemporary economies. Its pro-active elements promote entrepreneurial rather than regulatory styles in governance (Harvey, 1989a; Healey, Khakee, Motte and Needham, 1996). It suggested an end of planning, and the return of the market as the key organising principle of economic life. Yet this strategy is also running into problems. Flexible labour markets create impoverished and insecure workers, unable or afraid to spend on consumption. Individualistic competitive firm behaviour undermines the delicate relations between firms which encourage knowledge flow and creative innovation. Attention is now turning to the institutional preconditions for economic growth (see Chapter 5). The deregulation impetus itself has changed into a project of regulatory reform, changing the target and process of regulation (Vickers, 1991; Thompson *et al.*, 1991). This rediscovery of the institutional preconditions for market 'health' and 'vitality' has awakened interest once again in strategies which might foster economic *development*. Further, the increasing concern with environmental quality has created a climate within which there is more rather than less demand for the regulation of economic activity.

So planning and the strategic management of urban region change are once again being discussed with regard to the management of economies. The causes and forms of this are discussed in more detail in Chapter 5.

Underpinning the approaches are different social theories – of class struggle for the Marxists; of communitarian self-management for the anarchists; and of individualism for the Keynesians and neo-liberals. Despite their different emphases, however, the debates and practices of economic management have shared some common characteristics. Their focus has been on the material well-being of consumers and the generation of profits for producers. Their practices have drawn on the vocabulary of neo-classical economics, even in Eastern European economies, with its metaphors of utility-maximising, rational individuals making trade-off between their preferences. Through the science of economics, policy programmes can be developed objectively, without the need to test ideas out with the different interested parties. Governance becomes a technocratic exercise in economic management. All these assumptions are challenged by contemporary institutionalist analysis and the communicative approach now emerging in planning theory.

The debates on economic management provide a context for the discussion of the physical development of towns and cities, and the management of spatial change in urban regions, and hence for any exercise in spatial and environmental planning. But the connection between these two arenas has been persistently neglected. Economic analysis has focused on economic sectors, and has tended to neglect how economic activities occur in space and time. As a result, it has paid little attention to the co-existence of different economic activities in shared space, except at the level of the micro-analysis of labour market dynamics, or the agglomeration economies and diseconomies of particular clusters of economic activities. It was left to the field of regional economic analysis and regional location geography to articulate these connections through the elaboration of location models for urban regions. Drawing on principles developed by Von Thunen and Isard, urban region spatial organisation came to be understood as being generated by the regional economic base. This in turn created a service economy and distributed activities across space through trade-offs between transport costs and land and property values (Evans, 1985). These ideas were developed in the spatial planning field conceptually by Chadwick (1971) and McLoughlin (1969) in Britain, and more practically by Chapin (1965) in the US. They focused on the analysis and modelling of urban systems. It is the assumptions and findings of these models which have been comprehensively challenged in the fields of regional economic analysis and regional geography in recent years, contributing to the reintroduction of space, place and the institutional capacity of localities into both micro and macro economic analysis (Massey and Meegan, 1982; Harvey, 1982; Scott and Roweis, 1977). A critical contemporary challenge is to link these new understandings of the spatiality of economic process to the principles and practices of physical development planning.

Physical development planning

Whereas the economic planning tradition has been dominated by economists and political philosophers, the arena of physical development planning was shaped for many years by engineers and architects, and by utopian images of what cities could be like. Utopian dreams of urban form, and architects to build them, have been around since long before the Enlightenment. What modernity and industrial urbanisation brought with them was a more material and functional concern with the qualities of city development. These influences led to practical interest in building regulation and in the strategic regulation of the location of development. Land use zoning was introduced, aimed to prevent the pollution of residential neighbourhoods by dirty industry, and to limit development location to enable adequate services to be provided. Ways of providing infrastructure and measures for land assembly, to allow land pooling among owners, or the purchase by the state of sites needed for public projects, were also introduced in early planning systems. Urban master plans, layout plans for 'greenfield' subdivision and projects for the reorganisation of the urban fabric became part of the management of the physical development process in many places from the late nineteenth century (Ward, 1994; Sutcliffe, 1981).

This of course implied affecting the structure of land and property rights and the interests of land and property owners. However, until the 1970s, and even later, there was little discussion of the nature of the development process and land and property markets in debates on physical development planning (see Healey and Barrett (eds), 1985; Adams, 1994). These were relegated to an arena of 'planning practice', concerned primarily with tools (Lichfield and Darin-Drabkin, 1980). The tools available were usually presented by the physical development planners as inadequate for the task in hand. The tradition of physical development planning instead tended to focus on broad policy objectives, and on the 'ideal city'. In their Utopian dreams, the most influential thinkers in the tradition harked back to the pre-Enlightenment days. They were largely disinterested in an analysis of the *processes* of physical development unfolding before them (see Hall, 1995 on Abercrombie). Instead, the idea of modernity entered into their discourse through ways of thinking about the shape and form of cities and the qualities of neighbourhood organisation. Cities were seen as an amalgam of economic, cultural and household activities. The challenge was to find a way of organising activities which was functionally efficient, convenient to all those involved, and aesthetically pleasing as well. The objective was to promote and accommodate modern life, as both a project in economic progress and an opportunity to provide good living conditions for urban populations (Healey and Shaw, 1994). The aim was to build a functionally rational city for economic and social life (Boyer, 1983). There were vigorous debates on how this could be done, which reflected different attitudes to the nature of urbanity, the proper relation between people and nature, and how far to welcome new building technologies and motorised transport. In these debates, the 'British' tradition was often contrasted with the continental, the former celebrating a nostalgia for an urban form in a rural setting, and a life in balance with the natural order, as expressed in Howard's ideas for a social garden city; the latter emphasising the tradition of high density apartment life, as encapsulated in Le Corbusier's Ville Radieuse (Hall, 1988; Ward, 1994).

As a result of these influences, planning theory became in the mid-twentieth century a discussion about urban form. This generated some of the most powerful urban spatial organising ideas of the century (Keeble, 1952; Hall, 1988). The dominant idea in the British tradition has been the conception of the urban region as centripetal, focused on a city core, with a hierarchy of district and subcentres developed in an urban form which spreads out with radial routes, interlinked by concentric ringroads, and contained by a green belt to give a clearly defined urban edge. This image is particularly associated with the work of the great English planner of the first part of the twentieth century, Patrick Abercrombie (see Figure 1.1). These spatial organising ideas not only provided a vocabulary of urban spatial forms. The spatial plans for particular cities have in many instances provided enduring and popular principles in local debates on the development of particular cities, for example Burnham's plan for Chicago, Abercrombie's for London and Stephenson's for Perth. Such plans have had effects by *framing* how key players in urban regions have thought about place and location (Rein and Schon, 1993; Faludi, 1996; Healey, Khakee, Motte and Needham, 1996). This is currently recognised by politicans and planners in many places in Europe, in efforts to recast spatial planning policies and practices (see the example of Lyons in Chapter 3). The significance of these spatial organising ideas will be discussed further in Chapter 8. But by the late 1960s, the physical development tradition came to be heavily criticised, in part for the arrogant confidence of the planners who promoted it (Boyer, 1983; Davies, 1972; Ravetz, 1980), but also for the lack of any social scientific understanding of the dynamics of urban region change which the planning ideas set out to manage (Hall, 1995; McLoughlin, 1992).

In some countries, the tradition of planning as urban form dominates planning thought and practice to this day, for example in Italy. Elsewhere, the tradition has been relegated to questions of the design of neighbourhoods, or major projects, or urban design. Through this tradition, ideas about architectural style, and particularly the debate about modern and post-modern style, have infiltrated into planning discourse – the latter challenging the functionalism of the modernist pre-occupation with the spatial order of the city. Postmodern thinking has also challenged rationalist conceptions of the social science of city management (Boyer, 1983; Moore Milroy, 1991). The urban form tradition has nevertheless kept active an aesthetic consciousness within urban planning, repeatedly sidelined in more utilitarian planning traditions, such as the British. Even in Britain, however, physical development planning incorporated concepts of stewardship of the environment, which have salience in the light of contemporary

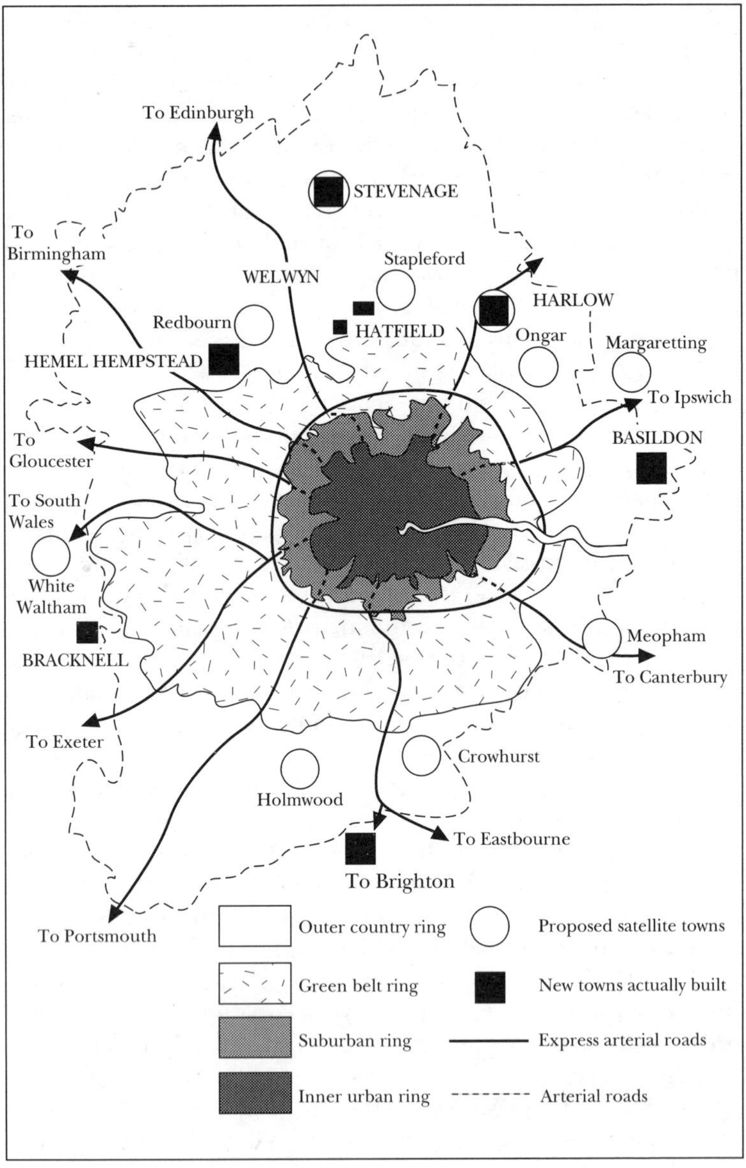

Figure 1.1 Patrick Abercrombie's plan for Greater London
Source: Wannop (1995).

concerns about environmental sustainability (see Chapter 6). Thus, despite its rationalising and modernist origins, the physical development planning tradition embodies a critique of materialist rationalism.

In countries where the architectural tradition has been dominant, research interest has focused on the study of the social relations of building form, in the search for principles of urban form through which to connect social process with physical form, as in the study of urban morphology (for example, in Italy). However, the primary focus of urban morphology has been on understanding the built form product and how to manipulate it (Madani Pour, 1990). A more social scientific tradition of spatial planning has developed in Britain and other Northern European countries which focuses on urban form and spatial organisation as a product of the dynamics of social forces. It is associated in particular with the movement of geographers into the planning field. Initially, as noted in discussing the economic planning tradition, their contribution was to bring regional economic analysis to bear on thinking abut urban strategy and spatial arrangement. They also provided a more rigorous understanding of the relationship between objectives of economic growth and quality of life, and how to manage the social processes though which these could be achieved. Such analysis had the effect of replacing discussions on idealised city form with an analysis of conditions and a prediction of *trends* which had to be accommodated, particularly in relation to accommodating the demands for better housing and for mass car ownership and use. Yet geographical analyses of the 1960s and 1970s neglected the dynamics of land and property development processes, nor was it common to recognise trends as expressions of 'market processes'. In more sophisticated analyses, the different dimensions of urban regions were integrated through the use of the urban systems models mentioned earlier, drawing on neoclassical forms of regional economic analysis and location theory. These were driven by the search for equilibrium relationships in urban region dynamics (Lee, 1973; Cowling and Steeley, 1973).

Such *trend planning* provided implicit support to the Keynesian demand management strategies being pursued at the level of the national economy. However, it became clear, as the stagnation of the 1970s set in, that trends could easily change. Many urban regions found their local economics undermined by the company restructuring occurring in the face of international competition (Massey and Meegan, 1982). This led to more interest being taken in how to create the conditions within which local economies could flourish rather than decline.

The increasing instability of many local economies also created problems for the process of land and property development, particularly where increasing reliance was put on private initiative, as governments began to cut back public expenditure programmes in response to their macroeconomic difficulties. This encouraged more attention to the mechanics of the property development process. Meanwhile, planners had been responding to both the increasing popular concern over environmental quality and the protection of nature, and to the realisation that welfare state policies had not eradicated poverty in the city, nor were they sensitive to the increasingly evident social diversity of urban life. By the 1980s, therefore, the physical development planning tradition was moving away from its utopian and aesthetic roots towards a form of policy analysis focused on the practical management of the dynamics of social, economic and environmental change in urban regions. Much of this tradition will be drawn upon in Part II of this book. What makes this tradition more than just a social science of urban region change is its integration with the tradition of policy analysis.

Policy analysis and planning

The science of policy analysis is of American origin, and grew out of a search for ways of making public administration more efficient and effective. In Britain, central and increasingly local government were transformed from the late nineteenth century by the development of an administrative class at national level, with substantial capability, good pay and a commitment to a service ethic. Local government was increasingly professionalised, challenging local politics with formalised expertise (Laffin, 1986; Rhodes, 1988). On the European continent, administration was formally governed by legal rules, developed from the Napoleonic code, which gave authority to administrative action. Both systems helped to constrain the play of political power games and to limit the subversion of administrative systems to private and political party objectives, except in places such as Southern Italy, where the administrative rules were typically bypassed or surrounded with powerful alternative practices.

In the US, however, local administrations were much more open to the whims of local politics. Many US studies of local politics describe alliances within which local politicians collude with local development interests to promote speculative land profits. Logan and Molotch (1987) argued that US local governance was dominated by property development and investment interest – a *rentier* politics. Stone (1989) develops the analysis of such alliances further to examine more enduring relations between local government and business. In their discussion of local politics, Lauria and Whelan (1995) refer to such alliances as *urban regimes.* Or local government could be driven by simple political objectives of maximising electoral advantage. This was described in a famous case study of Chicago, where decisions on the location of low cost housing were made entirely with electoral advantage in mind (Meyerson and Banfield, 1955). This led to pressure to make public administration more efficient and less corrupt (Friedmann 1973). The ideal local government balanced the demands of a pluralistic polity through technical analysis and management. Policy analysis offered rational techniques for this purpose. The core of the approach developed in the 1960s focused on identifying objectives, and developing and implementing appropriate means to achieve them. Its principles drew on Herbert Simon's ideas of management by objectives, rather than by setting legal rules for administrators to follow. This approach offered flexibility to address the particularity of decision circumstances while constraining corruption by clear accountability of actions to policy criteria. The decision model was the foundation for what became known as the *rational planning process.*

The resultant debates on planning as a policy process have been enormously influential, structuring the American planning tradition, and providing a point of reference for any planning culture open to American influence. They built on the pioneering experience in regional economic development of the Tennessee Valley Authority in the 1930s, and drew on ideas about efficient business management. Models for public planning and management were developed, based on the rational relation of means to ends (Friedmann, 1973, 1987). By 'rational' in this context was meant both a form of deductive logic, and the use of instrumental reason as a form of argument, drawing upon scientific analysis. As Davidoff and Reiner (1962) stress in their articulation of the approach as a 'choice theory of planning', a strict separation of fact from value was to be maintained. Values were seen as originating within the political process, and were provided by the 'clients' of the technicians of the policy process. Policy analysis work was seen to take place in a defined 'action space', cut out from the political and institutional context in which goals were articulated (Faludi, 1973). The planner as policy analyst was a specialist in helping clients articulate their goals, and translating these into alternative strategies to maximise, or at least 'satisfice', the achievement of these goals, through careful analysis and systematic evaluation.

This approach is discussed in more detail in Chapter 8. In the US in particular, it stimulated an explosion of work on the 'science' of decision-making, with much discussion on the forms the rational planning process could take and on the kinds of urban systems models which were needed to underpin analyses of the consequences of alternative actions. The model itself was challenged by those who argued that it was idealistic, with unrealistic expectations of the political willingness to stick to rational planning processes, and of the conceptual and empirical knowledge capacity to understand situations sufficiently to be able to identify and evaluate all possible alternatives. The most famous challenge was that by Charles Lindblom, who argued for an alternative approach of 'disjointed incrementalism' – approaching problems in small steps rather than big steps towards grand goals (Braybrook and Lindblom, 1963). Later he argued for a more negotiative approach, a form of 'partisan mutual adjustment' (Lindblom, 1965). Lindblom's ideas in this respect are an innovative precursor of the current discussion of interactive approaches to developing planning strategies.

Lindblom's arguments still propose a planning process dominated by the techniques of instrumental rationality (Sager, 1994). His approach looked rather like a sort of 'market adjustment' within the public sector, produced by a form of technical analysis which drew on microeconomics rather than management theory. Other American contributions to the debate on policy processes in the later 1960s raised more fundamental questions. These focused on questions of value. In the early post-war period, there was a powerful 'mood' in political debate that issues of value were no longer controversial. The West had chosen the capitalist path to peace and prosperity. Citizens were assumed to share broadly common interests, while arguing over the details of pluralistic interest conflicts (see discussion in Chapter 7). The planner or policy analyst was thus merely a technician of means committed to the values of scientifically-based and rationally-deduced policy choices, but neutral as regards ends. Davidoff and Reiner, writing in 1962, implied that this was indeed the case. But by the end of the 1960s, and linked to the reanalysis of poverty in American cities at this time, Paul Davidoff himself had come to a different view. In a famous paper, 'Advocacy and pluralism in planning' (Davidoff, 1965), he argued that it was impossible for the planner to be entirely value-free as regards ends, since planners as people had values. Implicitly, he acknowledged that these values divided people. In particular, the interests of poorer people in inner-city neighbourhoods were not the same as those of local business interests. He sought a way of planning which opened up the value diversity among the plurality of interests within a political community. In this context, he argued that planners should not stay value-neutral, given that they too had substantive values, values about ends. They should instead become value-conscious, declare their values and make themselves available to clients who wished to pursue such values. This approach had a powerful influence on American planning practice and thought in the early 1970s. The example from Boston quoted in Chapter 2 is taken from an example of advocacy planning inspired by Paul Davidoff.

Around the same time, the sociologist-planner Herbert Gans was arguing that planners had a moral responsibility to argue in favour of improving conditions for the disadvantaged. He argued, as Davidoff and Reiner had done, that planners needed to be aware of a double client, an employer, or 'customer' for the planner's services, and, more broadly, the citizens affected by the 'direct' client's proposals (Gans, 1969). Both Gans and Davidoff and Reiner were responding to the increasing political and popular interest in local environmental questions, and to the resultant pressure for more active citizen involvement in planning strategies and their implementation. In both the US and Britain, this led to ideas about the procedures for citizen participation in the planning process. This in turn generated critiques which challenged the pluralistic conception of local politics, presenting it instead as a power game, in which elites held on to power which citizens struggled to gain access to. This is encapsulated in Sherry Arnstein's *Ladder of Citizen Participation* (1969), with its metaphoric reference to the 1968 student protests in France.

Both Davidoff and Gans assumed a pluralistic polity as idealised in dominant US political thinking at the time. They also con-

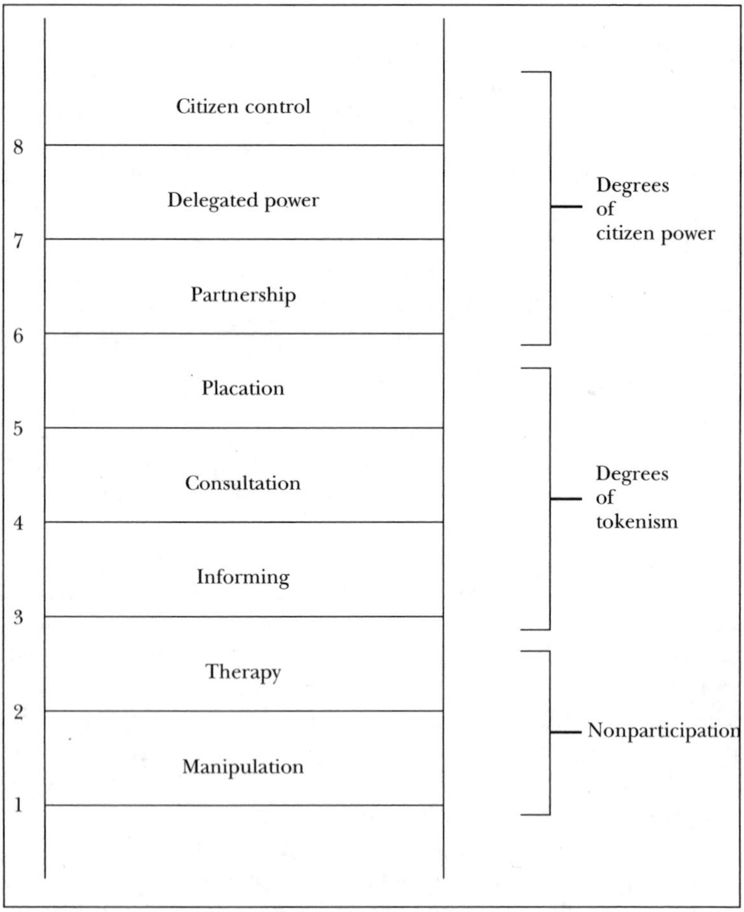

Figure 1.2 Arnstein's ladder of citizen participation
Source: Arnstein, 1969, p. 216.

tinued to advocate the techniques of rational scientific analysis. Their objective was to shift the approach to fit the pluralistic context better. In seeking to fit the planning model to the 'action space' of the institutional context, they thus shifted away from earlier conceptions of the transformative power of planning. For the urban designer planners, and for the early advocates of the rational planning process, planning approaches were in the vanguard of the transformation of cities, and the transformation of the management of local governance. Davidoff and Gans, in contrast, saw planning as a tool which citizens could use in extracting a more democratic pluralist polity from the clutches of dominant elites.

During the 1970s in the US and in Western Europe, the discussion of appropriate planning process models moved on from this position to question both the model of a pluralistic polity itself and the value of techniques based on scientific knowledge and means-oriented or 'instrumental' rationality. The first was most strongly developed in Europe, and drew on Marxist-inspired theories to analyse the structural bases for the unequal distribution of power (Castells, 1977). The second challenge reached planning from several directions and reflected a much broader questioning of the role of science and instrumental reason in Western thought generally. An early paper by Rittel and Webber (1973) argued for a more interactive and enabling approach to planning since facts and values were intertwined in people's consciousness. Others, interested in how policies influenced subsequent events, in how they were 'implemented', showed that policies were continually being reinterpreted by those involved in carrying them forward (Pressman and Wildavsky, 1984). British analysis argued that this negotiation and interpretation was an inherent dimension of policy work as practised. As a result, policies – that is goals, values and direction – were as likely to be articulated through the ongoing flow of events, decision and actions, as in formal exercises in policy-making (Barrett and Fudge, 1981a). The former were described as a 'bottom-up' view of how policies were made, to be contrasted with 'top-down' formal exercises. This work explicitly emphasised the interactive nature of 'doing planning work', and looked towards social exchange theory for inspiration. These developments are discussed in more detail in Chapters 7 and 8.

The interpretive, communicative turn in planning theory

All these traditions, as they have evolved, provide pointers to the development of institutionalist analysis and communicative approaches. The economic planning tradition, as it has evolved in both national economic management and local economic development, incorporates an increasing appreciation of the institutional preconditions for economic health. The physical development planning tradition has moved both to recognise the social processes underpinning spatial organisation and urban form, and the range and complexity of the demands for local environmental management generated by interconnecting social, economic and biospheric processes. The policy analysis tradition is seeking both to escape from its predominant emphasis on instrumental reason and scientific knowledge to incorporate greater understanding of how people come to have the ways of thinking and ways of valuing that they do, and how policy development and policy implementation processes can be made more interactive. But these directions were not unchallenged. A new reassertion of market liberal notions of governance was also emerging in parallel with these. The current period is above all one of tension between these two rapidly developing approaches in public policy.

Neo-liberal theorisation involves a reassertion of instrumental rationality, but in a narrow form grounded in microeconomics. The neo-liberal turn in public policy in Britain was promoted by the growing influence of economists in the public policy arena. This in effect abandoned the idea of policy formulation as a technical task, and concentrated instead on policy evaluation, both before policies were put into place, and in assessing their performance over time. This has generated a body of technique and evaluation criteria now used extensively by government agencies, particularly where neo-liberal policy interests predominate. It deliberately eschews a co-ordinative role with respect to public policy, leaving any necessary co-ordination to voluntaristic action, through the dynamics of market processes and community self-help. These ideas provide a foil against which the communicative approach developed in this book is developed.

The second direction shifts the conceptual ground firmly into a phenomenological interpretation of the relationship of knowledge to action. It builds on the realisation that knowledge and value do not merely have objective existence in the external world, to be 'discovered' by scientific inquiry. They are, rather, actively constituted through social, interactive processes (Berger and Luckman, 1967; Latour, 1987; Shotter, 1993). Public policy, and hence planning, are thus social processes through which ways of thinkings, ways of valuing and ways of acting are actively constructed by participants.

This recognition is part of a broad wave of reflection on identity (ways of being – ontology) and the bases of knowledge (ways of knowing – epistemology) which is influencing western thought in general these days. This intellectual wave has been building up in the planning theory field since the 1970s. It is now labelled argumentative, communicative or interpretive planning theory. It has many different strands, but the key emphases are as follows:

- a recognition that all forms of knowledge are socially constructed; and that the knowledge of science and the techniques of experts are not as different from 'practical reasoning' as the instrumental rationalists had claimed;
- a recognition that the development and communication of knowledge and reasoning take many forms, from rational systematic analysis, to storytelling, and expressive statements, in words, pictures or sound;
- a recognition, as a result, of the social context within which individuals form interests; individuals thus do not arrive at their 'preferences' independently, but learn about their views in social contexts and through interaction;
- a recognition that, in contemporary life, people have diverse interests and expectations, and that relations of power have the potential to oppress and dominate not merely through the distribution of material resources, but through the finegrain of taken-for-granted assumptions and practices;
- a realisation that public policies which are concerned with managing co-existence in shared spaces which seek to be efficient, effective and accountable to all those with a 'stake' in a place need to draw upon, and spread ownership of, the above range of knowledge and reasoning;

- a realisation that this leads away from competitive interest bargaining towards collaborative consensus-building and that, through such consensus-building practices, organising ideas can be developed and shared which have the capacity to endure, to co-ordinate actions by different agents, and to transform ways of organising and ways of knowing in significant ways, in other words, to build cultures;
- a realisation that, in this way, planning work is both embedded in its context of social relations through its day to day practices, and has a capacity to challenge and change these relations through the approach to these practices; context and practice are not therefore separated but socially constituted together.

This summary draws upon ideas developed by a number of contemporary planning theorists, notably Bengt Flyvberg, John Forester, John Friedmann, Charlie Hoch, Judy Innes, and Tore Sager. However, the planning theorists developing a communicative approach have given little attention in their work to the changing understanding of urban region dynamics evolving in regional economic analysis, urban geography and urban sociology (Lauria and Whelan, 1995). This too emphasises the active social processes through which everyday life and economic activity are accomplished. Intellectually, there are close links between the two emerging bodies of thought, grounded in the recognition of the social construction of meaning and the social embeddedness of ways of thinking and acting. A major objective of this book is to bring these two strands together and thus overcome the persistent tendency in planning thought and practice to separate the understanding of urban and regional change from the processes of governance through which political communities can collectively address their common dilemmas about what is happening to their neighbourhoods. The next chapter develops this challenge in theoretical terms.

2 An Institutionalist Approach to Spatial Change and Environmental Planning

The challenge

Conflicts over what we want local environments to be like are a routine part of our experience. If we are not actively concerned with the potential impacts of a new project in our neighbourhood, town or region, we hear of such conflicts, through street gossip, in newspapers and television programmes. Through this awareness, we have come to understand the impact of our own actions on conditions in other places. We fear the harm that we do to each other (Beck, 1992). The idea of progress, of the benefits of industrial and technological development, which so preoccupied people in the early twentieth century, now seems to be turning back on us, so that we are neither sure if there will be progress, or if there is, whether we will like the outcome. Local environmental conflicts affect us not just in terms of the defence of a particular material interest, such as the property value benefits of a particular view, or the increasing congestion on a road. They also have the potential to arouse fears and feelings about the way we live now, about the way our society is going. They touch our cultures, the 'taken-for-granted' frameworks and systems of meaning within which we make sense of the world around us.

Yet we view these conflicts from different cultural standpoints. In the past, local environmental conflicts in Britain were portrayed as manifestations of titanic struggles between classes, between 'capital' and 'community', 'big business' and 'ordinary citizens'. For many, the post-war welfare state was justified in order to protect people from the exploitation of capital (Ambrose, 1986). These days, such broad structural struggles are less clear-cut and less visible. The forces which structure the economic sphere are manifest as much in complex global financial flows as in the exploitative behaviour of a local industrialist. And they lead to very diverse interests in what happens in places, as companies have different strategies and different interests in land, property and the qualities of places. Similarly, the culturally homogeneous community with a common 'public interest' has been replaced in our imaginations by the recognition of a diversity of ways of living everyday life and of valuing local environmental qualities. This is captured in the idea that we live in 'pluralist' societies, which generate multi-sided interest group conflicts (Grant, 1989; Brindley *et al.*, 1989; Healey *et al.*, 1988). Contemporary social orders are often described as 'fragmented', reflecting a change from a 'modern' period of shared objectives, to a 'postmodern' time of lifestyle diversity and the celebration of difference (see Chapter 4).

But if the contemporary world is one where we both acknowledge difference and diversity, and fear the adverse consequences of our actions, difficult dilemmas arise with respect to coexistence in local environments. How is it possible to work out what the consequences of a proposed development are, and whether they are to be desired or feared, and by whom? How, if there is so much diversity, can agreement be reached? If powerful interests still have the potential to exploit and oppress, but yet are difficult to identify, how can their power be confronted?

In the past, one function of spatial plans was to provide a framework and ground rules to reduce and contain enviromental conflicts. However, economic and social change has undermined the bases upon which these frameworks were negotiated. In the US, the tendency has been to approach environmental conflicts on a project-by-project basis, arguing over the issues as they arise (Cullingworth, 1993). In Britain, conflicts have been managed by a form of pluralist interest group politics (Healey *et al.*, 1988; Brindley *et al.*, 1989). This approach proved time-consuming, as conflicts are repeatedly played out as the next project comes along. Such an approach also teaches people practices which encourage them to identify and defend their interests, in battles with others. It develops skills in adversarial conflict, and entrenches mutual suspicion, while masking the nature of the power relations which give rise to the conflict. In some contexts, and notably the US, this drives discussion of local environmental issues into the legal arena, which, in the US, further entrenches fragmented, adversarial litigation. This serves to reinforce popular perceptions that government is self-serving and untrustworthy.

The neo-liberal solution is to translate popular concerns with the impacts of projects into performance criteria by which projects can be judged. This tendency is well-illustrated by recent environmental legislation in the European Union, which uses norms, targets and principles to define the terms within which any development proposal should fit (Glasson *et al.*, 1994). Such an approach is in theory both transparent and efficient. It assumes that the criteria, and how they should be measured, are easy to define and to be agreed upon. Yet, in practice, indicators and measurements are all potentially contestable (Latour, 1987; Innes, 1990, 1995; Vanderplatt, 1995). This approach thus does not necessarily reduce the quantum of conflict. It also teaches people to treat issues in terms of rule-adherence, rather than identifying the actual impacts of a project on people and environments.

Other ways of moving beyond interest group conflicts are being explored drawing on principles of conflict mediation and consensus-building. These emphasise the potential for collaborative discussion of shared concerns about local environmental changes, through which people can come to learn about potential impacts and possible ways of valuing and addressing them (Susskind and Cruikshank, 1987; Innes, 1992; Innes, Gruber, Thompson and Neuman, 1994). Through such discursive practices, people learn about each other, about different points of view and come to reflect on their own point of view. In this way, a store of mutual understanding is built up, a sort of 'social and intellectual capital' (Innes, 1994), which can be drawn upon when dealing with subsequent issues. It also helps to build up, across the diversity of ways of living and ways of thinking, an institutional capacity to collaborate and to co-ordinate. It also serves to build 'institutional coherence' through which shared problems about the way urban region space is organised can be collectively addressed. The hope of the new ideas in planning theory is that, through such a process of 'learning how to collaborate', a richer understanding and awareness of conflicts over local environments can develop, from which collective approaches to resolving conflicts may emerge.

These ideas are being explored in several areas of public policy, at the present time. In some countries, long-established local governance cultures have encouraged the emergence of broad-based local collaborative approaches into the routine of spatial planning practice, notably in Scandinavia (Holt-Jensen, 1996; Khakee, 1996). But in other governance cultures, such approaches come up against some deeply embedded institutional constraints against collaboration, such as the hypercentralisation of the British state which limits local collaborative potential, or the dominant organisation of government into functional departments, which impedes spatial co-ordination. In such circumstances, local environmental conflicts present serious difficulties, because they are so multi-faceted, drawing in stakeholders across sectors and levels of government, and across divides between the state, private actors and voluntary organisations. 'Bringing in' space, co-ordinating through 'thinking together' and focusing on long-term impacts on places and people, flies in the face of neo-liberal philosophy and its underpinning aspatial economics. Yet many contemporary pressures are leading to a re-emphasis on spatial relations and the qualities of places. This argument is developed in Part II.

The challenge of addressing collective concerns with the quality of urban region environments demands an approach which both provides an account of the forces leading to change in the qualities of places in urban regions and offers ideas about the forms and processes of governance through which stakeholders and local political communities can come together to work out what to do and how to act. This book develops such an approach drawing on the *new institutionalism* as it is developing in the social sciences, in combination with the *communicative approach* in planning theory outlined in the previous chapter. This chapter reviews how the institutionalist approach grows out of precursors in both Marxian political economy and phenomenology, and discusses the contribution of two key thinkers, the sociologist Anthony Giddens and the philosopher Jürgen Habermas. The chapter concludes with a summary of the approach and a brief discussion of its implications.

'Structure' and 'science'

The new institutionalism is grounded in a relational view of social life, which focuses on people actively and interactively constructing their worlds, both materially and in the meanings they make, while surrounded by powerful constraints of various kinds (Powell and Dimaggio (eds), 1991). *Active agency* interacts with constraining *structures*, in Giddens' formulation (1984). This relational emphasis owes much to Marx's conception of the social dynamics of economic modes of production, and in particular, his interpretation of the social relations of capitalist production (Harvey, 1973; Kitching, 1988). Within capitalism, in this analysis, individuals are locked into a system which requires them to sell their labour power to bosses who seek to appropriate the fruits of their labour to themselves. Unequal relations between richer and poorer thus arise as a result of a structural relation. Marx and subsequent followers tended to overemphasise the role of structuring forces at the expense of the active role of agency. They were also committed to a belief that the forces of history could be understood as objective laws, driving human progress. Capitalist societies were thus both a progressive development from the past and an exploitative trap which locked workers into class relations where the value of their labour power was continually being appropriated by capitalists.

Marx appealed to workers to recognise their true, objective class position and overthrow the yoke of capitalist exploitation. To do this, they had to see through the liberal ideology of free individuals competing in a marketplace in order to identify their 'true' interests. Through ideology, workers lived with a 'false consciousness' of themselves and their social relations. The 'preferences' they expressed were thus not their 'real' preferences (Eagleton, 1991). The task of social transformation to a better society involved the stripping away of these ideological blinkers, to reveal to workers their true interests. When these were understood, workers, as revolutionary agents, would realise how much they had been exploited, and would seek to change society.

Scientific materialism provided the theory of knowledge which underpinned this political project. Like the capitalist world they sought to change, Marxist political activists believed in the power of science to provide an objective understanding of the world which could be used to resolve disputes between different ways of understanding. Prevailing economic and political relations could be criticised as a breach of principles of natural justice, and the cultural distortions and false perceptions generated by ideology stripped away.

Marxism, like liberal ideology, grew out of a western thoughtworld in which ideas of individual liberty and scientific objectivity were given a powerful role. Having rejected religious faith, socialism and liberalism became the two great secular faiths of the western world in the twentieth century. They were in effect two philosophies of how to achieve modernity and progress. By the 1970s, however, western intellectual thought was moving in a different direction. This slowly began to question the belief in the objectivity of science. Studies in the philosophy and sociology of science began to show that science itself was socially produced, framed by constructs which were held together only because groups of scientists believed in them. Thomas Kuhn analysed scientific progress in terms of shifts in such thoughtworlds from one paradigm to another (Kuhn, 1962; Barnes, 1982); and Latour (1987) have shown how these thoughtworlds are themselves carefully crafted social products. Furthermore, anthropologists described science and academic life generally as itself culturally constructed (Bourdieu, 1990; Geertz, 1988; Douglas 1992). Some sociologists went in search of the cultural underpinnings of organizational life, and began to explore the fine grain of social interaction (Clegg, 1990; Silverman, 1970). Feminist scholars, who grew in numbers and confidence during the 1970s, revealed the way contemporary life in western societies was infused with conceptions of the nature and role of women which bound women into inferior positions in the social order (Hayden, 1981; McDowell, 1992). Michel Foucault, the great French socologist/historian, seemed to bring much of this work together in his detailed work on the micropolitics of the organisation of the institutions of social control, such as prisons. He showed how every element of an institution – its formal routines, its informal practices, its physical structures, its discourses – 'carried' social meaning and the power relations of a social order. His central point, along with that of the phenomenologists and anthropologists, was that we inherently live within a social order, that we are culturally-bound. Foucauldian inspiration has lead to a rich seam of work on planning ideas and practices (Boyer, 1983; Tett and Wolfe, 1991; Huxley, 1994; Hillier, 1993).

These strands of thought have grown in importance as they have interrelated with the changing 'mood' of our times. As questions are raised about the possibility and desirability of further economic progress, about the nature of our ways of life, our identities and social orders and about the limits and biases of science, as we lose trust in what Giddens (1990) refers to as the 'abstract systems' of social, economic and political organisation which we had previously taken for granted, so we become increasingly aware of our cultural boundedness, our own biases and those of others. We recognise difference and differentiation in our systems of meaning, our ways of acting and our lifeworlds, and see around us not homogeneous values and ways of life, but cultural diversity. This leads to consciousness of differences between 'us' and 'others'. We reflect on the differences between our times and what has gone before. It is this mood which tends these days to be associated with critique of modernity. This critique has generated a rich intellectual debate on the presumptions and practices of 'modernity'. This reflects a broad-based shift in western thought, a shift in systems of meaning, and the parameters of dominant intellectual cultures.

One consequence has been that an awareness of the cultural embeddedness of social life, economic organisation and forms of governance has returned to western consciousness. 'Culture' in this context is understood not merely as ideology or political philosophy, nor as a particular dimension of social life, and still less as particular 'attributes' of a social group. Its meaning is more anthropological, implying the systems of meaning and frames of reference through which people in social situations shape their institutional practices. This conception of culture takes us beyond notions of values as 'individual subjective preferences'. Instead, values are seen to derive from models of thought. The recognition of diversity thus implies a realization that local environmental conflicts may involve encounters between people in different *cultural communities*. This contrasts with notions of place-based culturally homogeneous communities. The situation is rendered more complex in contemporary western societies by the way in which one person may live in different cultural communities. We are all linked by our networks, and by networks-at-a distance (Latour, 1987), through the media and processes of education, to all kinds of cultural communities (see Chapter 4). The result is not a reformed cultural homogeneity, though powerful networks seek to incorporate us in their cultural conceptions and ways of seeing the world. They are better understood, following Latour (1987), as overlapping centres of accumulation of 'local knowledge', items of information which are mapped and interpreted within the sense-making frameworks and purposes of particular social networks. As Geertz (1983) argues, this local knowledge is a mixture of systematised, formalised and calculated knowledge, and that acquired through social interchange and experience, a 'common sense' and a 'practical reason', a store of proverbs and metaphors, and of pratical skills and routines, conveyed as much in what is not said as in what is. Social networks, and the displaced networks of education and the media, develop 'a communal sensibility, present locally to locals, a local turn of mind' (Geertz, 1983, p. 12). This recognition has led to a re-emphasis in much western thought on the social situatedness of knowledge and action and the cultural frames of reference through which action is articulated. It represents a shift from a materialist to a phenomenological understanding of the nature of being (ontology) and the nature of knowing (epistemology).

Modernity and the postmodern 'turn'

The institutionalist approach develops this shift, specifically challenging the conception of people as rational calculating individuals, acting autonomously in the light of objective scientific knowledge, as in the liberal tradition, or in relations with each other which can be objectively understood, as in the Marxist tradition. Both philosophies arose from the intellectual inheritance now often labelled as 'modernity' (Giddens, 1990), which arose from the Enlightenment period (see Chapter 1). In this period, ideas from the earlier Renaissance of western thought and the classical ideas which informed them were drawn forward to our present day, as points of reference in politics and philosophy.

During the eighteenth century, and into the nineteenth, a new emphasis was given to the idea of the individual as autonomous of religious and governing structures, with capacities for self-reflection, and with rights which should be defended against the power of states. The constitution of the United States is founded on the struggle by emigrants to escape from a Europe of 'divine' monarchs and 'holy' empires to promote individual freedom. This history has provided a fertile ground for the flourishing of political and economic individualism. Scientific knowledge based on empirical inquiry began to reveal a world very different from religious myths. The world was seen to be round, not flat. The human species seems to have evolved from other species, rather than being created 'in God's image'. Through notions of the autonomous individual and the materialist focus of science, it was possible not merely to challenge and defeat the overweening monarchies and church hierarchies which had dominated economic, political and social life in Europe for so long. It was also possible to release the innovative forces of technological invention and economic organisation which lead to the industrial period itself (Hall and Gieben, 1992, Giddens, 1990).

While retaining many of the radical ideas of those times, such as the rights of individuals to life and respect, our sense today is one of betrayal. It is this sense which underpins the efforts to displace the thoughtworld of *modernity* with that of *postmodernity* (Harvey, 1989b; Giddens,1990; Moore Milroy, 1991). The liberating power of the idea that we are all 'free and equal', and that, by the application of scientific inquiry and technological invention, we can improve the material circumstances of everyone's lives, has been translated into governance institutions which have generated new bastions of power and new ways in which people are made unequal. The idea of the free individual in turn has been diminished into a narrow utilitarianism, in which what is materially useful is the primary measure of worth.

The problem with the project of modernity lies, as many now argue (Giddens, 1990; Harvey, 1989b; Habermas, 1993), in the way in which it was developed. The original materialism which helped to unmask the dominating power of religious organisation on people's lives and minds in an earlier era has itself displaced moral, emotive and aesthetic issues from public life. The objective nature of scientific inquiry, expressing a need to 'stand back in order to observe', was honed in the struggle with religious dogma into a belief in the objective nature of 'absolute scientific truth', replacing religious truths, as noted above. The free individual became an autonomous utility-maximiser, with material preferences and interests, disconnected from the social situations of existence. Drawing on these ideas, our lives became dominated by what Habermas (1984) also refers to as 'abstract systems', those of the competitive market and the hierarchical bureaucracy created in theory to organise the affairs of societies of free individuals. The first fostered individual efforts to compete in marketplaces driven by the search for competitive advantage. The second emphasised conformance to rules designed to 'protect' individual rights. The image of the first was the town market place. The image of the second was the paternalist family or kingdom, where 'representatives of the people', of 'elders', provided a protective framework for members in return for acceptance of the regime of rules. People, in these conceptions, were homogenised into a mass of similar individuals, with broadly similar behaviours. Such an undifferentiated conception of people was typical of the planning ideas of the early post-war period, as will be discussed in Chapter 4.

By the middle of the twentieth century, these ideas had become predominant in the western world. They were considered to be axoiomatic. The liberal conception dominated and ideology was banished. Through the scientific management of society, the 'rational' could master the forces of 'irrationality' (Mannheim, 1940). Bell argued that we now lived in a world without ideology (Bell, 1960). This meant we could carry on imagining a world of autonomous individuals with preferences, competing for material advantage and managed, at that time, through Keynesian demand management strategies. This conception was then vigorously projected onto other societies and other cultures in a form of cultural imperialism pursued through economic development strategies in the developing world.

The re-discovery of the cultural specificity of the conceptions of modernity, parallelled by research on the adverse impacts of the institutions of modernity on the material conditions and ways of life of many people and groups in our societies (see Chapters 4 and 5), have undermined this comfortable complacency. Along with a greater awareness of cultural specificity and diversity, more attention is now being given to how this specificity is shaped by particular histories and geographies. Through this shift, the early twentieth century geographers' concern with the cultures of places has been rediscovered, and recast into a conception of the local embeddedness and cultural rootedness of social relations.

The critique of the hegemony of modernity also fosters a move beyond the preoccupation with utilities and material things, to challenge the narrowness of scientism, by which is meant the faith in the material objectivity of scientific inquiry. As discussed in Chapter 6, we now see science as itself infused with assumptions about value, as both the potential provider of material benefits and as a threat to our welfare. Into the vacuum left by the loss of faith in scientific materialism has crept back not merely an increasing interest in metaphysical religious faith, but also a recognition that our material concerns are infused with our moral questioning and our emotive feelings, with what we care about about and what gives us aesthetic enjoyment. This recognition has been vigorously promoted in the critical philosophy of Habermas, the feminist philosophy of I.M. Young (1990), and many other studies on the nature of practical consciousness and practical reasoning.

Thus the project of modernity is now seen to have dominated our thinking with models of utility–maximising individuals, a narrow and 'cold' rationalism (Young, 1990), and competitive or hierarchical organisation. These models have crowded out the reality of diverse ways of being, of knowing and acting in relation to others. Modernity was in itself a cultural project, with significant political consequences, organising how we thought and acted as well as what we thought we wanted, our 'preferences'. Michael Dear argues that the characteristic quality of the present period is that this organising cultural force has disintegrated as we have lost faith in it. 'Modernity' has 'floated away', he argues, leaving us to see the diversity in cultures, understood as systems of meaning and modes of thought and action, which was there all along, but invisible to us (Dear, 1995).

But what does this leave us with? During the 1980s, a wave of philosophical and social scientific inquiry explored alternative conceptions of ontology, epistemology and social order. Drawing on an analogy with architectural debate, this search for alternatives became labelled as 'post-modern' (Harvey, 1989b; Goodchild, 1990; Moore Milroy, 1991). In reviewing the development of the postmodern debate in planning thought, Moore Milroy argues that postmodernism as a philosophical movement:

> ... is *deconstructive* in the sense of questioning and establishing a sceptical distance from conventional beliefs and, more actively, trying both to ascertain who derives value from upholding their authority and to displace them; *antifoundationalist* in the sense of dispensing with universals as bases of truth; *nondualistic* in the sense of refusing the separation between subjectivity and objectivity along with the array of dualisms it engenders including the splits between truth and opinion, fact and value; and *encouraging of plurality and difference.* (Moore Milroy, 1991)

This celebration of difference encourages not just the recognition of the diversity of ways we live and construe the world. It fosters individual efforts at differentiation, the assertion of distinctiveness, in dress, in opinions, in lifestyles. It could be seen as the ultimate development of the search for individuation set in train by the Enlightenment project through extending the meaning of individual liberty and respect (Giddens, 1984, 1990). The extreme individualist position encouraged by the post-modernist intepretation assumes that we can isolate ourselves from each other, creating a little 'culture' around ourselves. In this way, we seem merely to construct ourselves in the very language of neo-classical economics and liberal thought.

Postmodern individualisation generates severe problems with respect to the public realm, and specifically, for managing our relations of co-existence in shared spaces. How do we now think about our relations with others, as we try to assert our own distinctiveness? How can we begin to understand each other and why should we bother? Why get involved with 'development' and 'progress' if past efforts have brought so much damage to people and to nature? If we do decide to engage with others in trying to work out how to collaborate, how can we avoid falling into the trap of creating yet more 'orders' to bind our successors in structures which oppress them as we feel we too have been oppressed? How can we find agreement among us and between our differences if there are no general principles of objective or natural 'truth'? Much in the post-modernity debate in effect encourages an orientation away from public life and shared co-existence to the ultimate individualism – isolated autonomy.

The post-modern challenge is thus not merely a challenge to past planning practices. As many commentators have stressed (Dear, 1995; Moore Milroy, 1991; Beauregard, 1991; Goodchild, 1990; Healey, 1992a), it raises questions about the very enterprise of planning itself, as a practice of managing co-existence in shared spaces. It challenges any effort in collective debating and organising. Social co-ordination inevitably involves some constraints on people's actions. It will tend to stabilise the fluidity of social relations and reduce the diversity of ways of thinking and acting. It is therefore potentially oppressive (Boyer, 1983). It seeks to organise for the future in the name of *progress,* of making improvements. But who is to say what is improvement and why it is worth making an effort to change? A planning effort seeks to debate among a range of claims for attention with respect to local environments, but these claims come from different 'thought-worlds' and emphases and are particular and incommensurable. How then can they be discussed together?

Such challenges lead to several different possibilities. One response is to turn away, to an interior life, or to enjoyment of what we can while we can. Another is to engage in a perpetual effort of resistance and deconstruction, individually defending ourselves against the threat of 'abstract systems' against our own 'lifeworlds'. But these responses merely entrench our fears and our sense of isolation when faced with the real dilemmas of our social, economic and environmental relations. They also allow the tired practices of the old modernity to keep going for the lack of alternative ways of performing their work of organising the systems in which we unavoidably live. Rather than challenging the neo-liberal political project, and its reassertion of a narrow utilitarianism in public policy, such ideas provide a new dimension to the celebration of individual choice. The ideas discussed below, in contrast, provide alternative routes out of the political incapacitation to which the postmodern 'turn' in western thought can lead.

Transforming modernity: Giddens and Habermas

The opposition between modernity and postmodernity as concepts arises from debates in both philosophy and political sociology. Utility–maximising individuals and rationally ordered polities are contrasted with hedonistic, self-realising individuals and anarchistic polities. Underlying this is a shift in the intellectual tools with which we come to know ourselves and our social contexts, that is from scientific rationalism to a phenomenological and interpretive approach. The latter emphasises firstly, that individuals are not isolated from each other, but live in complex webs of social relations with others, through which cultural resources – ways of thinking, ways of organising and ways of conducting life – are developed, maintained, transformed and reproduced. Secondly, this social embedding draws together technical and scientific knowledge, with moral principles and emotive responses, in a flow of *practical consciousness* and *common sense* (Giddens, 1984). These constitute the *local knowledge* we have access to, and the cultural resources we mobilise when acting collectively (Geertz, 1983; Latour, 1987).

The challenge for public life in our present times is how to reconcile the individuation of cultural identity with recognition of commonality between individuals with different frames of reference, as well as different interests, in ways which do not trap us in modes of thought and practice which suppress our individual capacity to flourish. Such a challenge is utopian in reach, since in real societies, some always emerge more powerful than others, and the morality of majorities rejects some behaviours. But can we not find an evaluative position from which we can judge what helps to open up opportunity for diversity and what will lead in the opposite direction, to narrow moralising and growing inequalities in the distribution of material resources? Is it possible to reconstruct a public realm within which we can debate and manage our collective concerns in as inclusive way as possible?

Two major thinkers of our generation help in this task. The first, Anthony Giddens, drawing on Marxist and Weberian traditions in sociology, richly re-worked through the work of the phenomenologists and social interactionists, offers a social theory which helps to interpret individual ways of being in the context of social constraints, through a theory of *structuration*. The second, Jurgen Habermas, drawing on the German tradition of critical theory, provides a normative philosophy for the reconstitution of the public realm, built on a conception of inter-subjective consciousness and the *theory of communicative action*.

Anthony Giddens

Giddens argues that we are never as isolated or as autonomous as we sometimes think we are (Giddens, 1984, 1990). Firstly, our sense of ourselves is inherently constructed through interaction with other people and the natural world. We are born into social relations and we live through them during our lives. Through these relations we are linked to particular histories and geographies which constrain our material and conceptual resources and experiences. In this sense, our efforts in working out our individual identities and social relations are 'structured' by what has gone before. We are embedded within these structures. These 'pasts' are not just a benign collection of 'assets' which we inherit to different degrees. They are active forces, filled with implicit and explicit principles about how things should be done and who should get what. They carry power relations from one period to the next. Giddens (1984) argues that this is done through power over the formation of rules of behaviour, and power over the flows of material resources. These structures become abstracted from our daily life-making work in that, most of the time, we work within and use them as technologies or management routines, for example the telephone system, the system of dates, the educational system, the television networks, rules of the road, the financial and insurance system, and legal systems. Planning regulation over land use is typically just such a structure.

These structures operate in routinised and taken-for-granted ways, as we use them in the flow of daily life. They thus seem to have the quality of engineering and managerial techniques, abstracted from the flow of social relations through which we make our lives. Yet each element of such structures has at some time been actively made by human agency, and many are routinely remade, in the social relations of the classroom, the television station, the courtroom or the planning office. All engineering and organizational 'black boxes' have at some time been actively created by particular groups of people (Latour, 1987). As a result, they embody not merely technique, but modes of thought and sets of values. Modes of thought perhaps carry the greatest power of all, for example, the power to imagine that the public sphere was the domain of men and the private the domain of women; or that social status and position is inherited not earned; or that achieving material wealth is the prime objective of social effort and that those who succeed should be accorded most status in a society. In planning systems, these embedded modes of thought become the taken-for-granted assumptions of regulatory permitting or plan-making – the planning *doctrines* discovered by Faludi and Van der Valk (1994). These abstracted structures are thus infused with systems of meaning and carry cultural references forward in time. It is these abstractions from our social lives which filter back into the finegrain of our everyday lives, our life as human agents. A key principle in Giddens' theory of structuration is the recursive relation between structures and agency.

All this seems to suggest a world dominated by structural forces, by relations of power, as Marx described them in the nineteenth century. But for Marx, such structuring power over human existence was never absolute. People had the potential to challenge power if they could get sufficient understanding to reflect on their conditions of existence and see their 'structured oppression' for what it was. Foucault and the feminist deconstructionists (see above) help us to another insight, that these relations of power are not confined to the particular spheres of the world of work and of politics. They inhere in the finegrain of the social relations in which we live. Challenge and resistance is therefore a matter of daily confrontation.

Giddens builds on this kind of insight, but does so through the concept of the active agent. Marx and Foucault and their many followers present structure as external forces *acting on* individual subjects. Giddens argues instead that structural forces work through the relational webs within which we live, as we both use and constitute the structures which surround us. Our 'context' is thus actively constituted through our actions. Equally, we are implicated and constituted by the structuring forces which reach us through the relational webs within which we live. The structuring is therefore *inside ourselves.* Giddens believes, following Berger and Luckman (1967), that we are culturally made or socially constructed, and at the same time makers of cultures and social structures. But this is by no means a passive process. Without our active work, the structuring forces and the abstract systems of our lives would not exist. We ourselves make them (Shotter, 1993).

In this way, Giddens realises Marx's idea that 'we make history but not in circumstances of our own choosing'. We make history not just by acts of conscious resistance, but in the day-to-day way we decide about things, as we work out how to share a house, how to get on in an office, how to make a production line work out, how to share a public agency budget around, how to make a recommendation on a planning issue, how to organise a protest. As we do this work, we affirm our pasts, challenge them and change them. This is the meaning of Giddens' theory of *structuration.* We live through culturally-bound structures of rules and resource flows, yet human agency, in our continually inventive ways, remakes them in each instance, and in remaking the systems, the structuring forces, we also change ourselves and our cultures. Structures are 'shaped' by agency, just as they in turn 'shape' agency. Individual autonomy is thus always constituted in this interactive way, as, through the relations with others which we have, we individually and collectively maintain and change our social worlds. Structuring forces shape the systems of rules, the flows of resources and the systems of meaning through which we live. This creates our 'habitus', to use Bourdieu's term (Bourdieu, 1990). We live as social beings, through dense or diffused sets of relational webs, each one of which represents an active context for our lives. Our sense of individualisation arises as we face the challenge of managing the different demands of different relations. Thus, in the finegrain of planning practice, planners not only bring power relations into being, as Foucault describes. For Giddens, they also have the choice to change them. Thus the practice of planning, even in the details, involves delicate day-to-day choices about whether to 'follow the rules', or whether to change them, to transform the structure. John Forester's work contains many examples of planners reflexively making such choices (Forester 1989,1992a, b, 1994).

Giddens' ideas lie at the heart of the institutionalist conception of social life. As individuals, we live in webs of relations through which structuring forces bear in on us. Typically, we live in multiple relational webs, each with their own cultures, that is, modes of thought and systems of meaning and valuing. As active agents, and in the social situations of the relations within which we live, we construct our own sense of identity. Thus we may well experience the clash of culture within ourselves, and within the nodes of our relational webs, in the workplace, the household, the bar, the sports club, the community group. In our complex, globally-conscious contemporary worlds, our own selves, the nodes of our social lives, and local environments, can be seen as 'sites', layered over with different systems of thought and cultural meaning. Through our creative efforts, we are continually making and remaking our conceptions and meanings (Shotter, 1993). This active work of meaning-making is largely ignored in the utilitarian language of preferences.

Understood in this way, living with cultural difference is not something that is alien or new. We have been doing it all the time, with more and less success (Douglas, 1992). Negotiating among diverse thoughtworlds is part of our daily life experience. Some of us are more aware of this than others, partly because our particular histories and geographies, our webs of relations, give us more experience of being 'on the outside looking in'. We may be women in a man's world, blacks in a white world, working class people in a professional world, business people in a bureaucratic world, priests in a lay society. Others may be more used to imposing our worlds on everyone else and not realise that this is happening (Wood *et al.*, 1995). Yet we manage to 'live with difference' and to challenge and even change the culturally blind. Through this experience, we mould new cultural referents, for ourselves, those we relate with and, more broadly, the abstract structures which support our lives. We are active agents in a culturally dynamic world. We are thus accustomed to *making cultures* as we live within them.

If this is so, then it is possible to imagine that, through the attempt to recognise and respect our cultural differences – that is, the different systems of meaning which are layered over each other in the array of claims for attention in thinking about local environments – we have the potential to 'make sense together' (Forester, 1989), to arrive at a conception which works for us as a system of meaning, and which links, often in ways we cannot be clear about, to the other cultural referents we have. Thus managing our co-existence in shared spaces, in a way which draws in an explicit and reflexive way on the multi-cultural perceptions of the webs of relations which have some locus in a place, becomes an exercise not merely in consensus-building but in local *culture-building*, and in creating a public realm. It is an interactive and discursive effort, through which new understandings and institutional capacities may be built.

Giddens' theory of structuration thus emphasises that individuals are neither fully autonomous nor automatons. Powerful forces are all around us, shaping our lives, and presenting both opportunity and constraint. But structure is not something outside us. It is not an 'action space' within which we operate, as rationalist policy analysts tended to imagine (see Chapter 1). How we act in structured situations not only 'makes a difference'; our actions constitute (instantiate) the structural forces. We make structural forces, as we are shaped by them. So we 'have power' and, if sufficiently aware of the structuring constraints bearing in on us, can work to make changes by changing the rules, changing the flow of resources, and, most significantly, by changing the way we think about things. Conscious reflexivity on our assumptions and modes of thinking, on our cultural referents, thus carries *transformative power.* The micro-practices of everyday life are thus key sites for the mobilisation of transformative forces.

In this context, local environmental planning activity may be seen as providing a locale within which people act in constrained situations. They may merely play out well-established organizational routines. But they may seek to change them, shifting policies, or altering processes. In such situations, local planning activity becomes an effort in shaping or framing the webs of relations through which people give value and take actions with respect to the spaces with which they have some relation. Such framing work is an effort to *invent* structure (Schneecloth and Sibley, 1995). But how does this work of interactive culture-building take place? And how can it draw upon the richness of knowledge and understanding available to people in their different cultural worlds without oppressively limiting that richness through the dominance of particular ideas and power relations?

Jürgen Habermas

The critical theory of the philosopher Jürgen Habermas, though coming from a rather different perspective to that of Giddens, provides a rich seam of ideas about how to reconstitute the public realm through open, public debate. His work on the nature of communicative action is having a 'transformative' impact within the planning field on conceptions of planning processes (see Forester, 1989, 1993; Sager, 1994; Flyvberg, 1996). It is also influencing practical policy-making, as groups turn to the techniques of mediation and facilitation to deal with disputes and to organise discussion among different groups (see above). Habermas' work grew out of the German school of critical theory (Giddens, 1987; Low 1991). Habermas works with a social theory which has some parallels to the Giddensian one, but is more dualistic and static in its conception. He uses the concept of *abstract system* to identify the structures of economic order (the marketplace) and political order (bureaucracy) which constrain daily life. This is opposed to the *lifeworld* of personal existence; the daily, weekly and yearly going about and getting on in the life of personal experience. Normatively, Habermas seeks to reverse the tendency for abstract systems to penetrate into our lifeworlds, and looks for a reconstitution of the public realm as a vehicle for the redesign of abstract systems, more sensitive to our lifeworlds (Habermas, 1984, 1987).

Habermas' contribution to the challenge of 'making sense together' while 'living differently' lies in his approach to the concept of reason and the processes of public reasoning. Like Giddens, he rejects the regress of social life to an existentialist individualism, in which each of us focuses our attention on managing our present survival and enjoyment. Our consciousness is socially formed in interaction with others. Through these interactions, we develop ideas of responsibilities towards others, as part of our constitution of ourselves. What Habermas seeks to do is to rescue the concept of reason from the narrow instrumental rationalism with which it has been captured by the liberal economists, and to re-work it to provide a rich resource for democratic debate in our contemporary times. In this way, along with Giddens, he seeks to recover the progressive ideas of the original Enlightenment project from the narrow scientific materialism into which it had foundered. He effects this transformation, firstly by expanding the basis of reasoning, and secondly by providing criteria for a democratic reasoning process based on communicative practices.

Philosophers since Aristotle have noted the difference between the kind of systematised reasoning which they seek to formulate and 'practical' reasoning and *common sense*, such as we use to get by in our day to day lives. This often leads in academic thought to a separation between the world of theory and the world of practice in daily life. A major theme in contemporary philosophy has been to bring these worlds closer together (Young, 1990; Nussbaum, 1990). Along with Giddens, Habermas has been influenced by the philosoper Wittgenstein, who emphasised the hermeneutic understanding of language, and stressed that the meanings of words could only be understood in the contexts of their use (Wittgenstein, 1968).

This is good news for the study of the practice of local environmental planning, where the relation between systematised understanding provided by academic and professional endeavour and people's practical reasoning is a strong one. The interesting point about practical reasoning, however, is that we frequently do not separate 'facts' from 'values', or our emotional feelings from how we deploy our material resources. We mix together information about what we care about with what we think is happening, and what we would like to do. The whole process of reasoning and the giving of reasons, what we think is important and how we think we should express this and validate our reasoning claims, is grounded in our cultural conceptions of ourselves and our worlds. Habermas addresses this issue by identifying different forms which reasoning can take, and the 'validity' claims which each calls upon. He argues that there are three modes of reasoning which we mix together: *instrumental–technical reasoning, moral reasoning* and *emotive-aesthetic reasoning*. The first refers to scientific and rationalist reasoning, linking ends to means and evidence to conclusions. The second refers to reasoning focused around values and ethics. The third refers to reasoning derived from emotive experience. Just as we are accustomed to recognise different ways of thinking, different cultural moulds, so too we are accustomed, in conversation, to come across these different reasonings in our daily lives. Because scientific reasoning and instrumental rationalism have been strongly associated with the spheres of economic and political life, Habermas argues that their dominance in public discourse has been a tool to enable abstract systems to invade lifeworlds. Instrumental-technical reasoning has been allowed to 'crowd out' these other reasoning modes. They have been treated as outside reason, the irrationalities of the practical world. Our moral cares and emotional concerns have to be recast in the measured debate of technical analysis or legal principle.

Habermas argues, as does Forester (1989, 1993), that such 'purification' robs public debate of both the resources with which we can understand each other, and separates public policy from people's daily lives – their lifeworlds. Instead, we would understand each other better if we recognised explicitly that questions of moral value and emotive-aesthetic appreciation are part of public as well as private life, and should be debated explicitly along with our material concerns. Within the public sphere, therefore, we need to feel free to make claims on the basis of moral value and emotive concern, just as much as in the language of material interests and outcomes. So, the appeal to science, the appeal to moral value, and the appeal to emotional response should be given an equivalent status in debate, rather than privileging one sphere of reasoning – that is, the rational-technical sphere.

In this discussion, Habermas draws attention to the multiplicity of forms that the claims for attention which arise when discussing shared concerns about local environments can take. In an open society, which recognises different cultural reference points, not only is it important to acknowledge these different modes of reasoning. It is also necessary to develop an understanding of the processes of argumentation. In 'multicultural discourse', claims may arise from different systems of meaning and different modes of reasoning (see Healey and Hillier, 1995; Healey, 1996a; Macnaghten *et al.*, 1995).

In Habermas' public realm, therefore, participants engage in open debate through which they explore each other's concerns and the context of these concerns. This requires that participants recognise and respect different kinds of claims, as an aid to identifying assumptions and meanings, and that they acknowledge where different participants are coming from in articulating their claims This means that political communities need to work out collaboratively how to give validity and priority to different claims, in order to work out what action, if any, to take in a particular contested situation. How can such a process happen?

Here Habermas challenges the concept of an individual 'knowing subject' confronting a world of other knowing subjects, each one seeking to maximise their own interests. Instead, he presents an alternative conception of *intersubjective consciousness.* Like Giddens, Habermas believes our consciousness is socially constructed. Consequently, our understanding of the material world is structured by our social perceptions just as is our moral reasoning and our emotive feelings. If this is so, then we cannot resolve questions about collective action by using the language of any one form of reasoning. Neither scientific inquiry nor the economics of instrumental rationality can provide 'objective criteria' outside our debates to which we can appeal when arbitrating disputes. We must construct our ways of validating claims, identifying priorities, and developing strategies for collective action *through interaction*, through debate. These debates too are social constructions.

It is this idea that underpins Habermas' *theory of communicative action* with its *communicative ethics.* This focuses on how political communities communicate in public arenas, how participants exchange ideas, sort out what is valid, work out what is important, and assess proposed courses of action. In this conception, planning becomes a process of interactive collective reasoning, carried out in the medium of language, in discourse. Habermas argues that it is through our communicative efforts that cultures and structures are formed and transformed. Inherent in the communicative effort is the acceptance of a degree of collaboration and reciprocity. The metaphor of dialogue and conversation is critical in Habermas' thinking. In conversation, we must accept some common principles to allow this communicative exchange to take place (Habermas, 1984). Conversations imply the exchange of knowledge and understanding, of claims for attention. Their 'performance' requires some degree of trust and a preparedness for some degree of mutual understanding. It is only in the 'onesided' conversation that the hearer is dominated or marginalised. Habermas' focus is on the capacity for public conversations, debates about our shared concerns in the public realm. He is searching for ways of resisting the distortions of the one-sided conversation, and the ready made languages of abstract systems. It is through 'open' conversation among diverse peoples, through argument based on the available information, he claims, that we can arrive at 'truths' and 'values'. If based on principles of honesty, sincerity, and openness, to people's views and to available knowledge, then these truths and values can transcend the relativism of different persectives (Habermas, 1993).

Through reflexive dialogue, Habermas argues, through *monitoring* the mechanisms we create to manage ourselves, we can arrive at the richest conceptions of both what is 'true' and what is 'right' that we can collectively imagine, and agree upon, using all our resources of reasoning and all our cultural awarenesses. In the end, what we take to be true and right will lie in the 'power of the better argument' articulated in specific socio-cultural contexts (Habermas, 1984).

Reasoning in cultural context

Habermas, like Giddens, is criticised on many points by fellow philosophers and social scientists (Young, 1990; Clegg, 1990; Eagleton, 1991). In particular, the recognition of cultural differences in styles of 'conversing' need to be brought into Habermas' conception of debates (see Chapter 8). There are also problems with Habermas' notion of the desirability of achieving a stable communicative consensus in situations of cultural diversity and political hostility. But the contributions of Giddens and Habermas, the one emphasising active agency in the power of structures, and the other focusing attention on the processes of collective dialogue and how to confront the distortion of dialogue by the powerful, highlight both the cultural boundedness of ways of thinking and acting, and the possibilities for learning, for development, and for transformative action. They also address the cultural boundedness of scientific endeavour and economic rationality, the abstract disciplinary edifices which currently restrict our capacity for inter-cultural dialogue. As the anthropologist Mary Douglas writes,

> One by one the great logicians of our day are reluctantly coming to the same kind of answer. The ultimate and only authority for the way the universe is divided up has to be the community. Community is not seperable from logic: the mistake was to suppose logic had an independent existence, held up by its own bootstraps. The foundations of rational discourse are found in community commitment to stability and coherence. (Douglas, 1992, p. 251)

It is not that western society can manage without science and instrumental reason. Its development has been a great achievement. But it is important to understand the cultural context of their use, and to recognise the claims of other modes of reasoning. More recognition is needed to the assumptions and cultural referents of the communities within which reasoning work is accomplished. Such a recognition should foster a greater reflexivity within the context of dialogues about problems and possibilities in local environments. This should lead to more informed local planning and more capacity to resist the dominatory tendencies of the abstract structures and systems associated with the economy and the state.

The challenge then for collective action is to find ways of intercultural dialogue through which we can reflect on what we mean and understand, to 'explore the cage of our consciousness', as Mary Douglas puts it (1992, p. 267), in forms which offer respect to our individual and cultural differences. This could then provide the institutional capacity to address the difficult agendas discussed in Part II in ways which can open out opportunity, release creative energies and encourage respect for the natural world (see also Young, 1990).

Public policy-making, and processes of local environmental planning, may be thus reconceptualised as processes of intersubjective communication in the public sphere, through which dynamic mutual learning takes place. If such processes are to have the capacity to transform the public realm and to change structuring forces, they need to be capable of reflexive recognition of cultural reference points and evaluate the assumptions and conceptions built into the abstract systems created previously. They also need a creative capacity, to help build new 'transcending principles' and practices, which change the systems through changing the cultural reference points of all those involved.

An institutionalist approach

The institutionalist approach to understanding urban region dynamics and to undertaking collective action, that is, public policy work, can now be summarised. It rejects the notion that the social world is constituted of autonomous individuals, each pursuing their own preferences in order to obtain material satisfaction – the utilities of neoclassical economic theory. It is based instead on the conception of individual identities, as socially constructed. Ways of seeing and knowing the world, and ways of acting in it, are understood as constituted in social relations with others, and, through these relations, as embedded in particular social contexts. Through the particular geographies and histories of these contexts, attitudes and values are framed. It is in these relational contexts that frames of reference and systems of meaning are evolved. It is these systems of meaning, ways of valuing and ways of acting which become the cultural underpinnings of everyday life, for people in households, firms and agencies. The diversity and difference which causes problems in local environments is thus not just about individual interests – the noisy child versus the sleeping parent; factory effluent versus river wildlife. More difficult to address are the differences in systems of meaning, in *cultures.* Yet though social life is socially embedded, we are all active agents in the construction of our own lives. We reflect on, consciously adhere to, or actively set out to transform our conditions of life. Social life is thus both 'socially constructed' and actively made as we live our daily lives.

The approach acknowledges that this active work of social construction is not undertaken in 'neutral territory' as far as power relations are concerned. It is framed and interlaced by forces which impose structuring imperatives on social relations. For example, in our societies we need to find a job, or meet the state's benefit categories, to have any degree of material status and security. The structures of economic relations or of state organisation shape our opportunities and our values. We transact many relationships through the medium of money, which binds us invisibly into the technologies and dynamics of global financial systems. In our daily lives, in the playground, the home and the workplace, we draw on stereotypes about each other, about what men and women are like, about class position, about ethnicity, which are so culturally embedded that only a constantly reiterated effort at reflective confrontation can challenge them.

The recognition of the significance of structure is shared with Marxist analysis, and with work in the fields of feminist scholarship. For these traditions of analysis too, reality is seen as socially constructed. But the tendency in these traditions until recently has been to emphasise the power of structure, as some kind of external force apart from the social relations of the daily flow of life; the power of the 'laws of motion of capitalism' or of 'patriarchy', for example. The approach adopted here acknowledges that such powerful forces exist. But instead of treating them as external forces, the institutionalist approach recognizes, following Giddens, that they are present in, and actively constituted through, the social relations of daily life. The approach does not treat people as mere cogs in someone else's machine. It emphasises that the powerful forces which structure our lives are actively made by us as we acknowledge them in our doing, seeing and knowing, in our systems of meaning. It also acknowledges that we are reflective beings. As a result, we have choices about what to accept of our structured, social embeddedness, and what to reject. As we make these choices, so we maintain, modify and transform the structuring forces which shape our lives. Thus, as Giddens captures in his notion of structuration and the continual interaction between structure and agency, we are shaped by our social situation but we actively shape it too. One of the key themes to be pursued in this book is what the effort of actively shaping urban and regional dynamics to accommodate shared concerns about local environments could involve.

Institutionalist social theory thus emphasises the way, through the flow of the social relations of our lives, we 'make' our identities and our relations with others (Perry, 1995). Social life is an active process of continual 'making' (Shotter, 1993) in interaction with others. In these social relations, we make both our identities and our relational bonds with others. These bonds 'hold' through shared understandings and mutual trust which create relational resources, to be called upon at future times. The building of relational bonds thus creates *intellectual and social capital* (Innes *et al.*, 1994).

It is in the theory of such relation-building processes that the idea of *collaborative planning* is grounded. It focuses attention on the relational *webs* or networks in which we live our lives. It centres on people living in households, working in firms or agencies, taking part in interest associations. Each of these relations links a person to others, to ways of doing, seeing and knowing. These 'relational cultures' will vary in their spatial reach and temporal span. Some company managers will spend much of their yearly life travelling the globe, discussing with counterparts in other parts of a multinational company. When they come back to their household base, they may be required to negotiate parenting activities with their partner and their children, while pursuing leisure activities with family or friends which may take them travelling again. They may go to football matches or play golf with a friend or neighbour who works in a local authority, whose yearly life is spent with other council officials and, perhaps, working with residents. Some of these residents may be like the nomadic company manager, while others may rarely venture beyond the world of the estate where they live. The concept of relational webs and worlds can be extended to encompass our relations with the natural world. An ecosystemic view emphasises the ecological relational webs which link different species to each other, and within which the human species is interlocked.

All relational webs have points of intersection or *nodes*. These include the household, where members share a common space and resources; formal organisations, such as firms, agencies, or departments of government, focused around the production and delivery of particular goods and services; and associations, pressure groups, and informal groupings of friends and kin. The focal points of these relational webs act as nodes which provide the *arenas* where systems of meaning, ways of acting and ways of valuing are learned, transmitted and sometimes transformed.

The concept *webs of relations* is captured these days in the much-used metaphor of *networks*. Social networks overlap and intersect in complex ways. Many people operate in several networks at once, as the above examples illustrate. These relational worlds are framed and structured by the history of past power relations. In this sense, they are *embedded* in past experiences which structure relational opportunities and obligations. The power of structure and system is at its most forceful in these embeddings, in the deep structure of the 'taken-for-granted' assumptions which people implicitly draw upon (Lukes, 1974). But in their operation, as outlined above, these structuring power relations are continually re-negotiated and re-formed. This creates the possibility that the 'way things are' could be transformed into something different.

The metaphor of relational webs and social networks provides a descriptive way of capturing a conception of relational social dynamics. The driving forces of social change, though actively constituted within the interactions of daily life, arise through the mobilisation of networks. Companies mobilise to adopt new technology and new management structures to improve their market share. This creates pressures on other companies to change. Pressure groups campaigning on environmental issues develop their power base by making links with other groups and promoting ideas which capture the attention of other groupings. Broadly-based informal alliances and perceptions of common purpose provide the underpinnings for 'urban social movements' (Fainstein and Hirst, 1995). Families mobilise the resources for investment in their children's education, or a business venture, by seeking support from other family members with connections to money, power and influence. Such mobilisation involves both changing perceptions and understandings, and connecting people in one set of relations to others. Some nodes, such as annual general meetings, forums for discussion, council chambers, company boardrooms and clubs, have a key role in promoting or resisting such mobilisation efforts.

Governance, that is, the management of the common affairs of political communities, thus involves much more than the formal institutions of *government*. It may occur in informal arenas too (see Chapter 7). As Lukes (1974) argues, the visible power of formal government decision-making arenas is always complemented by the informal and less visible ways in which power and influence is mobilised. This less visible, informal power, in Lukes' model of three dimensions of power, is not just behind-the-scenes manipulation. It is also embedded in the thoughtworlds of the powerful. Governance processes themselves generate relational networks, which may cut across or act to draw together and interlink the relational webs of the life of households and firms. Governance activity may be aimed at sustaining relational webs, or at transforming them. Spatial planning efforts, as an example of governance activity, are inherently drawn into such processes.

But there is no necessary interconnection between the relational webs which happen to exist in a place. Instead of the integrated economies of urban regions typical of urban and regional analysis (see Chapters 1 and 5), and the parallel conception of neighbourhoods as united, socially homogeneous communities (see Chapter 4), the relational webs and social networks found in a place may vary enormously in their relational spread and their spatial reach. The relational web of one firm may be with East Asia; of another with Scandinavia, while a third may be focused on US markets. Families may have kin and friends around them in their neighbourhoods, but members may also be commuting monthly to work opportunities in the oil or construction industries in another continent. A neighbouring household may have two members working, but with daily commutes which go in opposite directions. Another neighbour may be 'hotdesking' from home and a car all over the country. One of the causes of local environmental conflicts is that people confront each other from often very different relational positions, without any past history of actual encounters, even when they are neighbours in space. People in such conflicts find themselves 'meeting with strangers'. Spatial planning systems aim to provide at least a framework for dealing with such encounters. They typically involve making connections between networks which co-exist in a locality, to enable conflicts to be resolved and to provide an arena within which people come together across different networks to work out what, if anything, needs to be 'managed' about local environmental change. As a result, they are forced to confront not merely conflict between individuals with similar values and ways of going on, but conflicts between *cultural communities* with distinctive systems of meaning and ways of valuing and acting. In this sense, spatial planning processes which seek consultation and collaboration are, in present conditions, unavoidably multicultural.

Local conflicts over space and place thus bring together not merely individuals with different interests and stakes, but people operating in different relational cultures, with different ways of doing, seeing and knowing. This will mean that they construct the issues in conflict in different ways, and have different ways of conducting discussion about issues and different ways of organising. A local environmental conflict may not just be about specific issues, therefore, but about conceptions of what is a problem and about organisational forms. Behind these often lie power relations – visible, behind the scenes and embedded in consciousness – which privilege not just some people over others, but some ways of discussing and some forms of organising over others. Any collaborative effort which aims to build understanding across culturally-different relational networks to address matters of common concern with local environmental change will require attention, therefore, to the ways in which issues are discussed, as much as to the substantive issues in question, and to distributional issues of who gets to participate in discussion.

These relational encounters over shared local environmental issues reflect power relations. But the potential always exists, however small, to transform them. In this transformative work, the realm of ideas and the discussion of ideas is a critical resource. Through the development of ideas in *policy discourses*, systems of meaning can be changed. Through changing ways of thinking, governance authority may be exercised in different ways, and material resources allocated by many parties in different patterns. Through the work of discussion itself, new ways of organising and new networks may be established, which add to the 'store' of relational resources available to those concerned about a place, whether living there, doing business, or caring about its landscape and heritage. In this context, spatial planning work could be drawn into deliberate governance efforts to maintain or to transform public discourses about the qualities of places. Where the emphasis is on transformation, planning could become part of an effort to build new relational links between networks co-existing in an urban region, and building up new systems of meaning, new cultural referents. It thus has a role in building up the *institutional capacity* of a place.

The concept of institutional capacity refers to the overall quality of the collection of relational networks in a place. It has been developed in the regional economic literature to refer to the social qualities which seem to make a difference to regional economic performance (Amin and Thrift, 1995). There is increasing recognition that the quality of this capacity matters, whether the collective objective is economic competitiveness, sustainable development, biospheric sustainability or quality of life. Since what people do locally adds up to what happens both nationally and at an international level, and has complex relational links to processes elsewhere in the globe, the institutional capacity of one place matters to others, and to national, transnational and global concerns.

Spatial and environmental planning thus becomes part of processes which both reflect and have the potential to shape the building of relations and discourses, the social and intellectual capital, through which links are made between networks to address matters of shared concern at the level of neighbourhoods, towns and urban regions. Collaborative approaches in this context are focused explicitly on the task of building up links across disparate networks, to forge new relational capacity across the diversity of relations which co-exist these days in places.

Spatial planning efforts have the potential to become sites for urban region, town and neighbourhood 'link-making work'.

Cultural embeddedness

The institutional approach focuses attention on the way in which our thinking about issues and our ways of organising around them is embedded in 'where we come from', our 'localised life-worlds'. This holds whether the focus of our lives is in our family relationships, in the making of a large scale business venture, in daily work at the office or factory, in engagement with some association, or in work in a scientific laboratory or an academic community. These provide us with a store of knowledge and values, and a range of skills and activity routines. It is through them that we make and re-make meanings. The store provides us with a repertoire of routines which we can draw upon when we undertake an activity, such as getting involved in a Local Agenda 21 meeting (about the environment) or responding to a questionnaire. This store is not just an individual bundle that we carry around with us. We share it and develop it with others, shaping and consolidating it through our relational interactions. In this way we build shared meanings and pass on 'taken for granted' understandings, images and metaphors. Embedded in cultural communities, we also build new cultural resources and create new cultural communities.

But our cultures are not fixed and given, nor are we their passive creatures. They are fluid and dynamic, evolving as we make and re-make them through our efforts to 'make sense' of ourselves and the world around us. Cultures are the consequence of our social relations (Latour, 1987), though powerfully shaping what we think and how we act. Nor do we necessarily live in one homogeneous culture. We are conscious that other people 'live differently' from us; we make distinctions between 'us', 'you', 'them' and even 'other societies' with which we have little to do. In our individual life trajectories, we may find ourselves pulled in different directions, as the principles about right conduct which prevail in some of the webs of relations in which we live pull us in opposite directions from the principles in others. In contrast to the densely interrelated *gemeinschaft* cultures of isolated so-called 'primitive societies', our lifeworlds are interpenetrated with multiple cultural 'layers'. The language of neoclassical economics encourages us to see these divergent pressures in terms of conflicts between our 'preferences', our preferences forming our interests. But, as the anthropologist Mary Douglas tells us (1992), it is silent about how these preferences are formed. The focus on cultures helps us to see the social processes behind the formation of the 'interests' over which we get into conflict. If we can see them better, perhaps we can change them more effectively.

The problem which arises in working out how to manage our co-existence in shared spaces through working collaboratively is that this typically involves intersecting with multiple lifeworlds and multiple cultural communities. In earlier periods, this was not as problematic as it is today. Either the reality of such diversity went unnoticed, through assumptions of homogeneous societies which shared a common 'public interest', or else the public tolerated leaving public policy to governing elites and their own cultural formation processes, or disaffected groups fought a class war, to displace one group of people and replace it with themselves and their culture. Today, however, diversity and difference is explicitly noticed. People from different lifeworlds are being forced to 'encounter' each other, as élite, class-bound societies experience popular pressure for more democratic and populist forms of organisation. If we recognise that this diversity is not just a matter of superficial interests, but arises from the implicit and explicit processes of cultural formation, then differences could be more deep-seated than pluralists and economists have bargained for. If we 'live' and form our lifeworlds in different cultural communities, within which we develop different 'languages' and different 'systems of valuing', how do we get to talk to each other about matters of common concern? And, when we get to talking across these divides, how do we get to decide what is right? If what we consider to be 'right' is determined by our cultural reference points, how can we defend ourselves from environmental disasters? Are there not some absolute priorities, such as a duty of environmental stewardship or of natural justice, which should override our 'little local differences'? Does not all this critical questioning plunge us into a cultural relativism which will end up as blind as the narrow instrumental rationalism and materialism that it challenges? How can the dominatory power of groups who command the definition of powerful abstract systems and who have the power to impose their interpretations on the rest of us be restrained?

The institutionalist approach argues that a way through the dilemmas of collaborating across cultural differences is firstly to recognise the potential cultural dimensions of differences ('where people are coming from'), and secondly, actively to make new cultural conceptions, to build shared systems of meaning and ways of acting, to create an additional 'layer' of cultural formation. Local environmental planning thus becomes a project in the formation and transmission of cultural layers.

Culture, in institutionalist analysis, is thus given a particular definition. It is the continuously re-shaped product of the social processes through which systems of meaning and modes of thought are generated. Cultures provide vocabularies through which we express what we think and feel. They shape our thoughts and feelings and our sense of ourselves, and our identities. They provide symbolic structures, in metaphors and rules of rights and responsibilities, which help to reflect and to arrange the relations within a social group – a family, a firm, a government department, a sports club, a pressure group. They provide a store of discursive resources, storylines and myths, and of organising resources, rituals and routines. They provide ways of thinking embedded in a way of acting, while the way of acting is infused by the way of thinking. We are constituted through our cultures. As we act we reaffirm and transform our cultures, as we do our sense of ourselves and our identities. Much of our cultural resources are so deeply embedded in our consciousness that we are unaware of them, or if aware, we assume they are part of the universal condition of being a person. Only when we 'travel', and meet strangers, as Latour (1987) explains, do we recognise other ways of being human.

This idea of culture has a long history in the study of 'other cultures' and the field of anthropology. In western societies this century, influenced by scientific materialism, we have often thought that we were 'beyond' culture, understood in this way. Culture came to be associated with segments of society and thought, with 'irrational' metaphysical conceptions, with faith and religion, which scientific knowledge made unnecessary, or with the 'high culture' of art and literature. It was also linked to ideology, understood as the biases and preconceptions which distort knowledgeable rational action. It seemed to bring in the personal and the 'irrational' to confuse modern thought and public policy. So the language of the modern period relegated culture to a sector of social life, rather than recognising the cultural embedding of all social life. The challenge now is to recognise the cultural situatedness of our knowledge and action and to work out ways of living in a multi-cultural world.

Spatial planning and multi-cultural consensus building

It is now widely understood in the planning field that planning is an interactive process, undertaken in a social context, rather than a purely technical process of design, analysis and management. Until recently, those planning analyses which emphasised the interactive nature of planning presented it either in the terms of class struggle, between capital and workers (Cockburn, 1977; Ambrose, 1986), or state and community, or as a form of bargaining among conflicting interests (Healey *et al.*, 1988; Brindley *et al.*, 1989). This chapter has argued for a different conception of interaction, which moves beyond theories of structure as aggregate class interests or individuals as subjects with sets of arbitrarily acquired preferences. Instead, it is argued that our interests are formed in social interaction through culturally-framed systems of meaning, through which we 'make sense' of our relations with each other and the natural world. In this effort in building understanding and 'making meanings', we draw on all our senses – our material appreciation and technique, our moral concerns and our emotive appreciation. Our different languages and discourses provide vocabularies of metaphors and reference points. Our understandings are shaped by and filtered through our thought-worlds, our cultural systems of meaning.

Once, in the romantic nostalgias which some people still yearn for, some of us lived in a place-based community, a 'habitus' where our social relations were tied to particular groups and places. Our 'group' contained all our relational resources. In British local planning practice, the romantic *gemeinschaft* community is often evoked in local debate on the qualities of places. In these globalising days, when our relational webs connect us to a huge range of possible social relations and stores of knowledge and understanding, the notion of a place-based community falls apart and we are plunged into a multi-cultural world. In such a world, we are conscious of different ways of seeing and knowing, of different languages and metaphors. One response is to attempt to simplify this diversity. The modernising effort of science and instrumental reason can be seen in this light – as a global effort to colonise our minds. This not only crowds out dimensions of the human experience which are important to us. It brings us harm as well as good. Another way of simplifying the diversity is to try to escape, by wrapping ourselves up in the language of protest, or by a politics of defence of 'our group'. One group confronts others with claims of 'I object', the other responds with cries of 'Don't disturb us'. Both are valid claims, but neither will make sense of our different claims. If we are to recover the original Enlightenment idea of respect for all members of the human species, and for the natural world, we need to adopt a different approach.

We cannot ignore that we live in a world which is heavily structured by powerful forces. They are the 'abstract structures' through which we get access to opportunity, to material resources and to rights of access. These often seem to fix the dimensions of our contexts – the impenetrable walls captured in Foucault's image of the prison. But these power relations are not *outside* us. They are part of us, and they exist *through* us. Through our relational webs, we continually reaffirm them, modify them and challenge them. We interpret rules, we make resources work in new ways, we re-think our ideas and assumptions, we turn our protests into transformative ideas. As human agency, despite the continual constraints on us, we thus have some power, the power to choose, to invent, to think differently. As we find the rules don't work and invent new techniques, so we come to think differently about things. As we think differently, so we want to invent new things and use rules in different ways.

Human agency thus changes abstract systems and structuring forces, but these transformations happen not by individuals in isolation. They are shaped and given meaning by the relational webs within which we live. These webs are held together by cultural referents as much as by instrumental purposes or ties of kin. They give us systems of meaning, languages and metaphors, cultural referents through which to articulate the implications of our re-thinking and re-making. But we are also transforming them as we live them. Cultures are thus dynamic.

In the public realm, the sphere of collective action, we come together not just as separate individuals, or groups clustered around a homogeneous interest. The challenge is to make sense of a multiplicity of claims for attention arising from the different relational webs which each actual and potential participant brings to the public arena. In this context, the *mobilisation of meaning* is a critical activity, as vocabularies and metaphors for describing issues and working out strategies are drawn upon and developed. In these situations, knowledge, arguments and ideas play a powerful role, but these are filtered through the frames of reference we use as we talk – that is, the discourses we use. Our problem is that some discourses have come to dominate our public arenas. This leads to cultural domination rather than inter-cultural communication. By critical reflection on the discourses which are brought to the public arena, it is possible to widen the understanding we have of how we experience issues, to see problems and make claims for policy attention. Through dialogue which reflects on the conditions for its own accomplishment, we can at least 'open a conversation' between our different cultural referents, and through this try to learn more about not just the claims we each are making, but why we think what we do and why we come to make our claims. In this way, we may be able not only to reach a better understanding of each other, but to find the bases for making public policy collaboratively. Through choosing an inclusionary dialogical style, political communities in a location may be able to generate the practices of reciprocal respect through which we can challenge the 'competitive babble' into which many policy debates founder and build a relevant and stable consensus.

Approached in this way, the power of dominant discourses can be challenged at the level of dialogue, through the power of knowledgeable, reflective discourse, through good arguments, through the transformations which come as people learn to understand and respect each other across their differences and conflicts, and as we learn to build consensus which respects difference. It is this possibility which is attracting the attention of philosophers and political scientists as they search for ways of recovering a new participatory realisation of democracy and reconstituting a public realm (Habermas, 1993; Dryzek, 1990; Held, 1987; Young, 1990). And it is these ideas which we can use to help us develop new approaches to local planning processes.

Spatial planning and local environmental planning, the practices of managing co-existence in shared spaces, are a particularly interesting arena for this challenge. Local environments may contain within them an enormous range of social relations and relational networks, bringing in ways of thinking and ways of expressing claims for attention in all kinds of ways. Any management of local environmental concerns raises both global issues and issues about the finegrain of detail of daily life for both people and other species. The range of issues which may come up is potentially vast. So some way to simplify them, to filter and order agendas, becomes essential.

In the past, this simplification has happened through a dominant discourse, or through deliberate exclusion. It is often said that in affluent western countries, it is the middle classes who dominate public consultation arenas. The approach discussed here suggests a different way. If we can learn more about the dialogical processes of inter-cultural communication, we may be able to build consensuses which have multi-cultural reach, making sense and giving voice to the different culturally-constructed claims for attention which arise in a place. Through this, we not only transform how we think about our claims, and even alter the cultural referents in our various relational webs. We also make new discourses, with the capacity to re-shape and frame, that is, to structure, the abstract systems which constrain our lifeworlds. It can also provide the opportunity to build new practices of democratic debate, and the chance, however small, to shift power relations. Thus how we go about managing our co-existence in shared spaces matters, for both its substantive agenda, and for its capacity to build practices of intercultural democratic collaboration.

A normative viewpoint

There is much in the traditions of spatial planning thought and practice upon which the development of the approach outlined here and developed in this book can build. But in most countries, there is a past to escape from. If the relational approach to social dynamics outlined above has merit as a way of understanding economic and social life and its relation to environmental processes, then the potential of spatial planning needs to be extracted from its various pasts, to pull out those strands which remain of value, and shift both ways of thinking and ways of organising to reflect new realities and understandings. Adopting a relational viewpoint is only part of the re-orientation. A view about power relations is also needed. It does matter what kind of institutional capacity is developed.

Spatial and environmental planning, understood relationally, becomes a practice of building a relational capacity which can address collective concerns about spatial co-existence, spatial organisation and the qualities of places. It focuses on making links between economic, environmental and social dimensions of issues as these interrelate in places. It potentially impacts on and links to a very wide range of people with *stakes* in a place, although the stakes are potentially very diverse.

But this 'link-making work' can be undertaken in many ways. How then should the quality of the institutional capacity-building contribution of spatial and environmental planning activities be judged? One principle is to assess whether the activity achieved the substantive objectives set for it – some combination of economic, environmental and social outcomes. This implicitly assumes the position of rationalist policy analysis, that ends are effectively met and the means are efficient (see Chapter 1). This is an important consideration, but assumes that the definition of what are desirable outcomes and how these may be achieved is easy to arrive at. The institutional approach outlined above would put more emphasis on how people changed their ways of doing things and seeing things, and thereby undertook their activities within a changed frame of reference. What the outcomes of this process are would be difficult to identify in advance. Specifying defined output criteria *a priori* also denies the process of creative invention in response to a changed frame of reference. Nevertheless, this criterion stresses that governance activity should be seen to work and deliver noticeable material results.

The normative criterion that aims are effectively and efficiently achieved needs to be moderated to allow for learning during policy development and implementation processes. The generation of *social and intellectual capital* is an important outcome of policy processes as noted above. This suggests a second criterion for judging public policy; that new links were forged and maintained, appropriate to the particular history and current circumstances of an area. Collaborative planning approaches perform particularly well on this criterion. Some analysts suggest there could be some kind of 'functional fit' or 'coherence' between the relational context within which spatial and environmental problems arise and the institutional capacity to relate to them. For example, Harvey emphasises the dynamics of the search for structural coherence between economic organisation and mode of governance. An economy which is driven by the dynamics of global markets and the global movements of finance capital may need a more flexible, 'entrepreneurial' approach than one driven by the organisation of 'Fordist'-style industrial production (Harvey, 1989a; Boyer, 1991). But the notion of functional fit assumes a mechanical relation between the external forces shaping the context of policy-making and the processes and contents of the particular instance. The institutional approach takes a less determinist stance, emphasising that responses are invented by people collectively learning about the issues, the context, each other and what they can do. The context may shape what they do, but how they respond helps to change the context too.

A third criterion would be that the spatial planning effort sought to recognise and reach out to all those with a *stake* in the locality. This is a distributional principle. The justification for recognising the full range of stakeholders derives from the search to find a stable, enduring and legitimate way of addressing the dilemmas of co-existing in shared spaces. This could be expressed as a search for *sustainable* practices for managing collective concerns about spatial change at the level of the neighbourhood, the town and the urban region. Unless all *stakeholders* are acknowledged in the process, policies and practices will be challenged, undermined and ignored. Unless participants learn how to build consensus across their differences, agreements about policy directions will not endure, disintegrating at every challenge. If stakeholders come from different cultural communities, however, building consensus in inclusionary ways will be socially and politically demanding, requiring careful attention to the communicative practices through which trust and understanding can develop. Spatial planning efforts should therefore be judged by the qualities of *process*, whether they build up relations between stakeholders in urban region space, and whether the relations enable trust and understanding to flow among the stakeholders and generate sufficient support for policies and strategies to enable these to be relevant to the material opportunities available and the cultural values of those involved, and have the capacity to endure over time.

In this book, all three criteria are brought into play, acknowledging the complex interplay of the content and context of planning work, the interplay of substance and process, to use a long-standing distinction in planning theory (Faludi, 1973). But the overarching perspective is that without the third, spatial planning efforts will make little contribution to addressing local environmental conflicts in sustainable ways. Developing understanding of what it means to build inclusionary, collaborative processes is a major challenge facing all those involved in urban region governance at the present time, and the theory and practice of the spatial and environmental policy field in particular. But through the process of developing and 'inventing' such practices, the field of spatial planning has the potential, because of the complexity of the issues involved and the range of potential people with a stake in them, to make a general contribution to the development of pluralist democratic practices for governance in our unequal, culturally diverse and conflict-ridden societies.

3 Spatial Planning Systems and Practices

Spatial planning: regulating land use rights and managing spatial organisation

The institutionalist approach emphasises the social relations through which collective action is accomplished, producing public policy discourses and relational resources through which material and cultural benefits are developed, and activities regulated. It focuses attention not only on the formal organizations legally charged with policy responsibilities, but also on the relational webs which connect these to wider arenas and networks and the collective managing processes which occur in these arenas. A 'field' of public policy is thus an aggregation of formal organizations and informal relationships through which collective action with respect to a set of concerns is accomplished.

Spatial planning practices may be considered as such a field. They constitute arenas where people come together to articulate concerns about the collective management of local environments and define and carry out sets of actions directed at such management. All policy fields are a mixture of new intitiatives, as new generations design different ways of approaching issues, and inherited organizational forms, laws, procedures, and informal cultures and practices. Spatial planning practices are no exception.

As a field of public policy practice, spatial planning has evolved from different origins in different places. It involves two levels of governance, as with any policy field, that of systems of law and procedure which set the ground rules for specific practices, and that of the specific instance, where various parties come together to undertake planning work. The first involves the design and operation of *planning systems*; the second involves the design and operation of *planning practices.* In Part III, these two levels are distinguished as the hard and soft infrastructure of *institutional design* for managing co-existence in shared spaces.

All societies have some kind of mechanism for dealing with issues to do with land tenure, land use and land development, though these vary according to the cultural contexts within which land is given meaning. For many farming societies in Africa, for example, land was, and to an extent still is, held in trust from past generations, to be passed on to future generations. In most western societies, land is typically seen as a commodity, to be bought and sold like any other. But even in our societies, owners are constrained in what they can do with their property by traditional rights, for example, of common access, as in rights to use public rights of way in England, or to roam on open land, as in Scotland or the *allemansretten* rights to roam and garner the fruits of the forests in Scandinavia.

Spatial planning systems have typically evolved in an urban context to set limits on what private owners can do with their sites and buildings. They are an explicit recognition that spatial co-existence at high densities leads to tensions. These may be between one property owner and another, or between people for whom a property is an attribute of their local environment and the individual land and property owners. In British industrial cities in the nineteenth century, public concern with environmental quality focused on health and hygiene, and the quality of housing. The solution advocated by the critics of private markets was that land should be taken out of the realm of private ownership altogether. Not only were there a host of interests in sites to be sorted out. Land and property in urban contexts grew in value as cities expanded and diversified. The owners of this land could just sit back and enjoy these 'windfall' financial gains. This drew the state into a role as landowner on behalf of the society. Others, such as Henry George at the turn of the century, argued that access to land was an inherent part of human well-being, so that everyone should be guaranteed a plot, to farm or conduct a business on. In this view, the state was necessary in order to ensure everyone had a reasonable land plot (Ward, 1994).

Other arguments for a state role in land policy, and hence a formal public policy towards the use of land and the location of development, grew from the increasing role of government in providing urban services, and particularly infrastructure. Through investment in urban physical services, such as roads, rail systems, water and sewerage networks, land values were increased for private owners, who then sought to develop to cash in on these values. Or land owners would speculate on the rate and direction of urban growth and the provision of public services, and allocate lands for development ahead of services. This then created pressures for public provision of services which might be costly to satisfy. Sometimes, greedy landowners short-changed purchasers with respect to development quality. The state might then get drawn in to improve the quality of buildings and local environments. In some instances, notably in the Netherlands (Needham *et al.*, 1993), the public sector is the primary land developer. A key role of planning systems may then become the direction of that development process.

As cities have sprawled out across regions, supported by motor transport and good rail systems, by increasing populations and, in western cities, by the search for higher quality dwellings and local environments, policy concern has focused at a more general level on the efficient functioning and quality of environment and quality of life of the urban region. This has led to an interest in critical urban region spatial relations, such as the costs of time spent in travel, the relation between workplace and home, the quality of life in different parts of the city, the availability of space for low value but necessary land uses, and with environmental quality and carrying capacity, from air and water systems to resource use and the quality of green spaces. The impetus behind physical development planning, with its preoccupation with urban form (see Chapter 1), arose because cities were changing so much. Issues of urban form and spatial strategy for the city are re-emerging at the end of this century as many cities are threatened by changed economic roles and decentralising pressures for spatial decentralisation from city cores.

These sorts of pressures re-focused the attention of public policy from regulating environmental quality at the level of the street and the neighbourhood, to the level of the town and the urban region, from managing land rights to managing the spatial organisation of urban regions. Contemporary planning systems tend to combine both dimensions, often uneasily. The challenge is a difficult one because it links objectives of market efficiency, to help the private land and property market work better on its own terms, with concerns for quality of life and biospheric quality. Further, the range of those with a potential interest in efficiency, in quality of life and environmental quality is potentially vast – all those with some kind of concern for the qualities of neighbourhoods, towns and regions. Addressing the concerns of these multiple stakes represents a very considerable challenge for governance. How spatial planning is undertaken thus reflects much about a society's capacity for collaboration across diverse interests.

Spatial and environmental planning systems

Spatial planning systems vary in their origins, their institutional arrangements, their policy tools, and their personnel (Sutcliffe, 1981; Davies *et al*,. 1989; Cullingworth, 1994). These variations reflect both distinctive styles of government and administration in different countries, and the purposes for which formal spatial planning systems were originally introduced. The discretionary British approach to land use regulation is often contrasted with continental zoning approaches. The first reflects British governance traditions which focus on the capacity of politicians, advised by administrators and professionals, to make good decisions. The continental approach focuses instead on clearly specified codes of practice, originating in the Napoleonic codes introduced to improve public administration two hundred years ago (Davies *et al.*, 1989). The British approach to spatial planning is also distinctive both in its centralism and its functional sectoralism. This too reflects a general characteristic of British governance. It allows national philosophies about land policy and spatial organization to be driven across local practices. For example, spatial planning in Britain since the 1970s has been forced by central government policy and practice into a narrow remit of 'land use matters' only (Bruton and Nicholson, 1987). This is a deliberate attempt to narrow down the potential range of interests in land development and spatial organisation issues and to avoid straying into the remits of other government departments. In other countries, where municipal governments have much greater powers, spatial planning is integrated with social, economic and environmental policy practices at the municipal level for example, in

Sweden (Khakee, 1996). There is much evidence that issues of spatial organisation are easier to address in such decentralised contexts (see Healey, Khakee, Motte and Needham, 1996).

These qualities contrast with the evolution of spatial planning in the US which has evolved locally, typically in response to local land management dilemmas (Cullingworth, 1993; Weiss, 1987). This localist approach was also found in Switzerland until recently. However, European planning systems, despite substantial differences, embody a stronger recognition of the importance of spatial organization and supra-local considerations. The result is an uneasy tension, noted above, between the regulation of the finegrain of changes to the built environment and wider considerations of the location of activities within urban regions. Another is a tendency to resolve this tension in a hierarchical way, with different levels of planning 'mapping on' to spatial levels. European spatial planning systems also tend to have a regulatory form which separates planning control and policy from the private sector and market processes.

One consequence of these European traditions is that planning systems in Europe have been uneasy bedfellows with neo-liberal public policy principles. These firstly challenge the possibility and desirability of strategic management approaches in the public sector. The only justification for planning systems is as a mechanism to set ground rules for market transactions in land development. Zoning ordinances are acceptable, but not spatial strategies. Secondly, hierarchical organisation, particularly in the public sector, is criticised as inherently 'bureaucratic', unresponsive to the dynamics of change, and probably self-serving to the officials within it rather than the consumer/citizen. Thirdly, forms of regulation should not be considered as apart from the private sector, but framed with the private sector, to help make the sector work better. The function of regulation is thus to address economic efficiency as well as social costs. Fourthly, much of the support for neo-liberal policy comes from the field of economics, which has had little recognition of the significance of *where* things are, or of the *institutional supports* which firms might need in order to flourish. Spatial planning could thus be dismissed as an irrelevant hangover from the hierarchical, paternalist welfare state (Thornley, 1991). In this interpretation, neo-liberal theorists were supported by critical urban political economists and postmodernists who have argued that spatial planning systems are the expression of an 'ordering urge' through which a particular capitalist order is maintained and through which the forces of modernism have dominated city life (Castells, 1977; Boyer, 1983).

That many current spatial planning systems and practices deserve criticism cannot be denied, whether in terms of neo-liberal principles, or the policy evalutation criteria set up at the end of Chapter 2. But this does not mean that there is no place for such an activity in the present evolving age. On the contrary, there are many pressures demanding more effective forms of land management and spatial planning. These arise because of the difficulties in contemporary societies in dealing with the problems generated by the co-existence in shared spaces of people living disparate lifestyles, caring about different environmental qualities and conducting diverse forms of business activity. As discussed earlier, in the past it was possible to imagine a world where most people's relationships were contained within a place-based community, the idealised village, the place-based social community or *gemeinschaft*, where everyone knew everyone else and shared experience and values together (Frankenberg, 1966; Mayo, 1994). Today, we share space, but our social relations are stretched across regions, nations and the world, and the biospheric consequences of what we do may affect people on the other side of the planet. Global relations infuse every element of the lives we lead in particular places. As a result, spatial and environmental planning has become an arena of governance not just for solving the problems of 'local' communities, that is, people-in-places, but for addressing the connections between what happens in particular places and global economic, social and natural environmental relations. The challenge of managing co-existence in shared spaces also requires the interlinking of the economic, social and environmental dimensions of contemporary life, from the point of view of people in households, firms and agencies, and associations of various kinds. It means bringing together on a territorial basis relations which have been separated off in many cases into institutionally distinct functional sectors – for example, economic development, housing, transport, education and health – in order to identify precisely where the points of strategic common interest lie, and to build on the institutional capability to address them.

Behind these pressures lie the restructuring forces which have transformed much of the economic organisation of companies, and re-shaped thinking about social life and environmental quality. Spatial planning systems and practices are struggling to escape from conceptions, modes of thinking and modes of organising which made sense in mid-century but have lost their utility in the social and material contexts of the 1990s. The challenge now is discover and develop approaches which are more appropriate for contemporary conditions. This is very evident in Western Europe at the present time, where there is a new surge of interest in strategic spatial planning in urban regions (Healey, Khakee, Motte and Needham, 1996). In the US, this is paralleled by a renewal of interest in comprehensive land use planning (Innes, 1992; Stein, 1993). Two cases from Europe illustrate the pressures for change and the tensions between new ways of organising and traditional spatial planning practices. The two cases shared the European Union/European Council of Town Planners Awards in 1995 for innovation in urban and regional planning.

Lyons: the power of a new spatial conception

Lyons in France is an agglomeration of 1.26 million inhabitants. Changes in the local economy have led to high levels of unemployment and increasing social segregation and alienation. During the 1980s, key public and private sector actors came together to develop ideas which consolidated into a new strategy for the metropolitan area. In this strategy-making effort, participants drew on a long tradition of public-private collaboration in promoting development. The new impetus in France towards decentralisation put the Mayor of Lyons in a key role with respect to investment and regulatory power. Consensus was built up across the various communes in the metropolitan region, with the spatial strategy being used to develop and articulate the consensus. The strategy, encapsulated in the rhetoric of a 'European city', was visualised in a way which both expressed the general spatial organisation, as with the plans of the physical development planners discussed in the previous section, and indicated the spatial dynamics which would guide change (see Figure 3.1). The use of a spatial organising idea in co-ordinating different actors and building consensus was a critical ingredient of the approach, which has now become a model and key point of reference throughout France (Bonneville, 1995; Motte, 1996).

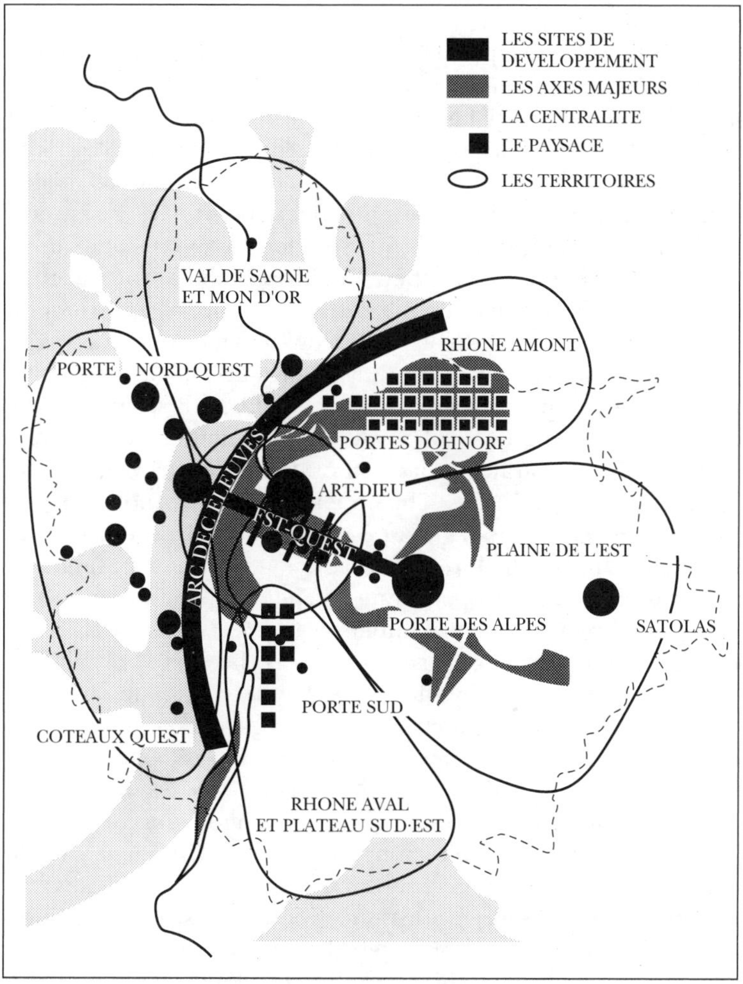

Figure 3.1 Lyon: general planning scheme
Source: Agence d'Urbanisme de la CURLY.

Lancashire: economy and environment: a sectoralised debate

In Lancashire, an English county of 1.4 million inhabitants, the planning department had for many years managed its land allocation and land use regulation functions with an inward-looking perspective. Its preoccupations were to redistribute opportunity from the more affluent west to the eastern parts of the county which suffered from industrial decline, to promote development in the core of the county and to protect the areas valued landscape and high quality farmland. In the late 1980s, this political and administrative consensus was affected by two new forces. The first was the growing concern with issues of environmental quality and sustainability, which developed as a diffused grass-roots feeling, but was given added force by local Labour councillors, who saw its significance as they sought to mobilise to challenge the centralism and neo-liberalism of the national government. This lead to the setting up of an environmental forum, drawing in discussion groups across the county, to produce an environmental audit and develop policies. Meanwhile, and largely separately, the county was drawn into North West Region initiatives to develop a regional business strategy – a collaborative effort between private firms and local authorities. The impetus for this was both the perceived weakness of the regional economy, and pressure from the European Union, which released regional development funds on the basis of a well-developed strategy. The problem for Lancashire has been to relate these two initiatives together. In its draft structure plan, the key mechanism for this is the spatial organising concept of transport corridors (see Figure 3.2). The corridors have an inter-regional function, expressing the county's location in a European context. They also provide a way of focusing development as far as possible within urban areas or near public transport routes. This provides some accommodation to environmental interests and builds longstanding distributional aims to concentrate resources in the older industrial areas in need of regeneration. However, with their greater basis of information and awareness as a result of the environmental forum work, many groups have challenged this attempt to combine economic development and bisopheric objectives. They claim it does not go far enough, as greenfield sites are still being released for economic development purposes. There is still no easily accessible forum where environmental and economic interests can discuss issues together (Davoudi *et al.*, 1996).

These two examples illustrate well the role of social interaction in building policies and spatial organising ideas, developing frames of reference and systems of meaning across diverse social networks which then have some prospect of enduring. If they endure, they then have the capacity to structure subsequent

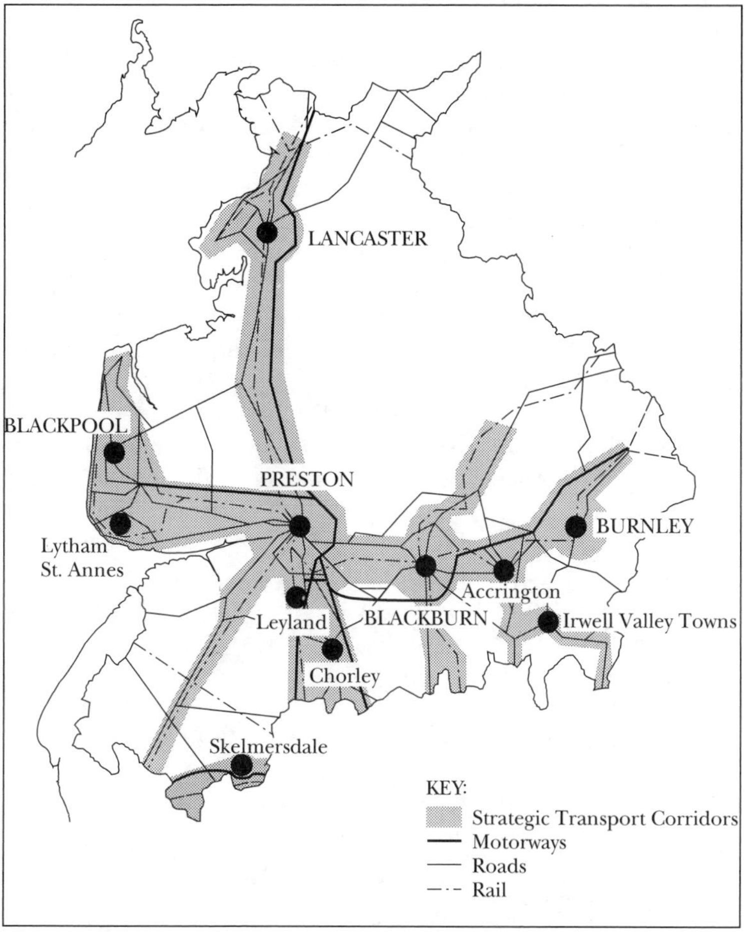

Figure 3.2 Transport corridors: spatial strategy in Lancaster
Source: drawn from Lancashire Structure Plan 1993.

investment and policy agendas in the future. They illustrate the kinds of pressures for change in thinking and acting which are faced by political communities in urban regions in Europe today. They also show the significance of institutional differences in shaping how pressures for change are met. Both countries have a history of centralism in government. In the British case, this is combined with a long-established functional sectoralism, which makes spatial co-ordination difficult, and with a traditional separation between the public and private spheres. In France, a strong spatial consciousness is well developed in the policy culture. In addition, powerful mayors took advantage of decentralisation in 1983 to take hold of and integrate areas of government policy, drawing on planning traditions, established in the 1960s, of regional co-ordination and partnership between private and public sectors (Barlow, 1995; Motte (ed.), 1995).

These institutional differences create substantial difficulties in defining spatial and environmental planning as a policy field, since its remit and nomenclature in each country is a product of particular institutional histories. It is therefore difficult to find a widely-recognised general term to describe the practices to be discussed in this book (Williams, 1992). In Chapter 7, in the context of the discussion of governance and public policy, planning will be defined as an approach to governance which embodies a policy-driven approach, a long-term and strategic orientation and which interrelates economic, social and environmental dimensions of issues in ways which recognise their complex space–time dimensions. The argument of Part II is that the new pressures in urban regions demand a capacity to interrelate issues to do with economic development, environmental quality and social quality of life within a framework which acknowledges the different and diverse stakeholders in the dynamics of urban region change. A *spatial* dimension is therefore crucial. The term *environmental* is taken to mean the qualities of places, as places to live, as places to do business, as part of natural ecological systems, and as an expression of cultural meaning. The term *planning* is taken to mean efforts in the collective management of shared concerns about spatial and environmental qualities, expressed in explicit policies which emphasize a strategic orientation to co-ordination between diverse actions and a relation between policy and action.

The phrase used in this book is therefore *spatial and environmental planning.* Implicit in this definition is a focus on the qualities of localities, regions and places. The practices encompassed in the term spatial and environmental planning could relate to any place or area which is recognised locally to have meaning. Such areas could range from the scale of the neighbourhood, where people physically co-exist as neighbours, to the region, where people share common facilities, such as infrastructure systems, or are tied into common relations, as in housing markets and labour markets, or in the ecological relations of water systems, and waste disposal arrangements. However, the particular organizational and legal form which provides the hard infrastructure for such planning practices, and the cultural communities which build up around the practices, will always vary from place to place, reflecting specific institutional histories and geographies. Nor is there any necessary connection between the practices of a formal system for spatial planning and the qualities embodied in the concept of planning as defined here. It is quite common for formal systems to lose track of the aims which led to their formation. The strategic emphasis on spatial organization may become separated from the detail of establishing land and property rights or even disappear altogether. New initiatives in strategic planning may then arise outside the formal institutions of the planning system (Healey, Khakee, Motte and Needham, 1996). The above definiton merely helps to define the scope of concern, and, in combination with the normative criterion for judging public policy articulated at the end of Chapter 2, to provide a perspective from which to evaluate how governance systems are responding and could respond to the challenge of managing co-existence in shared spaces.

Spatial and environmental planning as a social process

Spatial and environmental planning systems and practices are thus a part of the governance relations of a country, a region and a place. The nature of policy, and of planning as an approach to policy, is discussed in more depth in Chapter 7. Following the institutionalist approach outlined in the previous chapter, planning practices must be understood as both 'inside' formal government but also interrelated with business and social life. This interrelating happens through social networks which frame systems of meaning and provide intellectual, social and political capital which can help both to mobilize and limit policy and action in the area of spatial and environmental planning policy. In the cases of Lyons and Lancashire discussed above, strategies were developed by drawing together networks that had been going on separately before. They drew on knowledge resources, too, about trends, about issues, about data and measurement. They also drew on the cultural resources of the policy communities which had built up around the formal systems and practices of spatial planning activity. Both cases represent an attempt to break out of an established political-administrative way of doing things, to bring in new players and new perceptions.

Planning practice is thus not an innocent, value-neutral activity. It is deeply political. It carries value and expresses power. The power lies in the formal allocation of rights and responsibilities, in the politics of influence, the practices through which 'bias' is mobilised, and in the taken-for-granted assumptions embedded in cultural practices. Unpacking the power relations of any instance of planning systems and practices thus requires attention to Lukes' three dimensions of power (Lukes, 1974; and see Chapter 2). The way this power works, in privileging some interests, some stakeholders and some forms of knowledge and reason over others, structures the practices of individual instances, and expresses the systematic nature of the constraints on those involved. This is well-illustrated in the story of an advocate planner, one of Paul Davidoff's students, in Boston in the 1970s:

> We had gone to Boston's redevelopment office one summer morning back in 1966 to explain why our group was helping a neighbourhood organization oppose the city's official plan. That plan would have removed the neighbourhood in order to build a new city-wide high school. Our small contingent of four planners made our presentation to Edward J. Logue, the agency's director, in his office overlooking the demolition and reconstruction of downtown Boston. We said neighbourhoods should be able to choose their own planners and explained that such a process would make planning more democratic. He listened with a patient smile, asking only a few questions as he sat facing us from the end of his large conference table. When we finished, his smile vanished. 'So long as I'm sitting in this chair', he said, 'there's

> only one agency doing planning in this city, and that's this one!' (Goodman, 1972, pp. 60–1)

But structural power is embedded much more deeply than merely in these formal confrontations. It lies within the implicit assumptions about how things should be organised, what people are like and what they can do. When planning agencies take charge and resist consultation, citizens are forced into negative, oppositional responses. For example, people who want to be consulted about what happens in their neighbourhood are labelled as narrow minded NIMBYs (Wolsink, 1994). Some planners claim that citizens do not understand strategy, so there is little point in consulting them. But perhaps the problem lies in the way 'consultation' was conceived and carried out. For example, when business people meet residents' groups in disadvantaged neighbourhoods, they do not realise that a boardroom layout is alien and intimidating to many (Davoudi and Healey, 1995). To change systems, and to re-make structures, requires an effort to challenge the relations of power on all three of Lukes' levels, the formal, the 'behind the scenes' and the embedded dimensions of power, and a recognition, as Foucault argues, of the power relations of the finegrain of practices. This requires reflection on the process of organising to undertake planning work as well as on the issues in hand.

This means that planning work is not just about the *substance* or specific content of issues, for example, about how to produce adequate housing, or reduce traffic congestion, or conserve water supplies. It is also about how issues are discussed, and how problems are defined and strategies to address them articulated. Questions of *process* as a result are as important to local environmental planning as questions of substantive content. This is reflected in the preoccupation with process in the policy analysis tradition in planning theory discussed in Chapter 1. Process questions focus on the active work of *making* policies and strategies which endure (see Chapter 2). Process innovations are as significant an outcome of planning activity as are substantive outcomes. Interactive, collaborative planning processes are currently attracting attention in the spatial planning field because they offer the possibility of both mediating among the concerns of multiple and diverse stakeholders and building place-based institutional capacity.

The approach adopted in this book thus presents spatial and environmental planning as a social process within which those involved identify matters of collective concern, define problems, draw on knowledge resources, articulate solutions and develop ideas about how to put the solutions into practice. It is an activity conducted by, and in relation to, specific people concerned about specific places. How it works out is contingent upon the particular history and geography of these places. Further, it is a dynamic process. The activity of thinking about what the issues are and what to do about them itself changes the situation as people learn about what is at stake and what their own values and interests are. Spatial and environmental planning as an activity is not just a *response* to problems. It has the potential actively to shape, or *frame*, the ongoing flow of events and attitudes (Rein and Schon, 1993). It contributes to the enterprise of building up institutional capacity in urban regions, through ways of thinking and ways of organising over issues to do with co-existence in shared spaces. Yet it is not independent of the particular situation. The context of planning work is thus not just an external 'box' enclosing an 'action space' for planning activity. The context is actively present in the finegrain of planning activity, and is itself re-made through such activity. Spatial and environmental planning practices are embedded in specific contexts, through the institutional histories of particular places and the understandings that are brought forward by the various participating groupings, and the processes through which issues are discussed. Through this double activity of *embedded framing*, spatial and environmental planning practices thus both reflect the context of *power relations* and *carry power* themselves.

The spatial and environmental planning to be discussed in this book is therefore not just about technique and procedure. It is not merely about the technical capability in producing master plans or subdivision layouts, though this may be a part of a local planning process. Nor is it just about technical analysis, of local housing markets, or the impact of particular projects, or the condition of properties, or the capacity of water basins, though such analysis has an important place in local planning. Nor is it about a procedural practice undertaken by supposedly 'value-neutral' experts, apart from politics and interaction with stakeholders in urban region change. Instead, it becomes a social process built up from the particular social relations of a place. If this is so, then planning processes need to work in ways which interrelate technical and experiential knowledge and reasoning, which can cope with a rich array of values, penetrating all aspects of the activity, and which involve active collaboration between experts and officials in governance agencies and all those with a claim for attention arising from the experience of co-existence in shared places. It is this position which informs this book.

Part II

THE CHANGING DYNAMICS OF URBAN REGIONS

Introduction

Part I set the activity of spatial planning in the context of a specific viewpoint on social relations. This stressed the importance of individual agency, but not in the form of isolated individuals. Instead, individuals were presented as inhabiting and actively constructing everyday lives in interaction with others. Through the various social relations we have with other people, we develop systems of meaning and ways of organising which provide 'cultural resources' through which concerns about local environments are identified and ways of organising to address them are called upon. This interaction, though, always occurs in the presence of, and is shaped by, the powerful structuring forces which organise economic life, social mores and political habits and attitudes. Social change is the product of this continuous interaction between the creative activity of agency in relation with others, rethinking, affirming and changing situations, and the organising power of structural forces.

Planning, in such a conception of social relations, is understood as an interactive process, involving communicative work among participants, during which issues, problems, strategies and policy ideas are given form and meaning. It involves interpretive work. In many contemporary planning systems and practices, the interpretive work of earlier generations has become embedded into the practices of governance, in rules of procedure for zoning ordinances and obtaining planning permits. The challenge today is to assess critically these structuring processes inherited from the past, and to re-mould them to be more sensitive to the diversity of ways we live and do business these days, and to how we now perceive our relations with the natural world.

This challenge is particularly powerful and complex for spatial planning activity. The range of people with a 'stake' in a place – a neighbourhood, a landscape, a city, a village, an urban region, a territory – is potentially vast. Some of these people will be forceful and articulate. Others will be silent, or unaware of their stake. Some will be in a position to draw on rich 'relational resources', strong in knowledge and power, through which to argue for particular ways of identifying issues and arriving at policies, proposals and investment and regulatory decisions. Others may be skilled in calling up actual or metaphorical 'allies', for example the support of a government department, or a landowner, or the metaphor of 'future generations' or 'the findings of respected scientists'. Dissenting views may exist but have difficulty in getting leverage on debates, because their world view is too distant from the dominant discourses (Latour, 1987). The form and content of the communicative work of spatial planning is therefore a terrain of multi-dimensional power struggle between different social groupings, carrying different structuring dimensions into the arena of policy development and implementation. The outcome of these struggles is inherently locally distinctive, depending on the mix of key players and the viewpoints they bring into play. Yet it also expresses the power of systems to structure these viewpoints and the way 'local games are played'. There may be systematic tendencies to exclude certain groups, certain dimensions and certain ways of understanding. Individual instances of planning work may in turn generate new examples and principles which have the power to transform or become absorbed into wider systems. The case of the new planning in Lyons discussed in Chapter 3, which has become an exemplar for other planning exercises in France, is a case in point.

If local contingency and local interpretation are so important to how spatial planning work is done, then it could be argued that there is no need to 'know about' the social dynamics of social and economic change and our relations with the natural world. This will be revealed through the interactive and interpretive work of spatial planning itself. This position has been taken by many planning practitioners and some theorists. Some argue that those engaged in planning activity do not need the store of knowledge and understanding built up by social theorists seeking to interpret the dynamics of social relations. Rather, they should learn to interpret the social world in the particulars of specific situations, so as to develop theory-in-practice. Such a view underlies the arguments of Donald Schon that theory should be made in the context of practice, rather than *a priori* (Argyris and Schon, 1978;

Schon, 1983). It represents a struggle to escape and resist the continual simplification of the particularities of situations through broad spatial generalizations such as those of neo-classical economics, or Marxist theory, or postmodernism.

Yet our interpretations are shaped by our preconceptions as well as by the empirical reality we come across. The danger with relying solely on theorising-in-practice is that the 'deep structures' of power embedded in our ways of thinking and organising, will remain unnoticed. Such a failure to notice could have the effect of unwittingly reinforcing the power relations and driving forces which are constraining the invention of new practices. If spatial planning these days involves communicative encounters with people from very different social relations, with different ways of thinking and systems of meaning, then some tools are needed to alert those involved in spatial planning processes to the range of potential 'stakes' in local environments and the management of co-existence in shared spaces. Social science research and theorising provides such resources. It provides a store of theorizations and empirical investigations into the dynamics of social change, and the spatial and temporal dimensions of these dynamics. It offers intellectual resources which help us understand 'what is going on', and how our 'bits of experience' may be related to what is going on elsewhere. It helps us work out the relative significance concerns us in a particular context. In our globalising world, such understanding is of particular value in grasping the power relations within which our lives are embedded. Specifically, social theory assists in understand the structuring processes, the 'driving forces' which enter into our daily lives. It helps us to understand their dynamics, and our chances of challenging them, or using them to our advantage. It helps us to be alert for Lukes' 'power at the third level' (see Chapter 2).

The purpose of Part II is to provide such 'intellectual resources'. Specfically, it aims to:

- illustrate the strength of the institutional approach to the analysis of urban region dynamics;
- provide ways of thinking about the potential 'stakes' which people may have in local environments, the systems of meaning and claims for attention which these bring into play, and the relation between these and the structuring

forces which represent consolidated power structures which bear down on how people recognise their stakes and argue about them;

- examine the case, and the opportunity, for collaborative approaches to spatial planning activity, and particularly those which offer the possibility of broadly-based involvement by a wide range of stakeholders;
- contrast these approaches with earlier conceptions of social dynamics and local environments.

Organising such a review is a challenge in itself. It is easy to become caught inside the established structures of disciplines (such as sociology, economics and biology), or of traditional policy sectors (social, economic and environmental). The spatial planning tradition, as discussed in Chapters 1 and 3, has long struggled to overcome these divisions, recognising their interrelations in local environments. This appreciation of the interplay between social, economic and environmental dimensions of daily life, business life and attitudes to the environment is a major force in contemporary thinking. The institutional approach tries to capture these interrelations through the focus on the relational worlds in which people live, and which tie people into different spheres of existence.

Some division is necessary, however, to provide different 'windows' into the interlocking relations of the 'worlds' we live in today. Part II is organized around three perspectives – the world of 'everyday life', the world of 'business life' and the world of 'biospheric life' (Chapters 4, 5 and 6). Each is viewed from the point of view of the policy conceptions which have been used to grasp it, and the contemporary challenges being raised in relation to collective concerns about the management of co-existence in shared spaces.

This then provides the basis for the 'missing dimension' of this review of the social relations of local environmental change and our attitudes and actions towards it. This is the arena of governance, or the identification and management of matters of collective concern to political communities. Part III is devoted to the governance dimension, and specifically to developing the possibilities and implications of a communicative approach.

4 Everyday Life and Local Environments

The relations of social life

Organising our lives is an enormous challenge to each one of us. Yet its dimensions are strangely neglected in much policy literature, which cuts us up into bits of relevance to the organisation of government activity. Spatial planning touches us at many dimensions, however, as we move through local environments in our daily routines, or select where to live, send the kids to school and look for work. As we look out on the world, and on the environments through which we move, we view it from the point of view of our life strategies. What opportunities are there, what constraints and oppressions, what resources can we reach and how are we frustrated? Managing our existence has multiple time-scales – daily and weekly routines, yearly patterns, 'career' and personal development trajectories and generational time. As we think about what we need and what to do, we discover layers of 'stakes' in places – places to live, places to work, to go for holidays, places which symbolise aspects of our identity and culture, places we fear. Living is also hard work, as we seek out means of economic survival, manage household activities, provide social-psychological support to others, fulfil obligations to kin, friends and neighbours, take part in associations, get involved in creative activity or absorbing careers or pastimes. Some places provide a helpful context for all this work, others provide many hurdles, such as poor local transport or lack of playspace for children or lack of childcare. Changes in local environments – the creation of a new park, the building of a new road, the closure of a school – may have major consequences for the delicate patterns of everyday life which people build up. They upset daily life and may threaten people's sense of opportunity and identity. It is hardly surprising that there is much concern about the qualities of local environments and much complaint at changes to them.

We all recognise in ourselves and in others the immense diversity among people, yet we make generalisations too – about what people do, about men, women, children, the elderly. A major problem for policy activity is how to recognise diversity but yet act fairly as between people. One solution is to see each of us as autonomous individuals, with equal rights, to vote for example. In this conception, we vary according to our preferences. Neoclassical economics treats us in this way. It recognises that we have preferences, tries to observe or impute these, but does not ask where they come from. It looks to psychology for help in understanding how preference structures come about. Sociologists, in contrast, particularly ethnographers, tend to understand us in a different way. The sociological 'imagination' recognises that we are born into social worlds and that our ways of thinking and modes of being are constructed through interaction with the social relations in which we find ourselves as we grow and develop. It is this perspective on the 'intersubjective' nature of our consciousness which underpins both the notion of communicative action, as developed by Jürgen Habermas, and the institutional interpretation of social life, as developed by Giddens and others (see Chapter 2).

Institutional analysts seek to retain the sense of individual agency in referring to people, while recognising that our identities and 'sense of self' are constructed in relation to the social worlds in which we live. The approach emphasises that as individuals, we are formed and live our lives in social contexts, in interaction and continual communication with others. We construct our meanings and preferences in these contexts. This perspective is encapsulated in Habermas's concept of 'the lifeworld' (Habermas, 1984). But this lifeworld is not necessarily a coherent, integrated set of mores, expectations, perspectives and strategies. In our complex societies, open to multiple influences, we are exposed to all kinds of possible modes of existence. As the Italian sociologist, Enzo Mingione (1991) argues, we live our lives in a mixture of different types of relationship. Some are given to us, such as our family. Some are provided for us, for example, by governments, in schools and hospitals, or through the work we do. Others we actively construct for ourselves, as we seek out friends, clubs and likeminded others. Most of us live in multiple relationships these days, and we often face challenges as the demands of one relationship conflict with the demands of others.

Mingione argues that our problems in managing daily life and developing our 'life strategies' are not just about how to balance different demands. Even the principles on which these demands are constructed may be different. Many of the social relations of the contemporary world are based on associations, which we can choose to get involved with. The relations which build up in these associational forms rely on organizational rules and common 'interests'. But we are also involved in relations which we do not choose and in which we have 'given' responsibilities, such as our household, our family and our kin. These depend on reciprocal relationships among members. It used to be thought that modern societies replaced reciprocal social relations with associational ones. However, economic development research is showing the significance of social relations and obligations in creating or inhibiting the climate for particular types of economic activity (see Chapter 5). Feminist research, meanwhile, shows that women have frequently sustained reciprocal forms of relationships in the spheres of life over which they have most control (for example Hayden, 1981). Furthermore, as the formal economy looks increasingly less likely to be able to sustain us all, many are turning to reciprocal forms of relationship for livelihood as well as social welfare. We thus in our 'lifeworlds' shift around among our relational resources, transferring ways of thinking from one to another, or trying to resist the domination of one over another. Modern society is now often characterised as one where 'systems' and 'structures' take over much of the work of providing for our existence, but at the cost of increasingly penetrating our 'lifeworlds' (Habermas, 1984). Their withdrawal through economic restructuring and neo-liberal policies leaves many bereft, lacking both the economic means of survival and the social supports of family and kin.

Institutionalists, then, emphasise that we live in multiple relational webs which constitute our lifeworlds. Through our lifeworlds, we define ourselves and the way we relate to and live with others. Our attitudes and values, and the interests we have in our local environments, in where things are, and our demands and needs with respect to how we move around in space and make use of the built and natural environment, are defined in the context of our relational worlds. Through these, too, we develop interests in, and ways of, collaborating to do something about the problems we face as we co-exist in shared spaces and seek to turn spaces into places. We categorise and classify each other, making divisions between ourselves and others, particular others who we see as different in some way. Through these processes, we articulate the abstract structures which surround us, in our assumptions about what to do and how to do it. We carry power along with us. The result, where there are major differences in people's relational lifeworlds, may be the domination and exclusion of those who have fewer bases of power to draw upon. A great deal of the practice of land use regulation is harnessed to the attempt by some groups of people to keep different 'others' out of neighbourhoods, in the practice of 'exclusionary zoning' (Ritzdorf, 1986; Huxley, 1994). Some analysts have called this locational conflict or a 'politics of turf' (Cox and Johnston (eds), 1982).

In the present period, the vigorous flowering of the processes unleashed by the dynamics of modernisation has led to major changes in how we live our lives and how we think about our social worlds. It is difficult even to get a sense of the diversity of 'lifeworlds' in which people live these days. Yet any exercise in local environmental planning needs to attend to the dynamics and diversity of the way people live in places if it is to help meet needs and demands, avoid trampling unwittingly on people's interests and values and find ways of working together in place-making projects with the various peoples who co-exist in a place. This chapter explores how these issues have been thought about in the planning tradition. It looks at three shifts in conceptualisation: from the quantitative treatment of people and households to the analysis of social networks and lifeworlds; from the analysis of class position and the justice of resource distribution to the recognition of diversity and the multiple dimensions of domination and oppression; and from the concept of place-based community to that of 'everyday life'. In conclusion, the basis for a broadly-based collaborative approach to managing co-existence in shared spaces is assessed.

People and households

Traditionally, planners have assumed people were more or less the same – a standardised unit. The most extreme version of this is Le Corbusier's standard measure for building and urban design, his modular man (Jencks, 1987). Standardised individuals had standardised needs. Planning technique then dealt in numbers of people. Planners wanted to know how many people would live in a place, how many households they would form, how they would be distributed between age groups and how many jobs, schools and hospitals they would need. The great British planner, Patrick Abercrombie, had little to say on population and social structure. His proposal for a town survey prior to preparing a plan merely proposes a section on 'population', the content of which covers 'actual amount, with increase and decrease; occupation and diurnal movement; and density' (Abercrombie, 1933, p. 134). The preoccupation of these mid-century planners was with urban form (Gans, 1969; Boyer, 1983).

To provide information on people understood as quantities, planning analysts turned to the science of demography, to predict population change in terms of trends in mortality and fertility, in migration patterns and in household formation. Demographers tell us about general tendencies across the western world. People are living longer and longer. There will be many more people over 60 in our societies in the early part of the next century. Over 80, many of them will experience the health and care problems of extreme frailty. There may be fewer children, as working women decide to have lower 'fertility rates' (Champion (ed.), 1993). Such figures clearly have implications for potential demands and needs for services and facilities such as education, health, social welfare support and recreation. However, these tendencies in the numbers of individuals in different age and sex categories are the product of changes in the units within which we live as households. Again, demographers tell us about numbers, about falling household size and the relative decline of household units in the form of the traditional nuclear family. Average household size has been falling in most western countries for some time. In the middle of the twentieth century, this was seen as a consequence of falling numbers of children per family. Now there are falling numbers of households with children, and a rapidly rising number of single person households. This is arising partly because elderly people live on, with their children forming separate households, and death breaking up partnerships. But there is much more to this trend. Young people seek to set up home on their own if they can; partnerships break up, dividing households. Despite re-combinations of divorced partnerships, the numbers of single-parent households is rising.

These trends result in a seemingly relentless pressure for more dwelling units in aggregate. Further, the kind of dwelling unit that households want is often different in location and form from the stock of housing units available in an area. In the 1950s and 1960s, the housing policies of many western countries were driven by the overwhelming demand for housing for 'ordinary families', couples with children. Now policymakers and the housing industry in many countries are under pressure to move away from mass housing programmes and provide a different kind of stock, more relevant to smaller households in diverse financial circumstances. There are implications too for the location of housing and the provision of transport facilities. How are elderly people to get to the health and care facilities they need, and how are young people to get to the work opportunities that bring them income and seek out the leisure opportunities they enjoy? Is it sufficient to depend on the car? Will people move to be near the facilities they need? Will public transport riderships increase to meet new demands and needs? How, generally, are people 'making use of space' these days?

Two examples illustrate the significance of these questions for spatial organization. Certain people over the next twenty years will be in a position to exercise considerable choice about where they want to live and work. In the present age, the largest category of these people are the skilled industrial workers and the professional service workers. These people tend to be well-educated, and to enjoy rich opportunities in their lifestyles. They devote a lot of time to work and thus need environments which enable them to accomplish the tasks of daily and yearly life with as few time constraints as possible. Preteceille (1993) and Savage *et al.* (1988) argue that these groups, the new 'service class', are likely to concentrate in areas with a high job density, good services and facilities, including multiple transport options, and a high quality social, visual and biospheric environment. It is the areas which can deliver these qualities which will experience most pressure for growth in new buildings in the coming decades. Other areas may also need new buildings, but people in these areas will be less able to mobilise the resources to achieve this.

The second example relates to the significance of household projections. New projections were produced for England in 1995, drawing on the 1991 census data. These imply an increase in households. The housebuilding industry has immediately argued that this will require an increase in land allocated for housing in development plans. Groups concerned with housing for social needs have been supporting them. However, the housebuilding industry builds primarily for middle income people. The household projections suggest that the major growth now is in single person households. Not all of these will be in a position to buy a house. The growth in accommodation may well take place through an expansion of renting within the existing stock or increasing occupation levels in existing housing. In other words, the translation from household projections to the potential demand for new dwellings units of different tenure types, provided by different players in the housing industry, is a complex and contested process (Bramley, Bartlett and Lambert, 1995).

Demographers also describe and predict the consequences of patterns of migration. There are significant differences between countries in the extent to which people are prepared to move, within urban regions, between urban regions and between countries. Italians and Germans expect to carry on living in the same place and frequently in the same dwelling for most of their lives. British households move on average more frequently, and US households a lot. Nevertheless, there appear to be three broad tendencies in migration patterns. Households are moving within urban regions, typically from urban cores to the more rural penumbra of regions and they are clustering in neighbourhoods with others with similar lifestyles. They are also moving within countries from regions with economic difficulties to more buoyant regions. And they are moving from poor countries and areas of political instability to areas of affluence (Champion, 1992). Such demographic analysis provides an indication of changing amounts – of demands and needs which may become manifest in particular areas. It shows up something of the diversity of ways people live these days. But some trends are very difficult to capture in our demographic data sets. For example, some people, especially young adults, are not living in households at all, but 'roam' during the year between different bed-spaces (Campbell, 1993). Others, more affluent and often retired, 'roam' between different dwellings they own or rent, often in quite different places. Others again have no dwelling, except the street, while still others live a nomadic life, travelling in trucks, as encapsulated in the image of the 'New Age' travellers.

The diversity of lifestyles seems increasingly to be slipping out of the demographers' ability to categorise and capture in quantitative data. At the level of neighbourhoods and urban regions, the reality of this diversity comes alive in daily experience. Here, aggregate trends become local specificities. How people experience the social mix and tendencies of their area needs to come into analyses of amounts. Data on trends merely provides a useful backcloth to what people feel is happening, and how this makes them think about their place. Demography provides some clues as to the pressures which the changing social make-up of an urban region may produce and of the trends which may develop. Yet its predictions deal in the *outcomes* of social processes – the processes of producing more healthy living conditions and more health care and the active pursuit of healthy lifestyles; the social context within which people decide whether to have children and in what social relation, and how they want to live with other people; the processes which frame the way households come to live where they do; the context of opportunities for acquiring a dwelling, or a means of transport; and the production systems through which a supply of dwellings and transport opportunities comes to exist. Demographers predict trends which are the *consequence* of shifts in means of livelihood, facilities for living (access to dwellings, to utilities and services, forms of welfare) and lifestyle ideas. In contrast, an institutional approach seeks to identify the social dynamics of the relations through which people pursue their ways of living and their choices (or lack of choice) about where and how to live. It is these relations and processes which need to be understood if the dynamics of social change in a place and what this means to people are to be grasped.

Identities, networks and lifestyles

This recognition opens up a huge area of discussion, in sociology, in popular magazines, the media and in normal conversation. It is often said that the defining characteristic of our times is our recognition of social diversity and our reflexive concern with our own sense of self (Giddens, 1990; Habermas, 1993). This section will draw out four strands from the discussion which have particular significance for how we think about our local environment. The first is the change in women's roles and self-perceptions; the second relates to the meaning of home and family; the third relates to trends in lifestyle and cultures; and the fourth to the meaning of work.

Re-making gender identities

A major cultural change this century has been the re-evaluation of women's identities as equal socially and intellectually with men. In demanding equal opportunities, in work, family life, politics and leisure, women generate demands for the supports which will make this possible, and reduce their role as supporters of men and their working lives. The social consequences of this shift in terms of the household units in which people choose to live, in ways of working and demands on public welfare provision, are only slowly being understood (McDowell, 1992; Little, 1994a, b). Yet they have significant consequences for the way people use and value space and place, for who gets involved in collective concerns for local environments and the ways people prefer to go about organising their concerns. At present, women typically still bear a disproportionate burden of the juggling act between formal work, family care and household work responsibilities. This leads to long working days and complexly structured movement patterns. This is well-illustrated in Friberg's analysis of the daily lives of working women with children in Sweden (Friberg, 1993) (see Figure 4.1).

Where women live, the support facilities available to them and the travel opportunities they have access to have a significant effect on the weight of this burden. For this reason, women may make their choices about where to live and work to minimise the difficulties they face (Friberg, 1993; Hanson *et al.*, 1994).

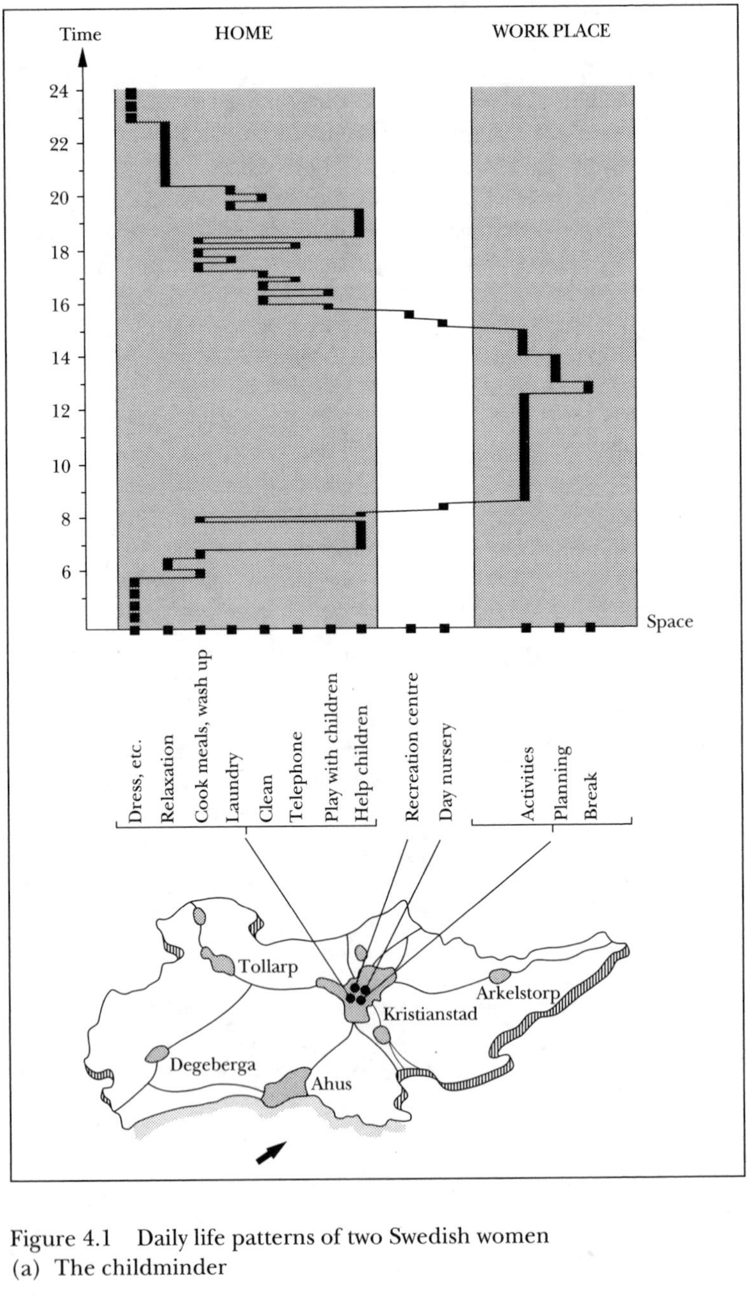

Figure 4.1 Daily life patterns of two Swedish women
(a) The childminder

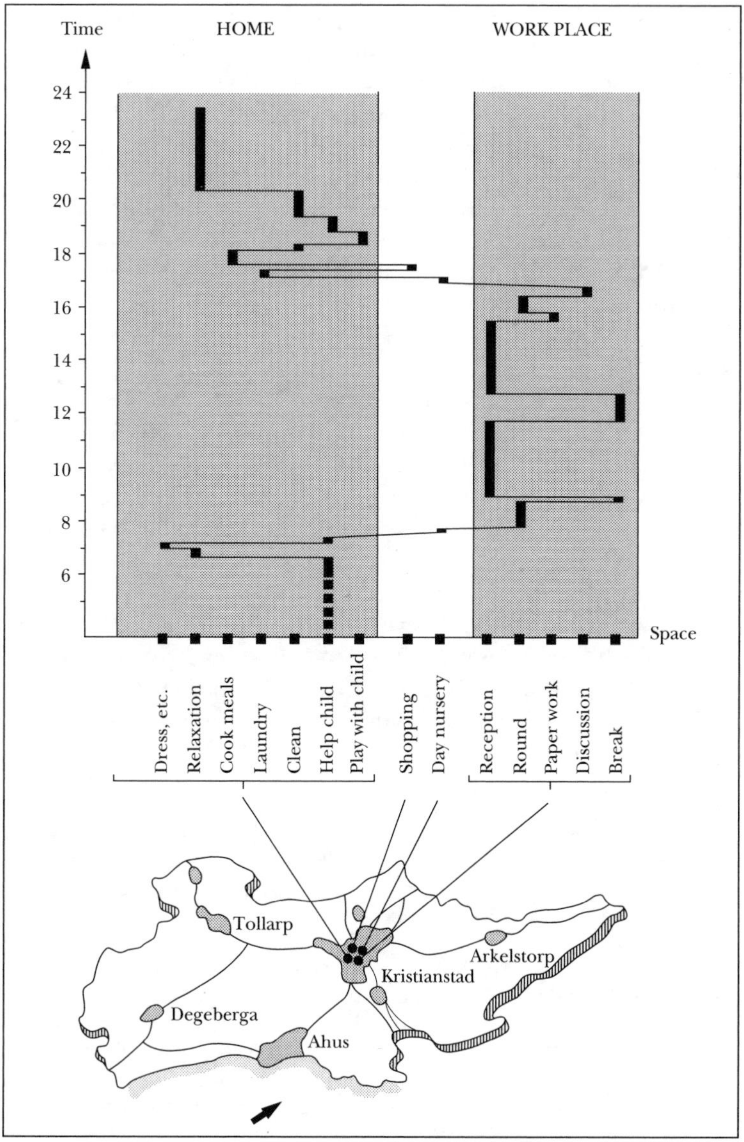

Figure 4.2 Daily life patterns of two Swedish women
(b) The doctors
Source: Friberg, 1993, pp. 155, 161.

Men, meanwhile, are faced with substantial adjustment problems in their expectations about how they should live in the household relation and who they should expect to work with. The result is considerable tension within households, and often conflicting demands on local environments. This is at its extreme in some neighbourhoods affected by high unemployment and reductions in welfare benefits, as may be found in many British cities. Women in such neighbourhoods often become involved in community development and talk of concerns for safety and security, for themselves and their children. Whereas in more affluent neighbourhoods, such talk may express fear of attack and burglary rather than direct experience, in poor neighbourhoods there can be no doubt that women experience a daily reality of threat (Campbell, 1993; Wood *et al.*, 1995). But the reasons for this threat are complex, and much more than issues of environmental design and management. They relate to the construction of gender identities. Men in such places, who once expected to leave their neighbourhoods each day for the social world of the workplace, now have to work elsewhere. They may seek out arenas where they can establish peer group position and the social contacts which work once provided. Bea Campbell, in her book *Goliath*, describes the explosive consequences in some riot-torn neighbourhoods in Britain.

> The crisis of public space on the (working class housing) estates was not caused by people's congress, but the extinction of their economy and the erosion of *co-operative* use of public space, its tyrannical appropriation and degradation by lads who terrorised the men, women and children with whom they shared space. .. Men, of course, were the traditional model for this capture of sociable spaces – they met in bars, pubs and clubs designed for their exclusive enjoyment. Men's relationship to estates tended to be like their relationship to home – not exactly a place to live so much as a place to leave, to return: to come and go. Work and pleasure were expected to be located somewhere else. Their social behaviour appeared in the contours of their spatial relations, and they provided the model for their lads. Mass unemployment changed the men's relationship to space because when their means of making a legitimate living was destroyed, then their licensed means of episodic escape – waged work was withdrawn. They were stuck at home. The lads, on the other hand, stuck to the streets. (Campbell, 1993, p. 320)

Re-thinking home and family

Women are re-evaluating the meaning of home and family. Work on women's positions in the home has identified the home as a site for domination and conflict as much as solace and support (Hayden, 1981; McDowell, 1992; Altman and Churchman (eds), 1994). This raises questions about the conception of household, home and family in public policy. Traditionally, planning conceptions have assumed that the household, the dwelling, the home and the family were the same thing, encapsulated in the model of the nuclear family, supported by a male breadwinner and by the welfare services of the state for health and education (Wekerle, 1984; Little, 1994a, b; Huxley, 1994; Gilroy, 1993; Gilroy and Wood, 1994). The home/dwelling in post-war policy in Britain and the US was the focus of social life and informal care, with households encouraged to invest their savings in purchasing and improving it (Hayden, 1981; Harvey, 1985). For many people in many societies, social life revolves around home and dwelling. For households with reasonable resources, dwelling units provide rest-space, playspace, workspace, a telematics communication centre, an arena for all kinds of hobbies, and a refuge. Investing in home building absorbs a great deal of many people's energies (sometimes called 'sweat equity' – see Hall, 1988) and incomes. Through the home, households tie themselves to specific places as the organizational base for social life.

But the erosion of state welfare support and the breakup of households has created new pressures on home life in many western countries. Resources now have to be found to pay for health and education services, at a time when a secure job cannot be predicted for a lifetime. As Mingione (1991) argues, this leads people to greater reliance on informal networks of support outside the immediate household, particularly kinship networks. There are enormous variations in the richness of kinship networks, in their social 'reach', in terms of the resources people can get access to, in the obligations which go with them and the spatial 'spread' of networks. While there are still many kin groups that are rooted in a place, most such groups have members somewhere else. In many kinship networks, resources earned in one place flow back to another. Family and kin act as a source of material support, through family capital and other informal services, through access to knowledge resources and social contacts, as well as by providing a store of experience of ways of organizing things, from tasks such as collaboration in child-rearing, house-building, managing a business and organising complex events, such as weddings and funerals.

If, following Mingione, kin networks are becoming more important in contemporary conditions, then a major factor leading to inequality betwen people may lie in the social and material richness of the kin networks to which people have access. These can be replaced to an extent by relations among neighbours and friends, and by associational relations in clubs and interest groups, but such relations are likely to be less stable and enduring. Professional and career-oriented people may often find it easier to 'buy in' the services they need, rather than rely on kin, although it seems common to build up local friendship networks to provide mutual support, particularly where childcare is involved (Mingione, 1991; Savage *et al.*, 1988). Such households are typically active in multiple dimensions besides home and work, and work to very tight time budgets (Friberg, 1993; Little 1994a, b) Their demands lead to pressures for retail opportunities which fit into their travel patterns and time budgets, and for services such as childcare and good transport. The 'two career' household, a key component of the 'new service class' referred to above, may seek out locations which are rich in work opportunities, leisure and lifestyle attributes, social networks based on common interests, with 'low' entry barriers, and support services. Households face significant problems these days in choosing how much time and effort to deploy in maintaining their kinship networks and how much in building up their work careers. The latter may bring short term material rewards (moving to follow a good job); the former may bring longer term security. How people work these tensions out will affect what they are looking for in their local environments and how far and how they are prepared to get involved in collective management.

Diversifying lifestyles

It is not just work, family and friends which define how we live now. We also make choices about lifestyles, in relation both to what we individually enjoy doing, and how we present ourselves to others. This shapes our choices about the dwellings we prefer (when we have choice), their furnishings, the goods we invest in and the leisure pursuits we follow. As in other areas of our lives, the lifestyle decisions we make are the result of a complex meshing of opportunity, particular social traditions and broad trends and fashions which sweep across the world through the media. Thus everywhere has become enmeshed in the glorification of the car as a lifestyle symbol, as well as a transport resource. The celebration of sport and healthy lifestyles generates proposals for new kinds of leisure developments and housing projects, and new facilities, such as marinas and cycleways. But new lifestyle fashions can also generate further conflicts. For example young people's clubbing and its association with drugs as well as alcohol can create a lively use of city centres in the evening, but in a form which older people find threatening and hostile. Consequently, young people come to take over particular places at certain times of day. And there may also be hostility between groups of young people. Therefore, the management of city centres in Britain these days is a complex balancing act between reducing theft from shops, cutting back on drug dealing, keeping order between different groups and encouraging lively city centres which will attract consumer spending and institutional investment (Bianchini, 1990; Montgomery, 1995).

Reviewing the meaning of work

All households need access to material resources to survive, obtain a dwelling and pursue their interests. The traditional assumption was that these would be provided by a job in the formal economy, followed by a pension on retirement. It was also expected that people would have a job in one firm most of their lives. As a result, home–work–leisure–welfare relations were lived out in one place. But this assumption has evaporated. Even the highly valued skilled workers of the dynamic new industries and companies may only have a limited period of their lives as a 'company employee' (Handy, 1990). As companies have had to become more flexible to survive, or have closed, people have experience of redundancy, and the search for new jobs. Many young people are finding it impossible to find work. Of the work that is available, much of it is part-time. Companies are encouraging subcontracting practices and new forms of homeworking. Flexibility for companies means vulnerability for employees. The new telecommunications technology encourages this, and those with more expertise and labour power in the marketplace often welcome the resultant liberation from office hours, just as those with parenting and other care responsibilities welcome part-time and flexible work opportunities. 'Waged work' is thus becoming a less frequent way to obtain material resources; and individuals can expect that some periods in their lives will lack such opportunities.

People are also being encouraged to set up on their own, selling anything from expertise to eggs. Such small business operations have the advantage of flexibility, combining income generation with household work. But they may also draw on the resources of several household members, in an informal way (Wheelock, 1990). There are other tendencies to the *informalisation* of work, as people try to put together a livelihood from several small jobs, or try to find ways of maintaining social welfare payments while supplementing these with odd jobs. There is also evidence in 1990s Britain that growing numbers of households in poorer neighbourhoods are supplementing their incomes through illegal activity, ranging from failing to declare income sources when claiming benefits to direct engagement in a criminal economy (Campbell, 1993). Still looked on with suspicion in the developed world, the 'informal economy' has traditionally provided business and employment opportunities at low entry costs (see Chapter 5). More households these days seem to be engaged in the kind of *pluriactivity* which was previously associated with the Celtic croft, or the Italian peasant farm. But this apparent flexibility is often combined with long hours and poor working conditions. In western economies, the standards established in the past to protect workers and ensure fair competition often make informal economic activities illegal.

Thus household budgets may depend on a mixture of wages from the formal economy, informal sources of income, transfers from kin, and welfare supports. Individual households may vary significantly in the nature of their strategies and the relational webs they use to get access to material resources. This too can lead to tensions between neighbours. One household may decide to invest their resources in building up the market value and social status of their dwelling. Another may decide to keep housing costs low and devote family savings to educating the children or to a business venture. The two households will react very differently to policies to improve the condition of their properties and their street. Such differences may lead to conflict between neighbours and encourage people to seek out neighbourhoods where others with their lifestyles and aspirations live. Public policies which seek to overcome socio-spatial segregation into neighbourhoods of different social status, by mixing tenures and house types, may encounter considerable resistance where people have experienced conflict with neighbours or fear that the value and social status of their dwelling will fall. Local environmental planning exercises need to pay careful attention to the way any policies and proposals might affect people's survival strategies.

The social relations of everyday life

These new understandings of social dynamics have two implications for the management of co-existence in shared spaces. The first relates to the recognition of the importance of the social relations in which people live for defining their aspirations and providing material, emotional and moral support. This involves looking beyond demography to the relations people in households have with each other, with kin, friends, associates in leisure and formal work arenas, through the formal work relation, through state support and informal opportunities. Spanning out from households, these relations may spread widely in both space and time. The household becomes a key node in social life, within which the various members work out how to bring together and deploy their resources, in relation to what they care about. In this work, collaboration and reciprocity are critical qualities, rather than competitive behaviour. Skills in this collaborative task are an important resource for wider collaboration in local governance. Given the traditional role of women in household management in many cultures, it is no surprise to find women playing a key role in community development programmes, in both the developing and the developed world (Moser, 1989)

The household is a key *economic* unit, recognised in the increasing use of the term, the *household economy* (Friedmann, 1992), as well as a unit of *care,* of social support. Accomplishing the combined task of resource management and mutual care is demanding work, and it still falls disproportionately on women. A dwelling is thus much more than a unit of shelter. It is a workplace, and it is often actively produced through DIY activity. It is a location for a household's material goods. It is a social setting. It is a lifestyle symbol and a base for many leisure activities. It is also a home, refuge and a solace from the difficulties of life outside, though within it may be hidden deep conflicts between household members. It is hardly surprising that the defence of the dwelling and its immediate environment from 'attack' – by new development, by change in the social status of neighbours, by burglary and assault – has become a major preoccupation of the management of local environmental change in many cities. But managing change in conditions of such delicate relations and social diversity has the potential to harm as much as it enhances. Land use zoning regulations in particular can be particularly damaging, by reducing both opportunity and flexibility for households, in the name of a particular view of local environmental quality (Huxley, 1994).

The second implication is that, through these various dimensions of household life, we learn different ways of thinking and different ways of organising. The 'management' of family relations, of household activities and parenting work, and of relations with friends and fellow-members of associations develops a rich store of skill in building agreements and organising activities. These skills, often underpinned by principles of co-operation and reciprocity, provide a valuable, though largely ignored, resource for collaboration in local environmental planning.

The power relations of social life

In the complex relational webs in which we live, we are not equal. Those who have more resources and who are surrounded by circumstances which allow them to pursue their lifestyle choices have more power than those who do not. But power lies in more than just possession. It involves power over the rules of social relationships, the power to define how other people do things and what they are encouraged to value. Sometimes this power to dominate is obvious, visible power at the first level, in Lukes' terms (see Chapter 2). But it may also be invisible, deeply ingrained in our social practices and modes of thought.

These relations of power in any situation derive from modes of thinking and social positions attained previously. They act as structures, which frame subsequent actions (see Chapter 2). Local environmental planning exercises are themselves attempts at 'framing' the rules for managing co-existence in shared spaces and consequently affect who gets what (see Chapter 3). Some exercises seek to express and maintain the power relations within which they are constituted. Others set out to transform them (Friedmann, 1987). One direction of transformation has been the redress of inequalities through redistribution of material resources. There is a strong strand of idealism within planning culture, which has argued that the primary objective of planning efforts should be to even out material inequalities and to reduce 'disadvantage' (Gans, 1969; Hall *et al.*, 1973, Ambrose, 1986). There is a close link between these objectives and the broad ideology of postwar welfare states. More recently, such concern with inequality has been modified with an emphasis on oppression, domination and exclusion, and the multiple systems of power which produce these phenomena (Young, 1990). Thinking about the forces which structure relations of power helps to identify which are the potentially powerful actors, interests and groups in any situation of actual or potential conflict over local environmental quality. It helps us not just in thinking clearly about what is obvious about power relations. It helps too in uncovering the deeper structures of power embedded in our thinking and acting.

There is a very considerable literature on how social relations and social life are structured. This focuses on the *dimensions* of power, what really divides us up into the more powerful and the less powerful, and on *social groupings*, and ways of categorising ourselves. Such categories are not merely of analytical interest, as they are used for policy purposes, for example, income or occupational groups. In local environmental planning, such groupings are often used in identifying demands, needs and disadvantage, in social impact analysis and in public participation exercises.

Pluralist power relations

An obvious dimension of power is our differential ability to get access to material resources to enrich ourselves and our kin. The possession of material resources gives us power to acquire goods, to buy influence, to realise our lifestyle ambitions and to exercise power over others. Some social theories assume our ability to get access to resources is the result of individual differences. Underpinning the assumptions of neo-classical economics is the notion that individuals are all competing for survival, and that the best interests of the human species are served by the 'survival of the fittest'. Such ideas have been translated into the political and social sphere in notions of societies composed of a plurality of groups, competing for space in local environments. Such groups could be seen as self-differentiating, based on income, lifestyle preferences, ethnicity and culture, an expression of the American notion of the 'melting pot' of immigrant cultures out of which their nation was seen to be composed. These pluralist ideas seemed particularly attractive in describing US local environmental politics, where the structure of local governance leaves local political communities with power over local land use regulation. The pluralist conception seemed to allow for diversity to be recognised in the conflicts between interests. It is in the context of such pluralist conceptions that Gans and Davidoff focused their attention on those groups who were disadvantaged in this competitive struggle (see Chapter 1).

Weberian power relations

But how do some individuals and some groups come to be disadvantaged? Two famous strands of thought challenge the pluralist conception by asserting the importance of classes and systems. Max Weber, writing in the context of Central Europe at the turn of the century, recognised the significance of social status and position. He saw society as divided into social classes of different ranks. Higher ranks had better access to material resources, but, as significantly, to the resources of social position. These discriminations were not the result of individual achievement, as in the American self-image, but of birth. Higher ranks exercised control over opportunity not just in the marketplace, but in control over access to jobs and, often, to local environments (Giddens, 1987). An example of such control is the way in Britain an administrative class of civil servants was produced through the channel of public schools and Oxford and Cambridge universities, which then provided priveleged access to jobs as well as significant networks of influence. Social life was not just a pluralist competition between groups. It was an unequal competition, in which the higher social ranks were able to maintain control of the best situations. At the level of local environments, in the pluralist United States, local communities have used zoning regulations to make social distinctions and exclude people from neighbourhoods who do not 'fit' a group's social image. In class-ridden Britain, élites could not only buy their way into exclusive environments, into country houses and village life. They could turn the whole planning system into a mechanism for the defence of the countryside, defending indirectly their privileged access to the lifestyle of the landed gentry (Williams, 1975; Marsden *et al.*, 1993). Such an approach to social differentiation encouraged a categorisation of people by income, occupational and educational status.

In both the pluralist and the Weberian conceptions, inequalities arise because some groups have captured control of favoured niches in social and economic life. Having achieved this control, they then find ways to hang on to it. Policies directed at reducing inequality could therefore be targetted at 'redistribution' giving those disadvantaged in the game of the market or of social position access to the resources and positions of the successful and the priveleged. A good example is the British post-war housing policy ambition of a decent home for all, as embodied in the building of dwelling units with high interior standards (the Parker Morris standard), and the related policies for universal access to education and health care (Ward, 1994).

Marxist conceptions of power relations

Marxist theory challenged this conception. In this theorisation, class positions did not just arise out of social history. They were actively produced by the processes of capitalist exploitation (see Chapters 1 and 2). It was in the interests of capitalist classes to keep workers' wages low in the early stages of the Industrial Revolution. It was in the interests of these classes to challenge the power of pre-industrial land-owning elites. It was in the interests of the capitalist classes in later stages of capitalist development to foster the development of a middle class benefitting from the wealth generated by capitalism and prepared to support governments which promoted capitalist interest. And it came to be in the interests of capitalists to support state provision of housing, education and health for their workers, as this reduced the costs individual firms had to pay out in wages. It was then in the interests of capitalists to support economic policies which helped economic restructuring and generated high levels of unemployment. The interests of the 'class of workers' was formed by the struggle not just to improve their status and living conditions, as implied in Weberian models, but to capture in their turn control over the machinery of government to limit the power of capitalist classes to define agendas and opportunities. Such conceptions set the interests of 'workers' against those of 'capitalists'; the 'people' against 'business'. Those campaigning to change this situation took policy aim at the relations of production, rather than at redressing balances between rich and poor, since such inequalities were seen as the product of the particular capitalist forms of production relations. The provision of housing and the management of local environmental change was to be taken out of the control of capitalists – the private, market-driven sphere – and given over to the control of governments promoting the interests of workers. This conception of course hugely homogenised people's interests, in terms of their structural relation to the means of production, that is to economic interests, and crowded out the diversity of situations of both capitalists and workers. Yet in the communist countries, and in socialist and social democratic strategies in Western Europe in mid-century, such conceptions of class interests dominated much policy debate and political ideology. This dominance reflected an important and ever-present reality, that those who control the means of production and the organisation of economies, have a significant interest in regulating the way the rest of us think and act. They have the power, through control of material resources, and through influence on government and through ideology, to structure the relations in which the rest of us live.

Challenging multiple structures of domination

Pluralist, Weberian and Marxist conceptions of social order competed for attention in social theory and public policy in the 1970s. These debates still live on in texts written about local environmental planning in Britain (Kirk, 1980; Cockburn, 1977; Ambrose 1986). But they have been transformed and overtaken by a challenge to the pervasive focus on power as arising within the spheres of economic and political organization. These other sources of power are characterised not by the language of material inequality but by concern with domination, with oppression and limitation and with obvious and subtle forms of discrimination and exclusion.

In most western countries in recent years, there have been many initiatives to overcome these discriminations. Opening up local environments to people with different forms of physical impairment is steadily changing the arrangement of our streets, the layout of our parks and the labelling of our lifts. Bringing women's voices into the worlds of business, of politics and of intellectual life is already beginning to have major consequences for both how we think and how we act, for, as already noted, women often bring along experience of collaborative practices into the world of business management and governance. Being in a majority, women can claim attention for changes to these conceptions and, slowly and over time, allow other ways of thinking and acting to come forward. Coming from all income and status groups, disabled people in organizations have been an effective pressure group, pulling at our democratic consciousness. This has helped to push forward the general case for a more sensitive recognition of the diverse dimensions of social division.

But these processes of change are slow, and there are vigorous debates about how past discrimination against previously 'invisible' interests has come about and how it should be changed. Some argue, like the Marxists, that the problems are deeply embedded in the dynamics of social structure; that Western societies are organised along principles which institutionalise structures like patriarchy or racism. If this is so, then policies to give excluded groups voice, resources and access to position will not help very much. Such perceptions, as with the Marxist analysis, lead to projects for revolutionary change, to capture control from those currently in charge, in order to reshape institutions and cultures. But others argue that, however strong the prejudices and discriminations may be, social change is a slow process. Particularly for many women, who have tended to retain values of supportive co-operation against the competitive thrust of economics and politics, revolution by slow collaborative steps could be more enduring and less likely to marginalise people than the aggressive promotion of alternative strategies. The challenge, following this line of thought, is to find ways of overturning one form of discrimination without producing another.

An institutional approach to power relations

An institutional approach to the power relations of social life seeks to avoid identifying power solely as an attribute of membership of particular classes and categories. It follows the Marxist focus on relations between people, but recognises much greater complexity in the forms and relations of power. It focuses attention in particular on the way the relational webs within which people live distribute power within them, and give access to material, social and cultural resources. Inequality is generated by differences in the richness of the webs people have access to. We can try to 'make our own fortunes' by building up links with networks with richer resources than ours. But our capacity to do this is affected by our inheritance. We are 'born into' relational webs in particular places, and into access to very different possibilities as a consequence. Further, many relational webs are infused with barriers, which, deliberately or not, serve to exclude relations with many who may seek entry. Such exclusion may be legitimate for groups clustered around a special cultural or religious project. It is inherent in the concept of kin. It becomes problematic where such exclusionary relational webs provide privileged access to resources that many would like to share. Social change may therefore be encouraged by strategies which aim at opening up relational links and challenging exclusionary ones where these reinforce inequality.

These multiple dimensions of potential social division, and the inequalities that are generated through them, raise enormous problems for efforts in managing co-existence in shared spaces, as the potential social diversity is substantial. Consultative strategies for developing local policy often founder on conflicts of interest, the power of dominant interests or the realisation that those actively involved in a consultative process in fact represent a minority interest.

The problems here are not just about conflicts of *interest.* If this were so, then the issues could perhaps be captured in an analysis of individuals and their *preferences,* in the traditional vocabulary of neo-classical economics. The differences lie deeper, in ways of being, of giving meaning and value to things and relations, and in styles of expression. The divisions cut across all our customary units of analysis. Even households are often riven by gender and generation divides. As Forester emphasises, to give power to the range of voices in a planning exercise requires a capacity to listen, not just for the expression of material interest, but for what people feel and care about, including the rage felt by many who have grown up in a world of prejudice and exclusion, of being outside, 'the other' (Forester, 1989). A recognition of the power relations of everyday life experience is of critical importance in developing the practices for collaborative local planning discussed in Part III.

Social diversity and social polarisation

That the rage of those who feel discriminated against continues to be justified is clear from the evidence of continuing tendencies in social inequality (Pinch, 1993). Much of our social policy inheritance grew out of Weberian and Marxist conceptions of societies in which large numbers of ordinary households did not have decent living conditions. The solution was mass provision, and it was hoped that this would redress inequalities. The failure of this conception became evident in the 1960s and later as academics and policymakers became aware of conditions in many urban neighbourhoods. Here, people were living at the sharp end of multiple dimensions of social discrimination and disadvantage. Despite efforts to improve the conditions of people in such situations, through national, people-targetted measures and urban place-targetted measures, evidence from the US and Britain at least shows that, through the 1980s, the scale of disadvantage between those doing well in our societies and those doing badly has increased (Pinch, 1993).

The persistance of tendencies for increased inequality in opportunity and access to the means of life and livelihood is a troubling phenomena for affluent western societies. The big effort in mid-century was to improve the conditions for the mass of the population. Why are some people not benefitting from this? If most people can enjoy a relative abundance of resources and opportunities, why is it that some do not? How this answer has been addressed by policymakers has had a significant effect on the policies which have been followed. Those who view social organisation in terms of individual achievement identify the problem as lying in traits of character and upbringing of those who do not manage to 'get on' in our societies. Many people who have put a lot of effort into 'getting on' will tend to support such a view. Many will have seen the differentiation going on as an active process in their neighbourhoods and schools, often without realising that their own views of what 'getting on' involves sets up labels and barriers which it may be difficult for other people in their neighbourhoods to accept or overcome. One of the main thrusts of equal opportunities policies has been to break down barriers over which people have no choice – the stereotypes of race, gender, physical ability and culture, and lifestyle (see Little, 1994b; Gilroy and Woods, 1994 on women's policies; Thomas and Krishnarayan, 1993; Thomas, 1995, on race).

However, the unequal distribution of opportunity and access to resources is a consequence of more than individual life strategies and neighbourhood labelling practices. It is also a product of the power relations discussed above. These power relations confront individuals with hurdles of very different sizes and burdens of very different weights as they seek to pursue a meaningful life. Each of us inherits a different mix of assets, burdens and hurdles, depending on the relational webs into which we are born and the places where we start out in life. The condition of inequality, as Weber and Marx argued is re-created through the generations, and is not easily overcome by individual effort. This argument reinforced by those who emphasise the reproduction of gender and race prejudice. This perception leads to policy targetting which seeks to redress inequality through attacking discrimination in ways of thought, through changing behaviour and language, as well as affirmative action to increase the presence of previously excluded groups in decision-making arenas. Redressing inequality thus becomes a project in cultural transformation, changing how people think about themselves and other people.

But such strategies, which have been pursued with some vigour in Anglo-Saxon countries since the 1970s, have benefitted primarily middle class members of previously excluded groups. Those without education, with very limited job market opportunities, who lack stability and richness of kinship relations, who live in neighbourhoods where they are exposed to opportunities to engage in crime and drug culture, who experience declining social welfare benefits, and progressive loss of urban services due to policies which require such services to be paid for, have found the hurdles to opportunity continually raised in front of them, and the burdens on them increasing, as the assets they have diminish. As Pinch (1993) argues, the mixture of factors producing this situation varies from place to place and country to country, depending on the health of local economies, the structure of welfare laws and labour hiring practices, and on culture and the way prejudice operates in getting access to benefits and jobs. But the phenomenon of growing numbers of people 'marginalised' by the 'mainstream' society has led to images of the growth of an 'underclass' of people, on the edge of or 'outside' the social mores of households who are busily 'getting on', or maintaining what they have (Jencks and Peterson (eds), 1991; Boorah and Hart, 1995). As the prospect of a secure job for life recedes for everyone, and as all households and kin networks have to give more attention to sustaining the conditions of their own survival and reproduction, many look with fear on the conditions that build up in the areas where such 'marginalised' groups tend to live. The fear has a double edge. On the one hand it is a fear of attack, and of corruption, by crime and by alternative values. On the other, it is a fear of sinking into a similar state. This fear sets up a powerful dynamics of differentiation and exclusion, through which social groups with opportunities seek out socially similar neighbourhoods in which to live, with consequences for the social composition of children in a school, patients in a hospital and who stands for and gets elected to local governments. This process of *socio-spatial segregation* at the level of neighbourhoods has a long history in American cities, characterised in the image of 'white flight' from downtown to the periphery. Similar tendencies are now evident in British cities, as those who can move in search of residential locations which provide their version of quality of life (Findley and Rogerson, 1993).

Such trends are intimately intermeshed with the politics and practices of local environmental planning, reflected in demands from local neighborhood activists for ways of defending their neighbourhood quality. Social polarisation is thus an active, ongoing process of socio-spatial differentiation, through which labels of difference and otherness are generated and imposed on the excluded others. Such processes may be exacerbated where public policy for help to those in need concentrates the most needy in particular places, as has happened in British housing policy since 1979 (Blackman, 1995). A consequence is that those with least opportunity for participation in the institutions of the dominant politics and economy tend to find themselves spatially concentrated. Yet to label those living in such neighbourhoods with a common category, as in the popular media term the 'underclass', is to mask the diversity of reasons why people find themselves living in such places, and the many reasons why people find themselves excluded from opportunity (Gans, 1990; Campbell, 1993). Any study of the 'neighbourhoods of exclusion' finds both great diversity in personal circumstances, life strategies and opportunities, and often many mechanisms for helping people to manage in difficult times (for example, Wood *et al.*, 1995). Community collaboration may be a vigorous process in places which are nevertheless 'redlined' by insurers and hire purchase companies because risks are high and the capacity to pay is low. Informal mechanisms may build up to provide mutual support, from helping out to pooling resources.

But diversity within poor communities may lead to tensions too. Racial tension is often at its most acute in such places, making daily life a misery for families from races targeted for abuse. And some mechanisms of community control are not so pleasant, with informal moneylenders holding a strong power position, and strong families or gangs in effect acting as a form of local governance, legitimated by physical force. Public policies which seek to offer opportunity to people living in such situations face both overcoming the reality of the exclusionary hurdles set up by previous policies, while recognising at the same time, the complex and often hidden dimensions of the social relations of the life strategies which people in such situations evolve to survive. Labels such as 'underclass' serve merely to re-enforce the exclusionary hurdles and mask the fine grain of differentiation in such neighbourhoods.

Community and everyday life

Some contemporary commentators argue that the problems of social polarisation and antagonism which seem to be growing in our present societies are the result of the breakdown of 'community'. Politicians, citizens and planners often talk nostaligically of a time when everyone living in an area knew and trusted each other. The metaphor of community is commonly asserted in discussion of local environmental issues in Britain. Proposals are judged in terms of their impact on 'the community'. Projects are resisted as likely to threaten the existing community. Communities in urban and rural areas are offered the opportunity to get involved with 'community development' activities of various kinds. Sometimes the word 'community' is used merely as a synonym for 'the people who live in an area'. But the metaphor carries more meaning than this. It brings with it firstly the image of an integrated place-based social world, the *gemeinschaft* of German sociology (see Chapter 3). Secondly, it carries connotations of community in opposition to business, or government (Williams, 1976; Mayo, 1994).

The idea of the place-based community has a long tradition in planning thought. It encapsulated an idea of village life, where the relations of living, working, raising children, relaxation and managing common affairs took place in a place-bounded world, in which people lived in densely interconnected social networks, and shared a moral order, a culture of common values, systems of meaning and ways of doing things. People might be different, individually, and in their resources and opportunities, but they were assumed to inhabit a common moral and perceptual world, a common 'habitus' (Bourdieu, 1990), in which 'everyone knew their place' (Williams, 1975; Wiener, 1991). Within the city, this rural idyll was replaced by the image of the urban neighbourhood, in which people helped each other out and shared responsibility, for street security or for the care of children (Wilmot and Young, 1960; Jacobs, 1961). Integrated place-based communities were also identified in mining villages, and other 'company towns', where people shared a common work relation and built up a culture of accommodation and resistance to it (Frankenberg, 1966).

This ideal of a place-based community culture, a moral order, is as much romantic illusion as historical fact, as Raymond Williams shows in his analysis of the actual social relations of many rural areas in the nineteenth and early twentieth century (Williams, 1975). Tension and violence were probably much in evidence in urban 'communities', as they are today, and as they were in the times of the nineteenth-century inquiries into the conditions of social life in cities (Hall, 1988). Where such integrated place-based communities existed, they were often limiting and stifling, serving to maintain oppressions of class and gender. To turn back to this ideal of social organisation would be both impractical, given the forms of mobility available to people, and unacceptable to many, cutting people off from the opportunities for developing a wide range of social relations.

Yet we nevertheless co-exist in shared spaces. We often do have important relations with neighbours. Collaboration among neighbours can provide helpful solutions to a lot of the challenges of accomplishing daily life. Neighbours – in the street, the neighbourhood, the city and the region – often share common concerns, even though they do not share a 'moral order', or many of their other relations, with their neighbours. So there are real reasons why people who share common spaces might find it helpful to collaborate to identify and address common concerns. This does not mean that they have rediscovered *gemeinschaft.* It means that they are re-working the meaning of a place-based *political community.* If those involved rely on an assumed commonality of values, a common 'moral order', they are likely to encounter immediate hostility. Building political community requires awareness of diversity and difference while building up trust and understanding.

The second image carried in the word 'community' is as an opposition to a dominating force. We talk of community, or community versus the state or business, or the 'forces of capital'. Just as the notion of *gemeinschaft* drew individuals into a place-based moral order, so this image draws individuals together into an aggregate interest, the citizens, or 'ordinary people', versus powerful external forces. It expresses our shared interests as human beings trying to live our lives, versus the spheres of business organization and political institutions. Of course, those who mobilise these spheres and articulate most forcefully the power of systems are people too, and presumably are citizens with 'ordinary' concerns about managing daily life, about kin and friends. They too have to manage the relation between the life of formal work and other dimensions of living.

Another way of expressing this common concern, though immensely various in its forms, is to emphasise not our interests as citizens, or ordinary people, but in a more specific way, as the strategies and interests we develop through the challenge of accomplishing *everyday life*. This term partly refers to daily life (Lefebvre, 1991). It can also be expanded to include those concerns which inform us as we organise and worry about what we have to do each day, the material needs, moral purposes and emotional encounters which shape our aspirations and expectations. It represents a point of view which challenges the separation of work from other aspects of life, and the sectoral divisions of the delivery of government services. This point of view, repeatedly asserted over the years, has been given renewed impetus by the contemporary women's movement (Ottes *et al.*, 1995). In Scandinavia, a collaborative research project among researchers in Nordic countries produced a manifesto for this approach called *The New Everyday Life – ways and means* (Nord, 1991). This argues that women are more aware of the problems of the present 'split-up everyday life'.

> It is partly a question of a concrete, physical split, which is the result of the functionalist way of urban planning. There is the dwelling, there is the day-care, here is the working place, here is the hospital where grandmother is. Each of them excellent institutions which solve the problems of dwelling, baby-sitting and care but which must be patched together in a complicated pattern of time and space.
> It is, however, not only a question of geography and physical distance. The split goes far deeper. The welfare-society is based on the necessity of somebody taking care of the work needed to tie together all these elements: homes, markets, public institutions. All of them with their special rules and logic which have to be learned. A great deal of women's time and energy is spent in the process of transforming these fragments of reality to something that at least reminds of a coherent whole. (Nord, 1991, pp. 11–12)

The analysis leads to an argument for an 'intermediary level', to tie together individual private lives and the formal public world (Nord, 1991; Horelli and Vespa, 1994). In this case, this informal *political community* is as much about the practical organization of living, working and caring activity as it is about making representations to formal government.

The appeal to 'community' can thus be reinterpreted to mean the assertion of the concerns of accomplishing life strategies and *everyday life* in the context of the forums and arenas in which *political community* finds expression, and in which collective activities are organised. It involves not merely the recognition of the integrated nature of living, working, reproducing and relaxing in the context of our lives, but the difficulty of accomplishing this integration in contemporary societies without huge organizational effort, an effort which still falls disproportionately on women. A key issue in local environmental planning in the coming decades is how urban region spatial strategy and neighbourhood spatial organisation can respond to reducing this burden. The market is already responding, as in the growth of large edge of town retail complexes, which cater well for the working, car-owning, middle-class parent.

This emphasis rejects ideal types of people's lives. It is linked to the recognition of social diversity in life strategies and lifeworlds. Yet people with different backgrounds and relational resources may wish to collaborate with neighbours, to ease the time–space hurdles they encounter, or to overcome isolation and build new social relations, or for some other reason. So, through the demands of the challenge of accomplishing everyday life, people may seek out a public realm in neighbourhoods, villages, towns, cities, regions, in which to discuss matters of common concern and combine with others similarly concerned to do something about them. The challenge of such activities is to finds ways of collaborating which can deal with different perspectives and priorities among 'neighbours', and develop the capacity to transform wider structures of power which make everyday life difficult. One of the rich areas of experience in collaborative consensus-building is in these arenas of community mobilisation.

Social life and local environments

The social tendencies at work in contemporary societies can be summed up as a shift from homogeneity to heterogeneity in our conceptions of possible lifestyles and household forms. There is now much more consciousness of social diversity and the differences among us within social scientific and planning thought than there was in mid-century. This has been accompanied by an increasingly diffused connection between people and places. Whereas neighbourhoods were once seen as places where different social groups intermingled harmoniously in a shared social order, containing most of the relational webs which people depended on for their survival, now our relational support systems spread across many dimensions. Neighbours live in different 'life-worlds'. The neighbourhood where we live may be little more than a collection of households connected only by passing in the street. Faced with social diversity and for fear of meeting with and mixing with different 'others', households may make locational decisions which will help maintain and reproduce particular lifestyles and life strategies, encouraging new forms of urban region spatial differentiation. Such active differentiation in turn encourages social fragmentation and conflict, and sets up barriers against those with least social and material resources to realise their life strategies. This becomes a mutually reinforcing process of social polarisation and exclusion, pursued through cultural labelling as well as unequal control over access to formal economy jobs and state welfare benefits. With the restructuring of economic activity to produce more labour flexibility, and the restructuring of welfare benefits to reduce costs to 'taxpayers', people are thrown onto the resources of household co-operation, and the support of kin, friends and community networks for both material resources and care. The burdens of these tasks fall disproportionately on women, because of the history of their social position, and on those with least material and social resources. One consequence of these changes is that the 'coping strategies' for accomplishing daily life, and the reproduction of daily life, are both diverse and complex, and often extremely sensitive to changes in the facilities and services available in local environments.

There are major implications of such social tendencies for local environmental planning. Firstly, we cannot address the diversity of our interests and values by the simple categorisation of people into the social groups of demographers and sociologists. Still less can we assume that similar kinds of people with shared systems of meaning and ways of organising live in particular places. In any place, there will be social diversity, both actively asserted and visible, and present but silent or invisible. Those living in a place will also draw in, through their relational webs, the concerns of others elsewhere. What it means to co-exist in shared spaces and what places could be made out of these spaces cannot therefore be approached in the formulaic ways of standardised zoning schemes or neighbourhood design rules. The challenge for the collective management of local environmental change is to discover what the diverse people in a place are concerned about and to find a way forward which will work for most people without excluding too many interests and values. Only then does it make sense to convert these ideas and understandings into the procedural, legal and financial tools available in planning systems. Even then these may need to be recast to serve particular local purposes.

The challenge of sharing spaces is made more complex these days not just by the degree of social differentiation which we now recognise. These differentiating processes are themselves dynamic. As people explore new lifestyle ideas, and find themselves exploring new ways of living, or try to cope with new limits to their material resources, demands are generated for new housing forms, in new types of location. People travel in different ways using new routes. They shop at different times in different places. The housing, retail and leisure industries respond to these shifts, and actively seek to push them along, by designing new products and offering them in new types of built structure in different locations. These not only produce conflicts as people living nearby object to the new. They may also change the spatial structure of urban regions. This generates an interest in re-thinking urban spatial structure; yet this too cannot be pursued in the imagery inherited from the past, with its metaphors of hierarchies of centres, land values radiating out from high value in city centres, and contained settlements surrounded by greenbelts (as in Abercrombie's strategies for the London Region (see Chapter 1)). Urban structure as read through how people these days use urban region suggests a fluid, multi-nodal and complexly-layered urban structure. Finding organising ideas with which to describe our dynamic urban regions to ourselves thus requires new efforts in imaginative capacity and socio-spatial understanding.

These socio-spatial dynamics in turn have the potential to generate substantial conflicts, over what places mean, over what environmental qualities are valued, over access to these. Wrapped up in these conflicts are the diversity of people's interests, life strategy objectives, and their relational commitments and their fears – fear of losing material and social resources, of encounters with different 'others', of burglary and of personal attack. Very easily, a neighbourhood playspace can be changed in people's imagination to an access route for thieves or a meeting point for threatening drug addicts. Fear, like moral outrage and aesthetic appreciation, cannot be reasoned away in the language of instrumental rationality. Ways of discussing issues need to be found which recognise these dimensions of people's concerns, and which allow the mediation and resolution of conflicts in ways which are at least seen as fair and legitimate by those involved.

But conflicts over local environmental change are not merely just between people. Wider forces carrying the power of economic and political organisation will permeate the way issues are constructed and debates conducted. These powerful abstract systems have paid little regard to the challenge of accomplishing daily life, partly because this has so frequently been rendered invisible – labelled as the private sphere and women's worlds. This suggests that public policy should give as much attention to social impact analysis as to environmental impact analysis and the interests of the business world. But such 'analysis' will barely capture the concerns arising from an 'everyday life perspective' if it is conducted through technical analyses of group interests or aggregates of individual preferences. It requires active discussion processes through which 'local knowledge' can be brought into play (see Chapter 2). This in turn needs a public realm, forums and arenas for discussion, in which there is sufficient recognition of diverse points of view, sufficent respect to allow many people to speak and be listened to, and sufficient trust to move from discussion of issues to doing something about them. Building the relational capacity to enable such discussion is a critical challenge in the re-building of *political community* in western societies.

However, in such discussion, it is not enough to make simple assumptions about who has membership of such discussion fora. A space is of interest not just to those who live there and those to whom these people are connected through their webs of relations. Its presence may be a potential resource or constraint on the life strategies of other people elsewhere. The images of such connections crop up regularly in local environmental planning, expressed in the terminology of LULU (locally-unwanted land uses) and NIMBY ('not in my back yard'). No-one wants a waste disposal plant near them, but there is a need for such a plant in every city. Some of us want to live in peace and quiet, and exclude the noisy bikers and ghettoblasters from our street. We would like to preserve our vistas and our open areas, but in doing so, we may be exacerbating the difficulties other people have in getting access to affordable housing. We want to keep our gardens green, cruise around in our cars and enjoy the huge variety of electrical gadgets now available to us, yet in doing so, we use up and pollute the resources which we and our children will need for survival. Many planning conflicts rapidly take on the form of 'us' and 'them', as if a conflict was between groups. This encourages strategies which are exclusionary. Local democracy, if it takes this form, rapidly becomes an exercise in the exclusion of weaker interests by dominant groups.

Yet these environmental examples make it clear that conflicts are as much *within ourselves* as between 'us' and 'them'. This recognition provides a basis for forms of democratic debate which are inclusionary and do not marginalise difference. The appalling conditions of inner city neighbourhoods in many American cities, and the active warfare and vocabulary of 'ethnic cleansing' in former Yugoslavia, provide images of the consequences of the search for an exclusionary escape from living with social diversity. Local environmental planning mechanisms are always in danger of capture by such forces, particularly where local governance mechanisms have considerable autonomy. This raises questions of the ethics of local environmental discussion processes, and the design of institutional contexts to safeguard rights. These issues are pursued further in Part III. The next chapter turns to the world of business and the economy, and discusses how concerns with local environments, and ways of organising to address them, appear from this powerful point of view.

5 Local Economies, Land and Property

Spatial planning and economic life

This chapter examines the concerns with local environmental qualities arising from the worlds of economic organisation and business life. A characteristic of western industrial capitalism has been the *separation* of economic life from everyday life, both in terms of time (work happens in factory or office time) and place (symbolised by the activity of going to work). In the context of western rationalism too, modern life has privileged material growth and technological development as a measure of welfare (see Ekins, 1986). Through the social technologies of skill development, company management and the development of the money form, and through engineering technologies, for transport and communications, and for labour saving devices, material resources have expanded around us, structuring our daily lives and our life strategies. These technologies have become systems which penetrate our 'lifeworlds'. The philosophy of the pursuit of material improvement, encapsulated in the strive for continual economic growth, provides the ideological underpinning for the dominance of economic organisation and priorities in public policy.

The relation between the pursuit of economic growth and concern for local environmental quality has always been an ambiguous one. Influenced by the conceptions of neoclassical macroeconomics, economic organisation has become the major preoccupation of national governments and international trade negotiations. Regional economies were interpreted as subsets of the national economy, structured by national policy (Richardson, 1969). The role of spatial planning was sometimes presented as promoting and accommodating economic activity, and sometimes as regulating it to safeguard other values, notably environmental conservation or social justice. In the language of economics, the purpose of spatial planning was to correct for internal market failures (economic costs) or to address external impacts of market activity (social costs) (see Bishop, Kay and Mayer, 1995; Harvey, 1987; Evans, 1985). A key theme of this chapter is that the local organization of economic life has a much greater significance for overall economic organization than this macroeconomic emphasis suggests, and that local environmental and institutional qualities have a key role in the competitiveness of urban regions in the present globalised ordering of economic life.

The interrelation of economic life with everyday life and the qualities of places was well understood by the planning tradition of the first half of this century. For Patrick Abercrombie, drawing on Geddes' conception of place–folk–work (Geddes, 1949), the key priorities for planning were the promotion of 'beauty, health and convenvience'. The term 'convenience' is used to encompass economic life, but as an integrated conception of utilities, presented primarily from the point of view of people as workers, but with an echo of the economic costs to government and taxpayers of different ways of building towns:

> Beauty and health stand condemned if they prevent commercial *convenience*; and it will be realised that convenience is the most clearly demonstrable of town planning advantages. The drawbacks of small ownership site-planning ... the impact of housing estates upon through-traffic routes: without some control of side inlets and riparian building most of the money spent upon new by-passes will have been in vain. Again, it is idle to attempt improved housing conditions for purposes of health without studying convenience of access from home to work. Town planning, in a word, intends to make the city in every way a more convenient place to work in, aiming at designing and remodelling its business quarters, manufacturing districts, railway facilities and water front, so as to save money to the business man and allow the citizen to go to and from his work with the least loss of time and energy. Scarcely of less importance is the question of determining the type of property to be erected, particularly in connection with the location of factories ... (Abercrombie, 1944, pp. 108–9)

This viewpoint, developed further in Keeble's textbook for planners in the 1950s (Keeble, 1952), put people first, the inhabitants of towns, and then sought to calculate how many jobs would needed (for male heads of households!), and how much land for industry and services should therefore be provided. Permeating the plans and planning texts of this period was the assumption that there would be enough jobs to go round. With Keynesian macro-economic policy to ensure 'full employment' (see Chapter 1) the right mix of regional redistribution policies and local activity in building factory units would ensure work for all. Theoretically, these ideas nested comfortably with economic base theory in neo-classical regional economics (Richardson, 1969). Regional economic models provided the basis for the urban systems models developed in the 1960s (see Chapter 1). These assumed an economic base, which then generated jobs, households, demands for services, and more jobs in the service sector. The modellers could then assume a hierarchical urban form, and play around with the consequences for traffic flows and residential location of locating industrial estates in different places (for example, Black, 1990).

Until the 1970s, urban and regional planners assumed that Keynesian policies had eliminated the possibility of recession aid that steady growth could be expected. Then, as another recession set in, local politicians, workers' representatives and local business groups in Britain were faced with the threat of local economic decline once again. Analysts now acknowledge that the 1950s and 1960s in Western economies were a distinctive period of sustained economic growth, during which it seemed less necessary to consider the preconditions for economic development. There is a much greater awareness these days of the periodicity of economic organisation, with interpretations of Kondratieff long waves of economic development, interrupted by periods of disorganisation and stagnation, or of transitions from industrial or Fordist economic organisation, to post-industrial or post-Fordist patterns (Amin, 1994). However interpreted, it is difficult to avoid the impact of *economic restructuring* on the landscape and social and economic life of many cities which grew rich in the period of industrial capitalism built on mechanical technology and fostered, in the British case, by the protected markets of the empire. Jobs ebbed away and obsolete factories and port facilities left vast areas of dereliction and pollution (Massey and Meegan, 1982).

The policy response in such urban regions has been to focus attention on ways of regenerating local economies. The existence of a stock of economic activity to be attracted to a place can no longer be assumed. This has led to the policy conclusion that it is not enough for local economies to rely on macroeconomic policy to generate work opportunities for people locally. The conditions for the survival of local economies have to be actively developed, to maintain existing firms and to attract what mobile investment there is. The perception that local economies need active development has been further fostered by the increasing mobility of economic activity. Even in the expanding sectors of economic activity, such as information technology and telematics, bioengineering, the financial services sector, and the leisure industries, urban economic interests find themselves in competition with those in other regions to capture and maintain companies (Harvey, 1985; Bacaria, 1994). This inter-urban economic competition began to emerge clearly in the United States in the late 1970s, and a decade later was vigourously developing in Europe. This creates pressure from local politicians, responding to lobbies for job creation and for the promotion of an improved local business climate, to develop an active role in the promotion of the local economy. Local economic development strategies aimed at building up local assets, accompanied by energetic urban marketting, have been promoted since the 1970s as a key 'trick' to play in the inter-regional competitive game (Piore and Sabel, 1984; Blakeley, 1989; Ashworth and Voogd, 1990). The place-making task thus became focused on urban quality as an economic asset.

This policy response to a new economic world now requires those concerned with economic activity in places to think much more carefully about how far and how it is possible to promote the survival and health of firms in an urban region through local strategies. It means thinking not just about spatial organisation and urban design, and about land and infrastructure, but also about labour skills and training strategies; about the quality of residential environments and cultural assets for the more skilled core workers of the new industries; about the development of skills in business management and entrepreneurship; and about the availability of finance for investment, as companies grow and seek out new market niches. It also means having a good knowledge of the competitive pressures and market opportunities which companies in different sectors face, and how this may affect what kind of local support they will need when. It also means understanding where and when firms are likely to cease operations in a region and how the consequences of this can be addressed. In Britain, Massey's pioneering work on the diverse reasons for job loss (Massey and Meegan, 1982) jolted thinking about local economies out of the economic base model within which the economy of a region was integrated with its core base industries, to a view of the urban economy as a complex collection of layers of economic relations linking companies to product inputs and markets with very different spatial ranges, and driven by different dynamics. Local economic development strategies in these diverse 'open systems' required a knowledge of the different competitive conditions in different economic sectors, and involved working out how to capture local benefits from companies during their sojourn in a region (Campbell, 1990; Cochrane (ed.), 1987). They also demanded a proactive approach to local policy, rather than merely the regulation of economic activities for social and environmental reasons.

This sectoral approach to local economic development seemed initially to leave the management of local environments and the regulation of land use and development on the sidelines. Such local environment management has come back into play for three reasons. Firstly, the provision of land, buildings and physical infrastructure remained important in keeping and attracting firms, and their supply was often one of the few tools which local governments could use to promote their local economies, especially in centralised Britain, given that subsidy and training programmes have typically been under the control of regional or national governments (Turok, 1992). Second, a 'good quality' local environment has been increasingly emphasised as an important part of the 'assets' which constitute marketable urban qualities in the competition for investment (Harvey, 1985; Ashworth and Voogd, 1990; Kearns (ed.), 1993). Thirdly, among the flows of inward investment to an urban region are those flowing into land and buildings. This brought land and property development activity into focus, as an important dimension of local economies.

Much of the literature on local economic development, in Britain at least, reviews the issues involved from the point of view of public policy. This chapter will set possible policy responses in the context of ways of understanding local economies from the point of view of firms. It will explore this through two dimensions – that of the *local economy* and that of *land and property development.*

The objective is to illustrate why local relationships are important for economic organisation, even though contemporary economic organisation generates pressures to 'disembed' firms from their regional connections. The chapter also identifies the potential 'stakes' which firms may have in a place, to illustrate what an institutional approach to local economies and land and property development activity involves and to develop the case for a collaborative approach in developing local strategies for managing co-existence in shared spaces, as a key element in building positive institutional capacities for proactive economic development.

What is a local economy?

Self-sufficient, export-base or open system?

There are many different ways of conceptualising the economic life of an urban region. These crop up in ordinary language and in local political debate, when problems and policies are discussed. From the point of view of people in households, the economy may mean a job, or the range of job opportunities. This was the dominant conception in British planning practice until recently. The task of local economic development was seen as the generation of jobs for local people. The measure of the health of a local economy was its unemployment rate. For those who own shops or have property investments, the economy may be seen in terms of the overall level of prosperity of a place. It influences how much spending power people have and how much rent shops and offices can afford to pay. Measures of local gross domestic product or consumer spending power may be more important for these groups than unemployment rates. Land use planning policies which use this understanding of an economy may emphasise 'the economy' or 'business'.

Increasingly, these two measures are diverging, as new technology realises the long-expected promise of 'job-less growth'. Restructured steel plants or engineering companies in Britain are now some of the most competitive and productive in the world. But they employ few people. Areas of job expansion are in the service sector, but much of this is relatively low-paid unskilled work. For this reason, there is often a political tension in developing local economic development strategies over the type of companies to support and the outcomes expected of such support.

Other ways of thinking about a local economy derive from regional economic geography. As outlined in Chapter 1, early regional economists often imaged a self-sufficient city economy, with agriculture and mineral exploitation as its base, generating manufacturing industries to meet the needs of farmers and workers. This in turn generated a service sector. Such a conception underpinned Howard's ideas of the 'Garden City' (see Chapter 1). It has been revived in some contemporary environmental thinking which focuses on developing local self-sufficiency, to avoid exploiting resources elsewhere and reduce the generation of exported waste (Beatley, 1994; Ekins, 1986).

The idea of self-sufficiency was soon replaced with that of an economic base formed from export-oriented manufacturing industry. This conception underpinned the regional redistribution and other industrial development policies pursued in mid-century. It also framed the planning analyses of both the physical town designers and the urban systems analysts, as discussed in Chapter 1. In British regional development policy of the 1950s and 1960s, industries were moved out of the 'congested areas', notably London, to provide the 'economic base' for new and expanded towns and to revive the flagging economies of the older industrial regions. A similar policy prevailed in France, focused on the promotion of 'growth poles' to counterbalance the pull of Paris (Perroux, 1955).

By the 1980s, however, jobs were falling in manufacturing industry due to the introduction of automation and the processes of economic restucturing. This encouraged the idea that the service sector itself could be the 'motor' of a local economy. Many analysts now divide services into 'producer services', provided on a national or international scale, and 'consumer services' generated by the people and firms in a place (Moulaert and Todtling, 1995). Thus the global financial capitals, New York, Tokyo and London, have as their economic base the production of financial services for the rest of the world. However, it is evident that these services are themselves also affected by restructuring, in response to technological innovation and a more competitive environment produced by deregulation policies at national level. The result is job loss in the financial services, and in many other consumer services where telecommunications advances have reduced labour time. The consequence for many office locations and town centres with a significant component of retail financial services is likely to parallel the impact of industrial restructuring in the generation of obsolete locations and premises. In the contemporary globally-open world, and in the context of an intense period of innovation in the new information and telematics technologies, a secure and enduring regional economic base seems hard to find.

These shifts in ways of identifying the economic base reflect the realisation that there is no one model for the economy of an urban region. Each 'depends' on a different mixture of key economic activities and networks. Each has its own specific ways of relating to its locality. The problem for contemporary urban regions is that the firms which make up its local economy may exist in relational webs within which the space of an urban region may be relatively unimportant. An urban region may merely provide, at a particular time, operating conditions which suit a company. The value of these conditions to a company may easily change as the market situation of the firm changes, or its relational requirements shift. Rather than being relatively fixed features of a local economy, firms must now be seen as transient and dynamic users of local assets and contributers to local employment and prosperity. But this does not mean that a firm's local relations are unimportant to it. Existing firms may prosper and new firms be attracted to locate in a place because something about the place 'adds value' to the firm's production relations. This effect could be produced by the quality of the labour force, the attraction of the local environment to skilled technicians needed for a firm, the rich base of knowledge, skill and contacts that may build up in a place, providing resources for research and development, or for recognising and opening up new markets, or for introducing new technologies. This shifts attention from economic analysis which focuses on particular industrial sectors, and how far and how to attract firms representing sectors to a region, to a conception of firms existing in a '*production filière*' or 'value-added chain', from primary production to final consumption. Firms develop niches in chains, but few can control the dynamics of the chain. Local economic development strategies can encourage firms, however, by finding ways to help existing and incoming firms 'add value' to their activities (Camagni (ed.), 1991; Camagni and Salone, 1993; Amin and Thrift (eds), 1994).

'Adding value' to open systems: the institutionalist perspective

Such an approach reflects the insights of an institutional approach to understanding the dynamics of local economies. In economic analysis, the institutional approach draws on the political economy of regional economic restructuring and on institutional economics (Hodgson, 1993). The first has analysed the way modes of capitalist production have changed, from the mass production vertically-organised firm captured in the image of 'fordist' production, to flexible production relations, with firms existing in horizontal networks of relationships (Boyer, 1991; Amin, 1994). The institutional economists focused on the institutional conditions for economic activity, meshing in with the political economists' interest in the changing institutional relations of production processes. In the political economy tradition, analysts emphasised the transition from fordist forms of production, based on hierarchically-organised mass production processes to more flexible organisational forms, with groups of firms in loosely-networked contracting relationships, able to produce differentiated products for more discriminating markets (Amin (ed.), 1994). There is more debate on the characterisation of 'fordism' and 'post-fordism', and the transition between them, than on the particularities of contemporary economic organisation, but there is general agreement on the increasing penetration of global economic relations in structuring the fortunes of individual firms, on the tendencies for greater flexibility in production relations, so that firms move away from vertically integrated companies to more flexible 'out-sourcing' arrangements.

There is also an increasing emphasis in the institutionalist literature on regional economies that a key factor 'adding value' to production processes arises from the social resources available in places (Granovetter, 1985; Amin and Thrift, 1995). Different places have different relational qualities, not just because of the working environment but because of the networks of everyday life in which people live. These generate knowledge resources, social contacts and cultural mores which may promote particular economic opportunities or restrict them. Such distinctive social environments, or milieux, have been identified in Amin's studies of the shoe industry (Amin and Thrift, 1992), in accounts of the economically dynamic Emilia Romagna region in Italy (Camagni and Salone, 1993; Harrison, 1994a, b), in Saxenian's comparison of Silicon Valley and Route 128 in the US (Saxenian, 1994), and in a number of other reports. These studies emphasise three key points about local economies. Firstly, that the locationally-specific assets from which firms benefit, and the difficulties they have, are linked to the social and political qualities of places. Secondly, that these assets are relational in form, producing an *institutional capacity* of a place, an embodiment of the relational resources available in the social networks of a place. Thirdly, this local institutional capacity is important for many firms, and the capacity to deliver it therefore matters to overall national economic performance. This recognition is now being given greater salience in economic policy, even in Britain. It is promoted as much by business groups interested in the qualities of their business environments as by local concerns with job provision and local spending power.

The contradictory consequence is that companies in flexible networks are less likely to be tied to a particular place for their sourcing and marketing, while at the same time valuing a supportive institutional context, rich in relational resources. These resources are partly long-recognised qualities, such as labour market attributes. They also include knowledge resources and relations of trust, to enable knowledge to flow easily around a local environment. Both draw on the wider social relations of places. They are 'embedded' in the specific geographies and histories of places, in the local cultures of meaning and organising. The concept of a dynamic industrial district, as symbolized in the 1980s by the regions of Emilia Romagna and Veneto in North East Italy, recognises the role of richness in such relational resources in promoting local economic growth (Amin and Thrift, 1992).

This conclusion could lead to an almost determinist conclusion, that competitive position in the global economy could depend on a region's past history and present location. This is to deny the active capability to remake ideas and build new relations. The institutionalist approach in effect shifts the emphasis of local economic development strategies from subsidising the provision of 'things' – specific jobs, training places, units of property, infrastructure projects, to building local institutional capabilities. This in turn focuses on building up new knowledge, new relations and new cultural orientations developing the 'intellectual and social capital of a place' (Innes *et al.*, 1994). Restructuring the institutional capacity of a place may then involve both disembedding and re-embedding the relation between everyday life and the business world.

The value of an institutional approach to a local economy in this context is that it focuses attention beyond firms and sectors to the relational webs within which firms flourish. It leads to a policy focus on building up the links which individual firms have with each other and with their places, through both specific measures such as local sourcing, and training arrangements, and generating a relational richness which makes one place more attractive to a firm and its key connections. It also focuses attention on the precise ways in which a firm's activities impact on a place, through flows of finance and through consumption of a region's assets, such as road space, water supply and environmental quality. The job market can also be analysed in a relational way, through examining the way firms find the type of workers they seek, and how people get access to job opportunities. An institutional approach further stresses that, in the networks within which firms conduct their affairs, the competitive struggle for advantage in the market place may need to be combined with reciprocal relations upon which firms can depend for support, in times of difficulty or when taking risks. This suggests that building up the relational richness which may encourage firms to stay in a place, and help them survive, may involve developing institutional infrastructures capable of building enduring relations of trust and support, particularly from local governance agencies. In return, the firms may be prepared to build a 'moral commitment to place' into their commercial interests, as they are already finding necessary with respect to their environmental behaviour. Thus firms may find it helpful to build up collaborative relationships within the locality of their operations, both for internal operating reasons, and to develop the relational richness of their local social embedding. In this way, firms are increasingly acknowledging that the economic sphere is not separate from everyday life

Informal economic relations

A local economy consists of more than its collection of formally-registered firms (Williams and Windebanck, 1994). If economic activity refers to all ways in which goods are produced and exchanged, other forms of economic organisation can be identified. In the retail field, there are many examples of informal retailing, from charity jumble sales, carboot sales and Sunday markets, to the traditional temporary markets which continue from a preindustrial age. Governments typically seek to surround such activities with regulations governing health and safety, traffic generation and fair competition. But new ways around these regulations are constantly being found. The same is true of both products and service provision, with activities often moving from an informal relation to a formal one either to get access to government grants or because formalisation is required to enter into a new market opportunity.

There is also a significant amount of informal exchange and bartering (Pahl, 1984). People may provide services for each other, in a reciprocal way. Or services may be provided through informal payments, for example for small scale building and decorating work, or cleaning and other household services. In some areas of high unemployment, barter may develop quite complex institutional forms, with, for example, paying for car repairs through the supply of vegetables grown on an allottment (for example, Williams, 1995). In the environmental movement generally, there is a growing search for alternative ways of conceptualising and practicing economic relations (Ekins, 1986).

Because they are informal, and 'outside' regulations, the scale and nature of such informal economic activity may be invisible. It is often undertaken with a mixture of economic and social motives. Reciprocity and collaboration may be critical ingredients. This is well illustrated in the tensions in the community business movement between the pursuit of economic returns as the primary business objective and social responsibility to community members (McArthur, 1993). It may also be kept deliberately small scale and invisible. Lack of trust (for example in a sympathetic understanding the game of balancing welfare payments against economic opportunities) may keep individual innovators from developing their informal 'market niche'. Such activities, typically ignored, are treated as marginal, or labelled as part of a 'black economy' (Williams and Windebanck, 1994), may nevertheless provide a significant source of income to poorer households and valued services to many more. In third world cities, where formal economic activity only employs relatively small numbers, it has now been recognised that informal economic activity is both a source of economic growth and a means of providing people with material support. International aid policies now regard such activity much more postively than in the past. If, in western societies, high levels of unemployment persist, governance may need to take a similarly positive attitude to this informal dimension of our local economies.

However, just as not all formal sector companies seek out local collaboration and follow self-interested and exploitive strategies if unregulated, so not all informal economic relations are benign. Some are technically illegal in that regulations are bypassed. There are other complex networks of criminal economic activity, depending parasitically on the formally regulated economy through the theft of goods, or 'insider dealing', or trade in illegal goods, most notably drugs. Those who practice corrupt business relations have been ignored in the discussion of local economic development, despite the adverse consequences of their activities, and the ever-present possibility that investment funds for land and property development may originate in profits from illegal activity. Criminal networks may not only provide access to wealth. They also tie people into modes of behaviour and interests which set them against both formal economic activity and local governance mechanisms. A 'politics of turf' may develop as such groups seek to control particular sectors of economic activity, for example protection rackets in the entertainment business, or the use of strategies of vandalism and theft from building sites to extort 'pay-offs'. Yet those who do well may look to their neighbourhood to invest their resources. An extreme example of this is the flow of Mafia money into urban development in Sicily, which became a 'safe haven' for drug-related and other 'profits'. These criminal economies are often very sophisticated and impact on local environments and on policies for their management in subtle ways. The planning community has been traditionally innocent of, or silent about, such situations. They are becoming more obvious in cities these days, with the widespread realisation of the interrelated nexus of the drug and criminal economy. This is having effects on the safety and security of town centres, business zones and some neighbourhoods. Addressing these effects has costs for economic efficiency. Attempts to address them may themselves be taken over by the power relations of informal activity, either directly or in a form of clientelistic politics (Eisenstadt and Lamarchand (eds), 1981). As dominant interests in political communities try to isolate themselves from the effects of the explosive mix of social disadvantage, drug penetration and criminality, forces for social-spatial polarisation are increased. But isolation serves merely to exacerbate the problem by widening social distance and hence the capacity for mutual understanding and communication.

A local economy, then, is not an integrated and self-contained set of relations, as posited in the neoclassical location theory literature. It is an aggregation of firms and individuals engaged in economic transactions, each with their own relational webs through which they get access to production inputs and to markets, and relate to the social worlds of the places where they are located. Sources of supply, markets and social networks connect firms and individuals to other firms, often outside the region where they operate, and bind them into power relations which it is difficult to control. In such conditions, firms learn to operate both competitively and collaboratively. The competition forces them continually to seek new forms of comparative advantage and to adjust production costs. This may lead to flexible labour hiring practices and flexible contracting arrangements with suppliers. The collaboration encourages firms to build up networks of mutual support. Public policy has a role in helping these positive networks to develop, in building local institutional capacity. A local economy may be fortunate if these networks are concentrated in its area, so long as the firms concerned are in a winning competitive position. But an urban region may suffer where its firms are losing their competitive position, where its local relations do not support dynamic economic innovation, and where its larger companies develop few intra-regional linkages.

Local economies, land and property markets and planning regulation

A key element of a local economy is its land and property markets, and the ownership relations, user demand, investment and development activity which shape the supply of built space.

As with the labour market, where firms draw on a regional 'store' of people with particular skills and particular rates of pay, the land market integrates the demands of diverse firms for space and property investment into comparative property qualities and values. Yet there has been very little economic analysis of how the land and property 'sector' fits into local economies (but see Turok, 1992). Similarly, within planning culture there has, until recently, been very little attention to the nature and functioning of land and property markets and how they are affected by land use regulation (Healey and Barrett, (eds), 1985). The reason was in part conceptual. In neoclassical economic theory, land and property markets are driven by consumer demand as reflected in price. Markets were therefore assumed to be responsive to changes in patterns of demand from the various economic sectors, and their behaviour could be predicted from analysis of local economic sectors. Marxist analysis highlighted the potential for landowner interests to act as a drag on the supply of land for capitalist production or worker housing. It was argued that landowners might seek to extract a share of the profits made in production for themselves, forcing up land prices and therefore wages and production costs. Workers and capitalists both therefore had an interest in restricting the power of landowners, by policies to bring land into state ownership or to regulate land owner behaviour (see Healey, 1991a).

Historically, the origins of land use planning systems in several instances can be traced back to concerns to contain land and property *speculation* and to produce more orderly markets (Weiss, 1987; Sutcliffe, 1981; Ward, 1994). In Germany, land use zoning was 'invented' in the nineteenth century to regulate urban extension and relate it to infrastructure provision (Sutcliffe, 1981). In Los Angeles, zoning was introduced to protect the 'community builders' who provided serviced plot layouts, from competition from speculators who sold unserviced plots in locations which were costly to service (Weiss, 1987). But the introduction of zoning schemes, especially where this deliberately limits land supply, as in the British town and country planning system introduced in 1947, distributes the benefits from development unequally among landowners. Those whose sites are designated for development make windfall gains. Those excluded from development have their prospects of appreciating land value gains wiped out. The British Town and Country Planning Act 1947, passed at a time when the property sector was largely inactive due to the after-effects of war (Ward, 1994), provided a 'once-and-for-all solution' to this problem by nationalising the right to develop, and removing the right to compensation for lost value, except where an existing planning policy is changed to one involving lower value uses. Most other planning systems retain compensation measures, although their impact is usually moderated these days by caveats of various kinds. Much more problematic in the British case had been who should get the benefit of the 'windfall' gains or betterment. This has become an ideological football, between those who argue that the benefits are due to private development effort and should therefore accrue to owners and developers, and those who argue that it is generated by the fact of public regulation and should therefore accrue to the public purse (see Healey, Purdue and Ennis, 1995).

Once introduced, however, the role of planning in market management was typically ignored. A deliberate mystification of the relation of planning to land and property markets often masked these origins, because planning regulation represented a fundamental state limitation on the rights of property owners. It was helpful therefore to present planning systems as acting fairly as between property owners, driven by planning and 'public interest' principles, rather than property market interests of any kind (Foley, 1960). This legitimation is particularly evident in the British case. As the quote from Abercrombie at the start of this chapter shows, the planning system in the 1950s and 1960s was typically presented in welfare state terms as concerned with the interests of citizens and factories, users of space, and with environmental qualities. In practice, it provided a sheltered, risk-free environment for property development and investment, and helped to foster the growth of regional and national development companies (Ball, 1983; Healey, 1994c). Rather than paying attention to the 'institutional capacity' of the property investment and development industry emerging in parallel with planning activity, most spatial planning exercises paid little attention to the nature of development activity, assuming that land markets would follow the patterns of use and intensity of development indicated in plans or that the public sector would step in to promote development where private action was not forthcoming.

Such assumptions have been challenged since 1970 by repeated cycles of property boom and slump. It often seemed that speculative development went hand-in-hand with planning regulation, as regulatory policies were relaxed in boom periods (Logan and Molotch, 1987; Berry and Huxley, 1992). As Barras (1987) argues, property development tends to be cyclical, producing short bursts of activity in response to shortages, followed by stagnation as a result of overproduction. This cyclicality internal to the development process may then be magnified by the broader cycles in economic activity and by investment cycles (Barras, 1987, 1994). These cycles have become particularly important as property investment has joined other investment media in the investment portfolios of financial institutions. As a consequence, property development and investment activity and property valuing has been increasingly linked with patterns of investment generally. This emerged with stark clarity during the international property boom of the later 1980s. This responded in part to the economic cycle, and the rise in the demand for space. It was fuelled to excess by international flows of investment capital, generated by production profits particularly in Japan. In Britain, this flood of investment finance was exacerbated by the deregulation of the banking sector, which encouraged competition within the sector, resulting in cheap loans to developers and to housebuyers. The result was rocketing land and property values and a massive increase in indebtedness in property for companies and mortgaged households. The overproduction that resulted coincided with the end of the economic cycle, and consequently produced a dramatic slump. This pattern has been repeated across Western Europe and in Asia, though in a less extreme form than in the UK.

The consequences have been far-reaching. The boom ratchetted property prices up, leaving companies and households with investments which they cannot now realise. The collapse in prices in many places has subsequently made households and companies very cautious about property investments, turning an excess of funds for development into a dearth. Construction industries have been catapulted into severe recession, as have all those retail services which benefit when families buy a new house. Further, in many countries, the over-enthusiastic funding of property projects by banks and savings and loans associations and other financial instititions has left bad debts on such a scale that the financial services sector itself has been adversely affected, with major consequences for national economies. With such a scale of economic impacts, it is not surprising that the functioning of land and property markets is now attracting much more policy attention. Land and property investment and development activity is now increasingly recognized as an economic 'sector', the production relations of which are defined in the term *the development industry*. One outcome of this new policy awareness is a slow realization of the role of spatial planning, in Britain at least, in creating the conditions for stable property development and investment conditions (Healey , 1994c).

This concern focuses attention on the variation in the way planning systems reflect and promote different interests in land and property development and investment. In some places, land and property markets are strongly managed by public sector control over the supply of urbanised sites (Netherlands, Sweden). In others, land use plans are the tool through which market values are established (as in Germany). In urban regions with a strong industrial tradition, planning systems are geared to ensuring adequate land supply in line with industrial and residential demand, essentially, the demand for property for its use value. But elsewhere the politics of planning systems can become driven by the value of land and property as an investment, a secure and appreciating asset. Logan and Molotch (1987) argue that such a *rentier* politics has dominated most American city government. Planning systems have then been geared to a local politics of growth promotion which would result in increasing land and property values. Such a politics not only encourages rising land prices, generating problems for the supply of affordable land for industrial activity and low cost housing. It also benefits from planning systems which establish land supply limits, and then tolerate selective breaching of the rules. It is this kind of 'growth promotion' politics which is highly vulnerable to speculative surges, arising where landowners, investors and developers compete to capture the benefits of a rising trend in demand and values. In Britain, the relationship is more complex. The planning system in certain respects has mimicked the strategies of the long-established large landowners, who have always managed a flow of land into urban uses in ways which ensured values remained high (Adams, 1994;

Coombes and Winter; Farthing, 1993; Massey and Catalano, 1978). The liberalisation of planning regulation in the 1980s and the vigourous and subsidised promotion of urban regeneration through property development on obsolete industrial and port sites tended to upset these strategies. The resultant market uncertainty for landowners, builders and developers is one factor behind the reassertion of the importance of plan-led planning in Britain in the 1990s (Bramley, Bartlett and Lambert, 1995).

Local economic development strategies in many places in the 1980s vigourously pursued investment in property development as a symbol of economic development. What these strategies failed to consider was that the investment flow was linked only marginally to real demand in local economies (Turok, 1992; Healey, 1991a). It was driven much more by the relative merits of different investment outlets at particular times, and by political philosophies which sought to make markets more open. Only when the flow of funds dried up, leaving unfinished projects, empty new space and a lot more empty space in older property, did it become evident that land and property markets were not necessarily driven by local demand conditions (Harvey, 1985; Fainstein, 1994; Berry and Huxley, 1992; Pryke, 1994; Keogh and D'Arcy, 1994; Barras, 1994).

A better understanding may be derived from the rapidly developing institutional approach to land and property development activity (Ball, 1986; Healey and Barrett, 1990; Krabben and Lambooy, 1993; Adams, 1994). This emphasises the social relations of the production and consumption of space. Its dynamics need to be understood in the same way as that of other economic sectors. This involves understanding the relational webs which interlink landowners, developers, investors, purchasers, leasers and renters in the development process, and how these interconnect with the regulatory and investment processes pursued by governments. It also concerns analysis of the driving forces of the processes, and how these vary in place and time. Finally it focuses attention on the institutional relations of the development industry and how these are both embedded in local specificities, such as landownership patterns, and open to national and international development and investment activity. The result is a 'land and property market', with particular capabilities to deliver sites, buildings and local environments, and therefore to create and maintain 'environmental qualities' of significance for economic development. In the context of such analyses, spatial and land use planning emerges as a key element in the regulation of land and property markets. The form of regulation helps to structure and frame the evolution of the relations they regulate. Such planning can no longer be conceived as primarily 'against' the market, as a countervailing force. It is actively involved in the *constitution* of markets. Local planning moves from being much more than protecting the interests of 'people' versus the 'economy', of needs versus demands, or environmental quality versus the drive for profits. It is actively drawn into the enterprise of managing local economies. One arm of this may be investment programmes, focused typically on land supply and infrastructure provision, though often linked to other aspects of local economic development, such as training and business development. The second arm is the power to regulate the location, form and timing of development.

The discovery of the late twentieth century is, then, that local economies are dynamic, delicate and differentiated, and that the land and property sector, and particularly the development industry, is a significant local economic player. Local economic and spatial planning policies can produce local economic assets, build supportive local economic institutional capacity and create local market opportunities. Spatial planning regimes, with respect to both the regulation and the promotion of development, have a key role in shaping the form of the development industry and the opportunities available to it. This is recognised by actors within the industry who learn to cluster around the decision processes through which regulations are articulated and resources made available (Adams, 1994; Healey, 1994a). This active role by local governance agencies in local economies is explicitly reflected in partnership arrangements between public and private sector actors. Interaction and collaboration between the development industry and local governments has a long history and many pressures encourage its continuation.

But collaboration is not necessarily a zero-plus game for local economies, local political communities or local environments. Within the industry itself, there are conflicts of interest, between owners, investors and users; between short- and long-term time horizons; between locations; between large and small operators;

between well-connected companies and others. A strategy which serves the interests of a few dominant firms in a locality may not help to build up the capacity to generate assets for the local economy. A strategy which emphasises the maximisation of economic benefits may not address the costs of development to everyday life and the biospheric environment. The challenge for local strategies is to find ways of working interactively with the development industry, helping it to reduce its own 'internal costs' of market failure, while resisting domination by particular interests within the sector. This challenge may be encapsulated in the approach to the 'entrepreneur developer', the symbol of 1980s economic dynamism in Thatcherite Britain and Reaganite America. Then, the entrepreneur was seen as the pioneer, to initiate projects and show the way to economic transformation through imaginative physical development, freed from regulation but liberally provided with subsidy (Thornley, 1991; Fainstein, 1994). But the consequence was destructive in terms of both economic costs, to the development industry and to the economy generally, and in terms of social and environmental costs. An alternative approach is for a deliberate shaping of the terms in which entrepreneurial opportunities can arise and investment offers be bargained over, an explicit strategy for moulding the institutional capabilities of the development industry in a locality (Healey, 1995; Bramley, Bartlett and Lambert, 1995).

Local economic development strategies and spatial planning

The case for local economic development strategies has been well-established for many years. It has a clear justification in terms of creating jobs for local people and sustaining local businesses serving the local economy. This chapter has argued that such strategies have a further rationale, to develop the economic assets of places, as a contribution to regional, national and international economic development. Among these assets, environmental qualities are important, including physical and social infrastructure, land and property supply and the social and environmental qualities of places. Less recognised until recently has been the quality of the institutional relations available in a place, through which knowledge resources can flow to and from firms. It has also been argued that land and property development and investment activity is a key element of a local economy. But the local economies of places, and their institutional relations, are highly variable, contingent upon their specific geographies and histories and the timing of opportunities arising from external economic and political conditions. The challenge for local economic development strategies is to build on the local distinctiveness of places, while escaping from the constrictions of local traditions, and to draw in outside opportunities, while limiting the potential for domination and exploitation. The result could then be the creation of new economic capacity, to add to the sum of human welfare, rather than the much-criticised inter-regional competition, where one region's gain is another's loss (Lovering, 1995).

Arriving at this ideal of a mutually beneficial strategy is no easy task. It requires a strategy with the capacity to 'add value' to the operations of most firms in a region. It must also bring benefits to the local economy in terms of increased prosperity and more jobs. As regards the first challenge, there will be conflicts between the interests of different sections of the local economy. Development interests and production interests are often in opposition, as discussed above. The interests of large inward investors may be very different from those of small service firms, while infomal sector activity may undercut the opportunities for firms providing similar services in the formal sector. If such conflicts of interest are not addressed, the economic opportunities for some firms, and the livelihoods which depend on these, may unwittingly be compromised. Further, the interest groups which support one sector may come into conflict with those of another, making it difficult to build up the kind of broad-based collaborative alliance whch could support a sensitive approach to local institutional capacity building. This suggests that a rich understanding of the range of economic life in a local economy and of its institutional supports is an essential quality for a sustainable approach to building up the capacity of a local economy.

The second challenge is even more difficult. Local interests want firms to be comfortable in their regions because this will generate jobs for local people and local spending power. But it cannot be assumed, as it once was, that this is an automatic consequence of the activities of a firm in a place. Encouraging firms to employ local people and to use local sourcing frequently requires active negotiation with the firms, as well as preparation of potential workers and sourcers to take up the opportunities. Institutional capacity building in an urban region, coupled with skilled negotiating, seems to help in 'drawing down' benefits from firms to the local economy generally. However, the activities of a firm are not all good news. Firms introducing new production processes may lead to the closure of plants, leading to job loss and derelict sites in a locality. They may place heavy demands on local infrastructure capacity and, in turn, on environmental capacities. They may directly lead to the loss of environmental assets, or disturb critical environmental relationships.

The preoccupation of local elites with the promotion of growth has frequently neglected these adverse impacts. Where local economies face a bleak future, it may seem that economic benefits must be given a higher priority than social and environmental costs. This may lead to 'fast-tracking' economic development projects through regulatory procedures. This approach is more difficult to sustain these days when the awareness of biospheric relations has led to a much higher consciousness of the adverse impacts of development (see Chapter 6). Competing local economic interests, as well as community and environmental groups, are likely to contest the approach, leading to conflict and crises of legitimation over government actions. This is destructive of local institutional capacity building. The rhetoric of 'sustainable development' which has emerged through environmental discourse suggests that there may be ways of achieving a 'positive sum' relation between economic and environmental benefits. So does the increasing interest in institutional processes which encourage collaboration and consensus-building rather than exacerbating conflict (see Chapters 7 and 8). Exactly how this could be done, if at all, will depend on both local particularities and national and international policy to constrain economic activity within environmentally sustainable parameters. Nevertheless, local governments have some leverage on the firms in their areas. If local distinctiveness and local institutional capacity are assets to firms, then building back benefits into the local economy and mitigating the adverse impacts of a firm's activities will not only bring a firm 'relational goodwill'. It may also bring it, indirectly, operating benefits. This opportunity should give local governments some confidence when negotiating with firms.

In recent years, the conversion of local governments to a proactive role in local economic development has been widespread in Europe, promoted vigorously by EU regional development policies (Batley and Stoker (eds), 1991). Spatial planning until recently was on the margin of these concerns. Planning systems were criticised as bureaucratic constraints on economic adjustment, in the language of neo-liberal ideology. As noted in Chapter 4, in opposition to this view in Britain the defenders of planning systems in turn claimed to be standing up for social justice or environmental values. The debate tended to be constructed in terms of planning *versus* the market, the economy and the forces of capital. This has led to resistance by some local politicians and officials to working collaboratively with the business sector (Cochrane (ed.), 1987).

Some neo-liberals now argue that, while a land use regulation system may be necessary, attention to spatial strategy is not (Thornley, 1991). In a world of dynamic firms in globalising relationships, locations and sites become assets – commodities to be 'traded'. In this view, localities are merely collections of assets for firms to exploit. Firms make choices about the package of advantages of one site in one region and country compared to the package of advantages in another. The question of the 'social costs' of projects, the balance of benefits and impact mitigation from a project, can be dealt with through site by site regulation, meshed in with economic development strategies. Simple zoning measures can be used to give each site a clear bundle of any necessary 'regulatory requirements', so long as the regulatory rules are both clear and clearly upheld. Such an approach appears to offer low 'transaction costs'. This approach is also favoured by environmentalists seeking to convert environmental issues into the language of economic calculus (see Chapter 6).

However, this argument ignores the impact of *where things are* on intra-regional relationships. Location is important both from the point of view of firms, and from the point of view of living with firms in a region. Some firms may seek particular kinds of locations, the large sites upon which big plant investments can be made, or the modern industrial and business parks which help to create an 'address' which has value in particular kinds of markets, or the locations where 'dirty' activities may be engaged in without too much hassle from neighbours. In open and unregulated land markets, such locations may just evolve. But most examples which provide the images which firms have in their minds when thinking about such locations are the result of active 'production' by local governments, which have used spatial strategies to get political acceptance of new types of activity in new locations and to coordinate the provision of infrastructure and development (see Needham *et al.*, 1993; Wood and Williams (eds), 1992; Healey, Khakee, Motte and Needham (1996). Firms also value the environmental qualities of places, especially where workforces and purchasers are discriminating about such qualities. These qualities include the ease with which people and goods can move around. But they also include opportunities for leisure, what a place looks and feels like, the availability of attractive informal environments for social encounters, and, most particularly, the quality of the city centre.

What emerges very clearly from the experience of development in places where there has been little effective spatial regulation is that the opening up of new locations and new types of production and distribution leaves in its wake a stock of obsolete premises, and devalues the assets of those who own such stock. This is a very clear trend in the retail and office sphere in Britain, where the ease with which retail and 'business' complexes were allowed on the periphery of conurbations has undermined the commercial viability of many city centres. Unregulated development may also potentially damage existing assets, for example where too many ill-designed hotel projects destroy a beach resource. Rather than building up the relational strength of the local economy, such trends undermine key competitive assets.

This argument indicates that the *qualities of places* within an urban region are important not just as assets, but as part of the relational capacity of an urban region. This suggests that, in a world of locational flexibility, there needs to be a capability to aid the continual reshaping of the spatial relations of neighbourhoods and access routes, to create new locales, to deal with areas left obsolete by new developments, support the development of new nodes in the urban structure, and defend critical nodes from the adverse consequences of changes in types and locations of activities. Local economic strategies therefore need a spatial component more than ever these days, just to address the internal economic efficiencies of firms. The spatial dimension of local economic strategy is reinforced if the need for legitimation to political communities concerned about the social and environmental costs of development is also taken into account.

Land and property markets and land use regulation

Spatial planning is also brought into the focus of attention in local economic development because of its significance in managing the opportunities for land and property development and investment and regulating the development industry from the costs of market failure. It has often been assumed that urban regions had integrated land markets, bound together by the competition for sites. Highest value sites were at the central node of a region, the city centre, and values then spread out evenly to the periphery. Land uses then distributed themselves through this market according to ability to pay. It is this model which is still conveyed in most standard textbooks in urban economics (for example, Harvey, 1987).

The contemporary reality of land and property markets is much more complex. They are not unified, but divided into segments relating to trade in different types of property. The form of this segmentation relates to the institutional history of particular national economies. In Britain, for example, there was until recently a clear division between the residential sector, the industrial sector and the commercial sector, the latter encompassing office and retail development. More recently, owners and developers have expanded into mixed use projects or switched a project from one use to another. Sectoral markets are in turn likely to contain different segments. In the residential field, high quality housing and small affordable units are quite separate markets for the consumer, though a developer may switch between them. Headquarters office accommodation and starter units for small service firms are similarly quite different products. The land and property market of an urban region is thus made up of a complex aggregation of micro-markets, each with its own product definitions and comparator values. Instead of being spatially integrated around the pattern of values within a particular urban region, the value comparators used in different markets reflect the spatial reach of the supply and demand conditions in each market segment. Some firms and some households will only look at property in a particular neighbourhood. Others will look at particular types of property and locations in a region, for example in the choice of high quality residential housing which will retain its value. Or a firm may compare business park premises in different regions in terms of quality and price. Even residential property may be compared inter-regionally, particularly where affluent employees expect to move with their job transregionally and want to protect the value of their housing asset as they move.

It is often assumed in the neoclassical literature that land and property markets are driven by consumer demand. Such an assumption allowed many landowners and developers to keep on building during the 1980s, rising property values being seen as a reflection of unmet demand. This ignored the role of land and property as an investment medium. The significance of property investment and its potential disjunction from the dynamics of the demand for property use was discussed earlier in this chapter. Land and property markets, even for a single property segment, may be driven by the sometimes conflicting dynamics of landowners, occupiers and investors. The agents of the market, the property investors, traders and developers, may also have diverse interests. While some properties may be built drawing on the savings of local households and firms, others may be owned by investors or developed by companies operating in an international arena.

The ebb and flow of investment interest in property on an international scale may therefore have a significant impact on movements in property values in particular market sectors and segments in an urban region. This may produce price movements which then filter into other market segments and sectors in a region, as owners try to 'capture' the new opportunities. Such filtering is not evidence of an integrated local market. Rather, it reflects the perturbations which ripple out from one set of relations to another. The result can be considerable instability and uncertainty. Where the result is an upward movement in value, such uncertainty provides fertile ground for the speculative entrepreneur, who seizes a new opportunity before others. The story of the development industry of the 1980s is littered with examples of speculators who grew big on such speculation, and then often headed into bankruptcy. The result of such speculative 'splurges', however, is often an oversupply of property and half-built sites. These may have the effect of reducing prices, thus creating uncertainty which may hold up further new development for a long time. Speculative, investment-driven markets, typical of the British case, thus tend to a form of volatility which creates not just extreme price hikes, but a slow reaction to real changes in demand (Barras, 1994; Fainstein, 1994). These may be contrasted with contexts such as the Netherlands where public policy has deliberately sought low and stable property values (Needham and Lie, 1994).

Land and property markets in a region are thus an amalgam of different relationships. Patterns of land value are not an even surface, sloping outwards from a central peak. They are actively constructed as owners position their sites and premises in particular market sectors and segments, hoping to 'catch' some of the value available for their property. As new types of business location or residential environment are created, and old ones rendered obsolete, 'chasing' value becomes increasingly uncertain. Just as the map of travel patterns and activity concentrations suggests that cities are increasingly becoming multinodal, rather than uninodal, or with a hierarchy of nodes, and as the pattern of activity nodes shifts in dynamic ways (see Chapter 4), all land and property market operators are faced with substantial uncertainty about both the value of sites and the likely demand for property. This is significantly affecting even the technique of property valuation, making it difficult to establish what is a fair price (Lizieri and Venmore-Rowland, 1991). It is also reflected in the demands for planning frameworks which help to stabilise market uncertainty. If market behaviour is itself 'socially constructed' by the active work of networks of actors in the development and investment process, then planning policy has the opportunity to play a role in shaping the social constructions of these players.

As with local economies generally, then, land and property markets are increasingly tied into wider and diffused relationships, rather than integrated within an urban region. Yet the movements of one market sector and segment affect others in a place. There are therefore often conflicts among land and property market interests within a region. The example highlighted by Marxist analysis, the struggle between landowning and production capital (Massey and Catalano, 1978), is the tension between many business occupiers, who may seek a reasonable choice of the type of property they are looking for at a low cost, and investors, who seek to maximise property investment returns. Many firms in Britain from the 1970s began to treat their property as an investment and increased its value in their company accounts accordingly. This helped to raise capital to maintain production during the recession of the early 1980s. But companies were then seriously hit by the collapse in value of their property assets in the slump of the early 1990s. Many firms, not to mention households, now realise that they benefit from measures to smooth out the volatility of property markets. Finally, those seeking to realise the development value of properties, or to get rid of property made obsolete by economic change, want a market context which provides opportunities and flexibility, but they may also seek assistance in removing 'blockages' to the development process, as manifest in problems of land assembly, infrastructure provision, and the clean-up of contaminated lands.

It has been argued in this section that local land and property markets are not sufficiently sensitive or integrated to manage themselves. It has long been recognised that they are particularly prone to market failure (Harrison, 1977; Scott and Roweis, 1977). It is now increasingly understood that local markets need help to encourage more stable conditions. The greater market certainty which would thereby result should encourage people to buy, invest and develop. It should also fill gaps in the supply of property types and locations, remove obsolete stock and recycle obsolete sites. These are not 'one-off' activities. Because of the transience of economic activity generally, as discussed earlier, it has become a continuous process, with new demands replacing old ones, continually reshaping the spatial organisation of an urban region, and hence its property values and market opportunities. This requires a finegrained understanding of the market relations of a place and of the development industry operating there. Developing the institutional capacity of local land and property development activity is thus a key ingredient of the 'place-making' challenge (Healey, 1995).

To take on this task requires a shift in thinking within the planning community. Planners have in the past tended to see their role as defending places against the wiles of the speculator and defined their role in contrast as champions of social needs or environmental quality. This chapter has argued that both local economies generally, and their land and property markets, need careful strategic management. This requires a deep understanding of the particular nature of the firms and economic relations of a place, including the characteristics of its development industry. The critical challenge for local governance capability is how to 'strike a bargain' with business, including property interests, which will constrain business where it could trample on social relations or undermine environmental capacities, while enabling business activity generally to flourish.

Local governance and local economies; a pro-active role

This chapter has argued that local governance, in some form, has a key role in contemporary economic relations. This is not a new phenomenon. There have always been relations between commercial interests and local government, depending on local political histories. What is new is its orientation and its organizational form. The emphasis today is on an overt and strategic approach to the promotion of the business world in urban regions in globalising economies. Such an approach has echoes of the urban promotion of the nineteenth-century 'city fathers' in Britain, who energetically promoted the development of cities such as Newcastle and Birmingham (Ward, 1994). This was displaced in Britain in the mid-twentieth century by a preoccupation with the delivery of social welfare and safeguarding environmental quality. This agenda was often presented as in opposition to, or deliberately constraining, economic activity. A key element of the current emphasis, in contrast, is in the constitution of the conditions for healthy economic activity. This means viewing the world from the point of view of the firms in a region or firms likely to be attracted to it. A major function of local governance is to help firms overcome hurdles and market barriers, to improve their internal operating conditions. The quality of the way this is done will affect the extent to which 'being in a particular place' adds value to a firm's activities. This in turn will affect the overall economic climate of regions and their contribution to aggregate economic activity at the level of nation states and international groupings.

Achieving such net gains in economic activity in a region over and above inter-regional competition for mobile investment requires a capacity for locally-sensitive and globally-aware understanding of the trajectories of the mixture of firms existing in a place, from which to identify the local assets and relationships which could help to 'add value' to their operations. This is recognised in the developing approach to '*production filières*' and value-added chains, which seeks to isolate the contribution which being in a place can make to the particular dynamics of such chains (Camagni (ed.), 1991; Camagni and Salone, 1993; Korfer and Latniak, 1993; Amin and Thrift (eds), 1994). This draws on an institutional perspective to examine the relational links of companies, between each other and with the social worlds from which company members are drawn. Research on technology transfer, technopole development and research and development work is highlighting the socially embedded nature of economic innovation, and the role of particular places in promoting innovative climates. Many examples of local technological transfer initiatives which have focused on providing physical assets, such as science parks, illustrate that such initiatives, without attention to the quality of the institutional relations of a place, led to little synergy between firms, and limited build up of 'local knowledge'. Such examples also show that the relation between economic innovation and land and property development is neither important nor straightforward. Land and property investment and development activity need to be included in the analysis of local economic activity and understood in the same kind of relational way as with other areas of economic activity.

The general message for local governance activity is that economic activity needs to be understood from the point of view of the 'business world'. From that point of view, the qualities of places in which firms are located are an amalgam of physical assets and particular environmental qualities, labour market attributes, company networks and market opportunities, spatial organisation and institutional relations through which knowledge about products, markets, opportunities and constraints flows around. Through this point of view, it is possible to build up some understanding of the range of 'economic stakeholders' in a place and their strategies, both these located there and external to a place. This helps to appreciate the driving dynamics behind economic actors, the power relations which they can mobilise to achieve their objectives. The economic development task for local governance is then to build up particular assets, and more importantly, develop the 'relational infrastructure' of places.

But this is a very problematic role for local governance. With respect to providing support for business, it requires developing good knowledge of the practical world of business in all its variety, and building up all kinds of joint working arrangements. This implies an interactive and collaborative role. It leads all too readily into a new form of 'corporatist' relations, between local political and business élites. These may have pay-offs for local companies, for job generation and for local economic health in the short-term. But if local economic development actively focuses on too narrow a range of the economic stakeholders in a region, they may well fail to be aware of, and stifle, other nodes of economic innovation and enterprise. There are many signs of new forms of a narrow corporatism in the regional economic spatial alliances being developed in many of Britain's urban regions in the 1990s. A more appropriate alternative for today's local economies is a more fluid form of institutional capacity building, open to new relationships, flowing knowledge around from a wide range of sources and capable of flexible adjustment. It also needs to be informed by an awareness of the sources of power of different economic networks, and the way these may influence bargaining strategies in collaborative contexts. It should further be surrounded by safeguards against too easy exploitation, by the company out to capture grant income, by insider dealing and by individuals who can see a 'market opportunity' in corrupt practice.

These problems of the institutional design of collaborative relations between business and local governance are compounded by the demands of paying attention to the 'social costs' of economic activity, to the social relations of everyday life and to biospheric systems. Because of their role in the production of material goods and the generation of material wealth through jobs and profits, firms wield a lot of power over political and popular imaginations. This power is recognised particularly clearly in the lack of trust which citizens have for companies. Motives are treated suspiciously; firms offering community initiatives are considered to be self-interestedly bargaining to cover potential exploitation. One way forward is to combine the positive promotion of economic activity with the negotiation of measures to mitigate social costs, or encourage firms to contribute 'benevolently' to their localities. But this by itself will not increase understanding if there is a deep lack of trust of business. This suggests that interactive relations need to be fostered through which business networks and the social networks of everyday life and governance may interpenetrate within the public realm, allowing understandings from one to flow through to the other. Such interpenetration already exists at the levels of the everyday lifeworlds of traditional business people. What is needed is an institutional framework which allows for much broader and two-way encounters across the relational webs of urban region life. This is not easy, as business people, especially in Britain, are not familiar with the world of government and have difficulty 'learning to speak in public' (Davoudi and Healey, 1995). But it is essential if new relations of trust are to be developed which will allow local governance to provide a supportive economic role to powerful stakeholders, within the context of the moral attitudes and material objectives arising from everyday life and concerns for biospheric environments.

This raises questions about both the form of interactive processes and collaborative practices, and about the systemic governance parameters within which appropriate local institutional capacity can be developed. These are discussed further in Part III. The outcome of local efforts in institutional capacity-building will be particular relational forms, particular ways of linking the economic, everyday life and biospheric dimensions of urban region life, distinctive cultures – ways of thinking and organising, and particular ways in which the various elements of a local economy are embedded in their locale. It is these which construct and 'frame' the economic assets of a place, the physical attributes and people's strategies. They also focus the attention of stakeholders from the worlds of economic organisation and business life.

6 Living in the Natural World

The environmentalist challenge

The previous two chapters have emphasised the material dimensions of social and economic life. They have highlighted the significance of the material qualities and social relations that develop in places for the quality of everyday life and the business environment, even though our social relations are not confined to particular locales, but thread in and out of the spaces of particular places. The 'natural world', with which we interact as we accomplish our social relations, is similarly organised, as we now understand it, as sets of biospheric relations which thread across places, sometimes tightly bound into densely-interconnected spatially-concentrated ecosystems; sometimes spreading across the globe, through the movement of airstreams, water systems and the patterns of movement of animals and plants. The environmentalist proverb 'think global, act local' could apply to all the relations of everyday life, the economic world and biospheric relations.

But the evolution of contemporary environmental philosophy raises questions ignored in material analyses of goods, of needs and demands, and their distribution. It focuses attention on moral responsibilities, for those who cannot speak for themselves, other species and future generations. It forces consideration of the interaction of economic activity, everyday life and the natural world, and carries the potential to demand limits on economic power and daily life relations. It confronts the power of the economic and political orders of the modern world with alternative conceptions of ideologies and strategies, and it raises difficult questions about priorities, between people here and now and people 'over there' and in the future.

Above all, contemporary environmentalism, though a broad church with many branches, challenges the materialist view of technological and scientific progress. Through scientific and technological progress, the predominant view in western societies this century has been that human welfare can be advanced by our increasing capacity to *control* the forces of nature to which we are subject. In such conceptions, the natural world appears as a *resource* to be exploited for our benefit, and as a source of *dangers* to be contained (Douglas, 1992).

Contemporary environmentalism stresses the limits to material development and the moral dimensions of the way we live now (Beatley, 1994). This challenge is not new. Throughout the modern period in western thought, there have been alternative conceptions of the relation of people and nature. In Britain, views of the natural world have been strongly influenced by the preindustrial culture of the landed gentry, for whom 'the countryside' was an inheritance, to be shaped and tended in its distinctive social relations and landscapes, and handed on to future generations (Newby, 1979). This attitude had a strong influence on early twentieth century planners. Within the field of natural science itself, conceptions of the natural world have oscillated between ideas which stress the complex interdependencies of ecological relations and the place of ourselves as a species bound into and living among these relations, and those which stress the trajectory of the human species as a progressive struggle to differentiate ourselves from other species, and increase our power, our competitive position, over the rest of nature (Worster, 1977). The first focuses attention on moral responsibility, on experiential knowledge and the rights of other species. The second supports notions of human superiority and command over 'nature', and competitive practices in social relations.

The second view is reflected in the scientific materialist conceptions of nature which underpin the dominant traditions in western economics (see Chapter 2). It came to dominate the science of ecology as it rose to prominence in the mid-twentieth century. Ecology treated the natural world as consisting not of a collection of separate natural species and physical forces but of species in habitats in relation with each other. The challenge of ecological inquiry has many parallels with that of geography and with the enterprise of spatial planning. It sought to examine how we should understand the interrelations between species in different local contexts. This has implications for the management of local environments (Worster, 1977; Simmons, 1993). The conception of the city as an urban system was borrowed in the 1960s from ecological precursors (see McLoughlin, 1969). But just as there are many ways of conceiving of social relations, so too have there been struggles between competing views of ecological relations (Worster, 1977). One resultant strand of inquiry has stressed the collaboration and harmonious interdepencies of species within habitats. The dominant strand in twentieth century ecology has, however, emphasised notions of competition, succession and survival of the fittest. By the mid-twentieth century, the emphasis in ecological research was to understand the dynamics of competition through the analysis of ecological relations. The majority view among ecologists was that that these were driven primarily by energy flow, derived ultimately from the sun. The emphasis in scientific inquiry was to measure the flows of energy through ecosystems in order to identify more and less 'efficient' processes of energy flow. The links between such inquiry and improving the efficiency of agricultural production are not hard to see.

This scientisation of nature and its instrumental purposes spoke with the language of objective knowledge. The objectification of nature was compatible with western conceptions of progress, of the autonomous preference-maximising self, and of a competitive market economy. Ecological science and neo-classical economics made comfortable bedfellows (Worster, 1977). But rumbling along on the sidelines of the dominant views were different conceptions of ecological relations. These stressed the importance of collaborative relations between species, echoing the recognition of reciprocity in social relations discussed in Chapter 4. Such perspectives have been sidelined in twentieth-century western thought by the dominance of utilitarian conceptions of autonomous individuals making rational choices. Alternative ecological views also emphasised that people, as much as any other species, exist *within* nature, and experience nature, not just in a material way, but in a spiritual way, as part of our emotional life. The natural world gives us 'solace', and a sense of splendour and awe. It connects us to the 'sublime' (Burke, 1987; also Myerson and Rydin, 1994). Our relations with the natural world thus take on a moral and metaphysical as well as a material dimension.

It is this broad view which has now once again bubbled to the surface of our thinking about the environment. It finds support in the challenges to 'objective' science and the 'technological solutions' which have arisen generally in social science and philosophy in the present period (see Chapter 2). It is not just that we recognise more clearly these days that scientific knowledge is itself socially constructed, and that the moral and emotive dimensions of human perception cannot be left out of our thinking about how we know and understand things. We now realise that science and technology are not just benign bearers of progress and welfare. They carry power and bring danger. Ulrich Beck, a German sociologist, captures this in his account of our current period as 'The Risk Society', within which we have exchanged the ordered and certain parameters of industrial capitalism for a world where, as more autonomous individuals than ever before, we live at the risk of dangers produced both by natural forces – earthquakes, volcanic explosions, hurricanes, droughts and tempests; but also by science itself – nuclear explosions, poisoning by pesticides and drugs, the collapse of dams, the shipwreck of oil-tankers and pollution incidents (Beck, 1992). It is the adverse impacts of our activities that now strike us, turning the word 'risk' from a connotation of the possibility of high gain and high loss to a word which is interchangeable with 'danger' (Douglas, 1992).

Late twentieth-century environmentalism, which has had such a significant effect on environmental politics and environmental policy in western societies, has developed its leverage on our thinking through its role in the critique of 'objective' science and of 'rational' economics. Scientific inqury has helped in this process, showing how actions in one part of the world effect environmental conditions elsewhere (for example, the impact of British power station effluent on acid rain and tree health in Northern Europe) and undermine the conditions for life on the planet as a whole (for example the impact of pollution on the ozone layer). Such understanding has been greatly promoted by the presentation through television of programmes about the wonder of the natural world, and the destructive effects of human actions of all kinds. The new environmental mood emphasises that there are material limits to our capacity to exploit our environment (resources we need for life support can be destroyed), and there are moral limits to our rights to despoil our environment (a disrespectful attitude to our environment undermines our ability to respect ourselves). We understand that action by individuals, by companies, by local communities, can make a difference to global conditions. Through environmental politics, debate about local environmental qualities has become infused with much more than natural science knowledge. It brings moral and aesthetic issues firmly into the arena of argument in new ways. It focuses attention on wide-ranging *impacts* of changes in local environments. It emphasises the significance of biospheric ecological, hydrological and climatological relationships when assessing the links between an action and its impacts. It forces us to think about why we care about some kinds of impacts, even though such care will lead to limiting what is in our material interests. It makes us aware of our own physical, moral and aesthetic relations with the natural world. Through this awareness, we also come to consider the rights of other species with whom we share our local environments.

All these new claims for our attention jostle with all the other considerations and claims outlined in Chapters 4 and 5 when it comes to the challenge of managing our co-existence in shared spaces. 'Stakeholders' in local environmental issues proliferate before us. Powerful lobbies seek to tie down this range and diversity in the language of economics or that of natural science. But the issues keep breaking out of the confines of these expert languages. How then do political communities concerned with local environments identify the issues they should address and how?

This chapter examines the various ways that the relations between the social and the natural worlds have been constructed, and how this has affected consideration of the significance of the biospheric relations of natural environments and the role of spatial planning. It focuses in particular on debates in Britain where concern with the environment has been a longstanding concern in spatial planning. It illustrates a continual struggle to confine debates into familiar powerful languages, and the repeated failure of these strategies as the assumptions of materialist science and economics are challenged. The challenges are thrusting new issues onto policy agendas, about the sustainability of current practices, about the complex interrelations between people, and between people and the natural world, and about rights and duties, towards each other, towards our inheritance from the past, towards other species. The chapter concludes with a comment on the challenge for governance created by these new conceptions.

Conceptions of the environment in spatial planning

It is often argued that spatial and local environmental planning has inherently been the guardian of concern for the environment, especially in Britain, where the planning tradition is infused with the objective of the conservation of a particular kind of rural landscape. (Newby, 1979; Marsden *et al.*, 1993). In thinking about places, planners have always been conscious of the 'physical' environment. For Patrick Abercrombie, this was expressed in notions of the 'beauty' of physical form and natural landscape (Abercrombie, 1933).

How planning traditions have interpreted environment and the natural world has itself been shaped by the ebb and flow of the wider debates about ecosystemic relations and the relation of people and nature. However, until recently, concerns about the natural environment have typically been relegated to the margins of a preoccupation with the built form. The natural world, the countryside and rural life have been most commonly conceptualised as a backcloth or setting for the city (Healey and Shaw, 1994). This conception can be readily linked to the tradition of planning as urban form (see Chapter 1). The planning thinkers and practitioners of the nineteenth century and early twentieth century were preoccupied with the problems of managing burgeoning cities. Strongly influenced by architectural and engineering traditions, their attention focused on the arrangement of physical structures. Yet ideas about new ways of organising and managing cities were infused with ideals about a better world in which citizens had access to a natural environment with space for recreation and free of pollution. Some, such as Abercrombie, looked back to a preindustrial era for models of urban life, encapsulated in Howard's ideas for a 'garden city', with urban nodes interconnecting across open landscapes. Others following the modernist planner, le Corbusier, looked forward to a modern, technologically advanced and car-based city, where buildings were so arranged as to leave plenty of open space on the ground, and a free flow of air and light around high rise structures (Hall, 1988).

In these images of urban form, with their preoccupation with creating new ways of accommodating urban life, the natural world played an important, if often underemphasised, role. Natural systems – clean air and clean water – were seen as a precondition for good health. 'Open space', usually interpreted as places open to the sky and populated by grass, flowers, shrubs and trees, was seen as an essential amenity for neighbourhoods and as a strategic necessity for cities. Children needed open spaces for play, and urban dwellers needed 'lungs' of open air, from which to escape the pollution and stress of the city. A major justification for the first of Britain's greenbelts, around London, was promoted as 'a lung for Londoners' (Ward, 1994). Urban plans of the mid-twentieth century recognised the need to safeguard the resources needed for urban life – food supplies, building materials, energy supplies. The natural environment was thus considered as a store of resources and amenities, to serve the needs of urban dwellers. But it was also more than this. Patrick Abercrombie, in his Greater London Plan (see Figure 1.1), refers to the need to conserve the countryside for 'the visual solace of man'.

These ideas are a long way from a scientific and materialist view of the environment. Abercrombie held a more metaphysical notion of the relations between city and countryside, man and environment. Depending on nature as a man depends on the nurture of a mother, the city as an adult (and male!) must take on the moral duty of care and stewardship for the natural environment, as a husband should to a wife (as Abercrombie understood gender relations!). This justified strong policies separating town from country, the control of urban sprawl and the designation of greenbelts.

> The English countryside ... is a Ceres, a well-cultivated matron, who duly produces, or should, her annual progeny! If therefore it is true that the town should not invade the country as a town, the regularising hand of man has nevertheless sophisticated the country to serve his needs ... (Abercrombie, 1944, pp. 178–9)

The natural world for these British physcial development planners was thus conceptualised as both a resource and a setting. As a setting, however, it was much more than an aesthetic landscape. It had a constitutive role in underpinning the vigour of city life; it was a haven to return to. As a consequence, urban dwellers had a moral responsibility to safeguard its integrity, for the present and for the future. 'Man' was presented as 'in charge' of nature, just as, in western thought and legal practice of the time, men were responsible for women's lives. This inflection co-existed with a concept of stewardship derived from the estate management tradition of the British landed gentry (Lowe, Murdoch and Cox, 1995).

In the interrelation of material, moral and emotive-aesthetic conceptions of the natural world, in the concern with a moral responsibility to nature, and in the notion of a stewardship responsibility to care for the natural world as an inheritance for the future, these early ideas foreshadow many contemporary environmental concerns. Yet they are also deeply imbued with modernist notions of technological progress and the advance of the human species. Man is 'in control' of nature, as well as reponsible for it. Having grown up and out of the womb, he is no longer 'within nature'.

In the post-war period, in any case, the moral dimensions of environmental concern were progressively sidelined, as the planning community became preoccupied with the challenge of accommodating economic growth. Planning technique addressed natural environmental systems in terms of constraints and thresholds. This is clearly evident in the sub-regional studies of the late 1960s and early 1970s in Britain which sought to identify new growth locations (Cowling and Steeley, 1973; Ward, 1994). Development was seen to be constrained by factors such as drainage, infrastructure availability, landscape features etc. Natural capacity constraints were viewed in terms of 'development thresholds' which represented cost barriers to urban growth. Options for locating development were therefore reviewed in terms of the comparative costs of overcoming constraints.

Parallelling the dominance of scientific ways of analysing ecological systems, urban systems too were analysed as sets of activities linked by communication channels, using the analyses of regional science (Chapin, 1965; Chadwick, 1971; McLoughlin, 1969; see also Chapters 1 and 5). The conception of the natural environment narrowed down to a collection of material and aesthetic resources needed for modern life which should be conserved and provided. Yet by the end of the 1960s, the costs of a material preoccupation with growth, to which the planning community had become vigorously attached, were beginning to command public attention. Fears of global pollution by nuclear explosions, the imagery of Rachel Carson's powerful depiction of the costs of growth in *Silent Spring* (Carson, 1960), and the evidence of the complex transregional effects on climates and the hydrology of resource depletion and pollution began to claim public attention. This coincided with the end of steady postwar economic growth in western economies, raising questions about the sustainability of economic growth itself.

1970 saw the publication of an influential report on *The Limits to Growth*, produced by a group calling themselves the 'Club of Rome'. In the US, the first evidence of public policy leverage arose in the National Environmental Protection Act (1979), which required environmental impact assessments (EIAs) to be undertaken for major public projects. In Germany, environmental ideologies were promoted in the political arena with the vigourous development of a 'Green Party' politics (Galtung, 1986), and in Australia, the trade union movement picked up environmental issues, banning construction work on environmentally insensitive projects (Stretton, 1978). By the 1980s, the new environmentalism was a powerful political force in Europe, poised to influence the policies of the European Commission. Its content, however, was rather different to the established British preoccupation with the rural landscape. The new preoccupations were with biospheric systems, their qualities and their sustainability; with ecosystemic relations, with water systems, with air pollution; and with the interconnections between localised activities and planetary conditions, symbolised by the concerns with acid rain and the ozone layer (Beatley, 1994; O'Riordan, 1981).

In Britain, these influences were more muted in the 1970s. There were few debates on environmental issues at national policy level. Concern about both the limits to growth and the technological and materialist emphasis in public policy were challenged primarily at the local level through the machinery of the planning system and the requirements for public inquiries into the siting of power stations and roads. As Grove-White has argued (1991), the planning system was made to 'take the strain' of the tension between economic development and environmental concerns (Lowe and Goyder, 1983; Grant, 1989; O'Riordan, Kramme and Weale, 1992). The professional planning community at this time tended to construct its debates about the nature and purpose of planning in terms of social justice, focusing on redistributive questions (see Chapters 4 and 5). The more pragmatic avoided discussion about the purposes of planning altogether, emphasising instead the professional role of making projects and programmes work – 'getting things done' (Healey *et al.*, 1982). The planning profession in Britain was thus ill-prepared to consider recasting the overall conception of the purposes of planning in the terms of the emerging 'new environmentalism'. Yet ecological conceptions of the environment were entering British planning practice through a new interest in the active management of 'countryside' resources.

The countryside has a peculiar place in British culture. It embodies and symbolises some essential qualities of what it is to be British, just as the city centre means civic culture in Italy and France. The countryside, for British people, means both a landscape and a lifestyle. The landscape is that of the English heartlands, with their greenfields, hedges and scattered tall trees, grazed below by cattle, wherein nestle villages of thatched cottages, a manse and a church. Within the idealised village, people live in harmonious, collaborative relations, tending the fields, and their cottage gardens, and enjoying country walks and village ceremonies, a romanticised *gemeinschaft.*

This image as it is now used is the dream of a highly urbanised country, 'invented' by poets, tourist guides and landscape designers in the nineteenth century, and promoted since then by the professionalised middle classes (Williams, 1975; Marsden *et al.*, 1993; Wiener, 1981). Its defence is embodied in powerful pressures groups, most notably the Country Landowners Association and the Council for the Protection of Rural England. This 'dream' has underpinned the powerful support for landscape conservation policies in Britain, for greenbelts and national parks, areas of outstanding natural beauty, wildlife sites and sites of special scientific interest. However, as noted in Chapter 4, it bore little relation to the actual conditions of rural life in nineteenth and early twentieth-century Britain, nor does it reflect contemporary social realities (Williams, 1975). The idealised village is now most likely to be the home of urban commuters and business activities technologically freed from the need to be in the city, while the countryside is increasingly a site of struggle by farmers to find new commercial endeavours to meet the economic challenge of agricultural overproduction (Marsden *et al.*, 1993).

This was the 'countryside' which Patrick Abercrombie and his fellow planners in Britain in the 1940s sought to defend. Combined with the national policy concern to ensure a high level of home agricultural production, it lead to a strong commitment to protect agricultural land against development. By the 1970s, it had not only become clear that urban growth was springing across the greenbelts placed around cities to contain it. In addition, the farmers, who once were seen as the stewards of the countryside image, were now found to be its despoilers, grubbing up hedgerows and trees, and polluting watercourses with fertilisers and pesticides. Meanwhile farmers were complaining that urban visitors to the countryside were not quiet respecters of landscapes, but liable to vandalise property and disturb crops and stock. This led to the growth of countryside management as a practice, which in turn required a degree of ecological knowledge and brought natural scientists into the planning field. By 1980, the management of the 'urban fringe', and strategies for conserving agricultural land while preserving its landscape features, had become major themes in British planning policy (Elson, 1986).

In certain respects, these British traditions of planning thought and practice provide a good basis for addressing contemporary environmental agendas. They contain an understanding that the environment is more than a resource to be exploited or conserved; that it has a moral and aesthetic role. They emphasise the significance of the *local* management of natural environment relations, land use planning being justified as a form of stewardship of the natural world. They acknowledge that other species need protection from human activity. (The defence of habitats is a familiar exercise in British planning practice.) But, despite the flirtation with ecological systems in the development of urban systems theory in the 1960s, the planning tradition, even in Britain, has had little understanding of the nature of biological, climatological and hrydrological systems, that is, of biospheric relations. And the conceptions of the relation of people and nature have been deeply infused with the view that the human species can and should command and control the natural world. These assumptions are now being rearticulated and challenged in the light of the new environmentalism. But this is not a conceptually homogeneous and coherent point of view – it is riven with internal debates.

Debates in contemporary environmental policy

The environmental movement which has swept across western thought in the later years of the twentieth century is an amalgam of many, often conflicting, strands. Different discourses compete to dominate policy debate. The elastic quality of contemporary environmentalism is one reason for its influence on politics and policy. It can appear as a radical attack on the forces of capitalist production, on the materialist emphasis in western thought and on social and individual behaviour which treats the environment as both goldmine and rubbish pit. Or it can be presented as merely a modulation to our strategies, helping us to steer economic and social development with more care for our longer term interests. The former view is often presented in apocalyptic terms, urging that we make radical changes to our systems and behaviours now if we are to save ourselves and our planet (Giddens, 1990). In another guise, it can be seen as a task for technology, to find ways of carrying on as usual but with less waste of resources and production of pollution (Stretton, 1978; Sandbach, 1980; Sagoff, 1988).

Tim O'Riordan captured these dimensions of the environmental debate in his conception of two polar extremes, the *ecocentric* and the *technocentric* views (O'Riordan, 1981). This division continues to find expression in environmental debate. 'Deep green' environmentalists argue that the cultivation of harmonious relations between the human species and the natural environment should have first priority in public policy and individual behaviour. Human behaviour should be radically altered to replace its current exploitative and damaging practices. The 'technogreens', in contrast, seek an accommodation between the priority of environmental care and other policy objectives, in particular, economic growth. This debate echoes the conflicting positions within ecology about the relations between people and nature.

As the environmental debate has moved to centre stage in public policy, its concepts have been re-defined as powerful policy communities have come to recognise its potential influence and the scale of the challenge to their established practices. In parallel, the construction of policy debate has tended to shift from O'Riordan's polarity, to what appears as a more inclusionary project. This is encapsulated in the concept of *sustainable development.* The concept of sustainability, as developed in the environmental arena, has many precursors. Its most influential expression has been that of the Brundtland Report, *Our Common Future* (WCED, 1987). This argued that, while economic *growth* should be restrained, it is possible to reach a beneficial accommodation between economic development and natural environmental systems. This is expressed as sustainable development.

> *Humanity has the ability to make development sustainable – to ensure that it meets the needs of the present, without compromising the ability of future generations to meet their own needs* (WCED, 1987, p. 8)

The report explicitly linked questions of the condition of natural environmental systems to the economic and social relations which were exploiting them. Taking a global perspective, it emphasised the interrelations between the practices of the so-called 'developed' world and the 'developing' world. The former tended to export the adverse effects of its affluence onto the social and environmental relations of poor peoples struggling to find the means for survival in the third world. This generated a moral *imperative* to first world communities to reduce their production of adverse environmental effects and provide resources to help the third world deal with the burden of externality effects.

The sustainable development concept reflects social considerations as as much as ecological ones. It presents environmentally respectful economic development as a possible trajectory. It has overtones of the ideas of stewardship as an inheritance of environmental resources upon which planners such as Patrick Abercrombie drew earlier in the century. And it echoes the moral philosophy and customary practices of many non-western societies.

This encourages the view that it is modern western culture which is peculiar in its silence on both the role of intergenerational resource husbandry and its concern with the sustainability of its own means of existence. This peculiarity arises because of the combination of the modernist belief in the power of human invention to overcome constraints and the focus on profit-maximising behaviour as the central dynamic of capitalist economies (see Chapter 2). In this context, it is not surprising that the struggle to accommodate the challenge of the new environmentalism leads both to confused responses and real power struggles about alternative definitions. It raises important *general* questions about the viability of our cultures and societies, while bringing to the forefront of our thinking the relations between our social and economic behaviour and the natural world understood in terms of its biospheric relations (Jacobs, 1991).

In Britain the influence of the new environmentalism had, by the end of the 1980s, moved from the terrain of pressure group politics to a mainstream political preoccupation. As a consequence, civil servants, professionals, experts and politicians have now increasingly taken control of the discursive agenda, as they seek ways of tieing down campaigning concepts into policy rhetoric and operational programmes, within the context of their other political concerns. The dominant discourse and precise content of the new environmental agenda varies from one policy community to another. Within Western Europe, where national policy debates are significantly interlinked through the European Union, which has played a major role in environmental policy, four strands, or discourses, of policy debate appear currently to be struggling for policy attention. Each is grounded in established languages, though often opening up quite new directions. Each leads to different policy priorities as regards the management of change in local environments.

The environment as a stock of assets

One conception derives from neoclassical economics. It sits comfortably with utilitarian modes of thought and with contemporary neo-liberal tendencies in public policy. The environment is construed as a collection of assets, a stock. Sustainability is taken to mean the maintenance or enhancement of this asset stock rather than its depletion (Pearce *et al.*, 1989). This allows economic development to proceed, so long as any losses to the asset stock are compensated for by the creation of new ones. In line with principles of the responsibility of private individuals, *polluters* should be made to pay for their adverse impacts on the natural environment. Environmental problems are thus addressed in economic terms as adverse externality effects. Environmental regulation is one measure which can be used to negotiate such compensation, through agreements with developers (Healey, Purdue and Ennis, 1995). The calculation of losses and gains can be made in the established vocabulary of economic cost–benefit analysis, this being extended to encompass the valuing of non-monetary goods, such as wildlife reserves and heritage landscapes (Cowell, 1993). Environmental audits perform a key role in identifying the asset stock of a locality (Glasson *et al.*, 1994).

Calculating the relative weight of gains and losses to the asset stock has demanded all the ingenuity of environmental economists (Turner, 1993). Such calculations deal in the language of balance and trade-off. Policy may also seek to act more systemically, encouraging people in firms and households to consume fewer resources and produce less waste. This can be done by pricing policies, such as price incentives to encourage the use of unleaded petrol, or the use of road pricing to ration access to congested and polluted town centres. This form of *demand management* policy aims to achieve behavioural shifts, but sets no quantum targets for overall environmental conditions, thereby avoiding the specification of limits to growth. Those governments concerned about the distributional consequences of such policies, which tend to raise costs for poorer people and smaller firms who have fewer resources with which to adjust to new price situations, may help these groups out with grants for conversion. New behaviours in turn generate the demand for new products and practices, creating opportunities for innovation in economic processes, and thus promoting growth. In this way economic 'growth' can co-exist sustainably with care of the biosphere, using both regulatory and financial policy tools. Local environmental management has a role in regulatory policies, setting the terms for alleviation and mitigation requirements, although there are difficult questions about the spatial scale across which an asset stock should be calculated and hence its depletion by development compensated for.

This approach has considerable advantages in that it highlights the adverse externality effects of development activity and works through market behaviour. But such a commodification of the environment is neither technically simple nor morally easy to accept. The technical problems focus around the definition of a constant stock of environmental assets. Debates focus around what counts as an asset and how assets are valued. Can all assets be exchangeable, so that the loss of an ancient woodland can be replaced with the creation of some sportsfields? Or are some assets 'unalienable', critical to our survival? Pearce *et al.* (1989) argue that some assets should be treated as 'critical natural capital' and hence unalienable. The vocabulary of heritage sites could be seen as having such qualities. But what about greenbelts, or areas of 'outstanding natural beauty'? How do these come to be unalienable? Is greenbelt a tool to protect a natural resource around cities for all time, or is it merely a mechanism for managing urban growth and urban fringe land markets? (Elson, 1986). Are our notions of what is critical to be derived from economic analysis, or natural science, or do they in fact arise because of our cultural traditions, our *beliefs* about what is important. If so, how do we bring such dimensions into our valuing? Further, is it possible to treat biospheric relations in the language of stocks and assets when it is the ecological *relationships* which are critical. Can the quality of a hydrological system be treated as a commodity, or the interdependence of tree cover, pollution levels and bird life in cities? (Owens, 1994; Beatley, 1994; Goodin, 1992). And how can an economics which deals in individual preferences address questions of cultural beliefs and systems of meaning? These difficulties in addressing environmental problems in the language of economics provide policy space for other styles of argument.

Environmental systems and carrying capacity

Natural science, and particularly ecological analysis, provides an alternative vocabulary. The central focus of ecology is a relational one, emphasising the relations of species to habitats, the interdependencies between ecosystems, and between ecological, hydrological, climatological and geological systems. Science offers no simple answers, and there are vigorous debates within ecology about the driving forces of the relationships examined and about what relationships exist. However, the approach has pushed into policy debate the language of systemic limits to the capacity of biospheric systems to absorb exploitation, depletion and pollution. This leads to an emphasis on the 'critical natural carrying capacities' of local environments and urban regions. This is linked to a moral attitude in the face of scientific uncertainty. If it is not possible to be certain about the amount and scale of damage to carrying capacity which a project or a strategy will produce, it is better to be 'on the safe side'. This is embodied in the precautionary principle. If in doubt about the scale of environmental damage, it is better not to proceed (C. Williams, 1993).

In the terms of these debates, the objective of environmental sustainability focuses on the maintenance of environmental *systems.* Such systems, webs of biospheric relations, have the capacity for self-renewal and evolution, but can be destroyed if their habitats are adversely affected, or they are used up in absorbing too much waste matter, or if they are depleted by over-use. Policy research is then needed to identify critical natural thresholds, which should be safeguarded by both regulatory policies and by positive environmental management. It is these thresholds that become the 'unalienable' element of the environmental inheritance which one generation should pass on to the next. Environmental audits using this policy language focus attention on the causal chains between system quality and adverse effects. An interesting example is a Californian case of Natural Communities Conservation Planning, where the approach shifted from a species-by-species approach, to a focus on 'natural communities', informed by a panel of scientific experts (Innes *et al.*, 1994). From this point of view, localities become an important focus of attention to the extent that they co-relate with key natural systems, such as water basins. A central emphasis in public policy becomes the management of economic and social activity within areas so that adverse impacts are reduced, and where possible, drawn back within the critical natural thresholds. The language of limits replaces that of trade-offs (Owens, 1994; Healey and Shaw, 1994). Demand management thus takes on a more radical meaning, potentially involving reductions in overall levels of activity. It leads to a policy emphasis on setting targets aimed to reduce levels of pollution within the capacity of locally-specific natural systems and which contribute to supranational and global reductions in pollution. Recent British innovations in local air quality and waste recycling targets reflect this approach (see, for example, Petts, 1995).

Where natural environmental system thresholds within an urban region are vulnerable to further development, then their protection should have priority over all other policy objectives. Obvious examples of such situations can be found, such as the creation of a state planning system in Florida to ensure the maintenance of the delicate water balances of the Everglades swamps (DeGrove, 1984). A political community concerned with distributive consequences should then provide funds to help those adversely affected by the imposition of necessary limits on development.

This approach seems to have more affinity with the 'institutionalist' view in social science, in that it emphasises relations rather than 'things'. It forces attention to the way phenomena are interconnected in ways which the economistic approach neglects. It requires some form of collective action and community responsibility if the actions of individuals are to be limited within natural constraints. But it too encounters problems. Ecologists, climatologists and hydrologists find it hard to identify and agree upon key natural thresholds (Worster, 1977). To the exent that such threshholds exist, they are contingent on the particularities of specific circumstances, and therefore require considerable scientific effort in local investigation (O'Callaghan, 1995). One reason for this scientific difficulty is that natural systems are no more static than human ones. They evolve and adapt to changing situations. This raises the question of what particular form of a system is to be regarded as natural. Are unusual weather patterns experienced in the mid-1990s the result of 'global warming' or just 'natural'? What kind of landscape can be regarded as 'natural' in Britain, or the Australian bush, and what justification is there for measures to conserve them?

These kinds of issue illustrate the cultural dimensions of concerns about the natural world. Views about the 'integrity' of nature are not merely scientific. They arise from our metaphysical and aesthetic appreciation of landscape and the natural order. In using the language of contemporary natural science, which appears to deal in objectively-established facts, we seek to mask this relation. Nature can be treated as 'out there', to be managed rather than damaged by human activity, in the same way that economics converts nature into commodifiable assets to be used rather than abused by profit-maximising humans. But these languages of natural science and economics are infused by values, by conceptions of individuals, and of the relations between people and nature which their search for objectification renders invisible. They are the product of carefully-crafted social processes of 'fact-production' (Latour, 1987). Yet in the arena of public debate on environmental policies, such objectification is continually contested, both explicitly and implicitly. A key issue for managing our co-existence in shared spaces in acknowledgement of the natural world is the ability to combine scientific contestation with public debate without getting caught up too deeply in the internal processes of scientific contestation.

The environment as 'our world'

The ecocentric or 'deep green' view has leverage in this context as its starting point is a moral position, rather than scientific evidence. The human species is conceived as but one among the many natural species co-existing within the natural world. It draws on the collaborative rather than competitive strand in ecological traditions, to emphasise the harmonious relations between natural species, and the importance of sensitive adaptation to local environments. The image of 'planet earth', or 'Gaia', as a set of delicately balanced ecological relationships, as promoted by James Lovelock (1979), is an important metaphor in this thinking. Preindustrial conditions are often taken as an ideal, within which people lived much closer to the earth, tending the soil and caring for animals. The core of the ecocentric view is not a form of analysis, but a moral attitude of environmental respect and care, reflecting the feeling of belonging with nature and needing to be in balance with natural systems. Other species, and the local relations between species, are to be accorded the same respect as we give to human relations. The only distinctive quality allowed the human species is a capacity to reflect on our conditions of existence. The moral responsibility of this capacity is the requirement to treat our common natural world in a way which sustains rather than damages its interrelationships and means of survival. Sustainability thus means that we move beyond the demand management strategies of the ecological scientists and the economists to reconstitute our thinking about ourselves, our modes of economic production, our ways of life and our relations with nature. The clear implication is that the relations of capitalist social organisation and all its technological and material benefits are largely *unsustainable*. Local environmental management is thus not merely a question of careful attention to the flourishing of natural species, the conservation of resource use and thoughtful waste recycling practices. It means we have to be prepared to live quite differently. This construction of environmentalism also raises the importance of rights. If humans have rights, so too do other species. This position has been strongly advocated by animal rights groups in Britain, and by organisations such as The Royal Society for the Protection of Birds, which claims to speak 'on behalf' of bird species.

Such a perspective has long antecedents in radical communitarian movements (Beatley, 1994; Beevers, 1988). Ebenezer Howard reflected some of these ideas as he dreamed of his 'Garden City'. Its value in the present period is that it speaks unashamedly in the language of moral imperative, infused with the sense of an emotive and moral relation with nature rather than a material one. It enters the political arena with strong arguments and robust convictions. But its very radicalism leads to its limitations. Because it rejects so much of 'the way we live now', it has little tolerance for the values and ways of life of most people in western societies. It tends to speak with the voice of fundamentalism, entrenching differences with the unenlightened others. It offers a radical vision, but the path towards it seems hard and destructive of present worlds. Thus while it brings into local environmental policy debate a wider array of interests and concerns, particularly the 'voices' of the different natural species, it does so at the expense of hostility to many people in our own species.

The environment as a cultural conception

The fourth strand of environmental debate recognises that how we view the environment is not the result of objective facts or fundamental principles of our planetary condition. It arises from the way we look at the world and our place in it. Our conceptions are socially-constructed, and interlinked with our other preoccupations and ways of understanding. It is this perspective which dominated the Brundtland Report itself. This attempts to interweave the biospheric dimensions of environmental care with a concern for the sustainability of *human* social relations. It is infused with a concern for the distributive consequences among people of human interaction with the natural world. It asks firstly how far 'the way we live now', both globally and in our different places, communities and classes is *reproducible* over the long term. Secondly, it is infused with a moral notion of how we ought to live. Our concern should be not just to maximise general human welfare as some aggregate, in the conceptions of neoclassical economics. It should be to enable the 'flourishing' of all human life in its individual particularities and social contexts. Human life is conceived as lived in social relations and cultures within which relations with the natural world are framed. Enhancing the quality of life is not just a matter of material welfare. It is also a matter of spiritual and emotional richness, and involves discourses about rights and responsibilities.

Such a conception can be viewed as an extension of the humanitarian socialist project which has had such a powerful political influence since the nineteenth century in western societies. According to such a view, the new environmentalism is transforming this project from the doldrums of a political preoccupation with promoting the interests of workers over capitalists in which it got becalmed in the post-war period, to a richer understanding of the nature of the ways people exist in the natural world and the value which a respectful and collaborative attitude to the natural world contributes to our own well-being. Unlike the ecocentric fundamentalists, this perspective is deliberately inclusionary, ecompassing a recognition of the diversity of forms of social relation and culture in contemporary societies, seeking to accommodate the plurality of ways of living and understanding in the modern world. The challenge it sets itself is to discover ways of co-existing, among the cultures of the human species and within the relations of the natural world, in ways which are mutually sustaining rather than collectively destroying (Blowers (ed.), 1993; Beatley, 1994).

This perspective locates the new environmentalism as a *cultural* project, rather than a technological or scientific one. Before we can decide whether and what to measure and calculate, we need to understand how we think about ourselves, our place in the natural world, our societies and our values. We need to work out why we have become so sensitive to environmental threats, and why we consider some attributes of the environment as 'unalienable', that is as sacred. We need to work out how collectively we give priorities to certain qualities of our local environment before we set out to devise policies to protect these priorities. Such debates about how we should think crop up regularly in any arena of public debate on environmental issues – in disputes about the siting of power stations and motorways, in debates on water management or energy policy, in discussions about the quality of urban life or the conservation of the countryside. The value of such a perspective is that it explicitly links our biospheric concerns with our other cares. It offers the possibility of addressing environmental issues 'in the round', as material, moral and emotive-aesthetic, reflecting the ways we as humans interact with the biosphere. It brings 'everyday life' back in as part of the ongoing flow of social relations interlinked with ecological ones (Nord, 1991). Following the institutionalist perspective of this book, it allows us to see our 'relational webs' with the biosphere as an integral dimension of our other relational webs, and it helps us see how what we do in social contexts impacts on our environmental inheritance. The project of sustainability thus becomes an explicitly moral project – to maintain the conditions of human flourishing among ourselves and between the generations.

These environmental debates have clearly both extended the range of policy considerations and recaste many issues in new terms. They have also added to the range of policy discourses with which local environmental issues may be discussed. By policy discourse here is meant not merely the language of policy debate, but the organising conceptions, the key metaphors and the storylines brought into play (Hajer, 1993; and see Chapter 8). There are clear dominant tendencies among the discourses, promoted by governments and policy élites seeking to accommodate the pressure for greater environmental sensitivity through modification rather than transformation of policy agendas and practices. These emphasise the possibility of technological solutions ('technofix') and economic accommodations (compensating trade-offs). These approaches dominated British public policy in the mid-1990s, drawing on the asset stock and natural capacity approaches, grounded in economics and natural science. These traditions provide quite radical principles for contemporary western economies, as in the principle of environmental mitigation; the polluter pays; the notion of demand management within natural environmental limits, and the precautionary principle.

But they deny the *cultural* dimensions of our perceptions of environmental issues, and the moral and aesthetic questions they raise (Hajer, 1995; Owens, 1994). Such questions have, however, proved ever more difficult to exclude, both because of the problems of deciding what it is, specifically, about natural stocks and capacities which makes them of value and because of the wider tendencies in our societies to loose faith in the wisdom of science and technique. But including them opens up the potential, already evident in many environmental disputes, for conflict over strategies, policies, indicators and the terms of policy evaluation. It is in recognition of this, combined with the realisation that any real progress on the policy agendas raised by contemporary environmentalism means persuading everyone to think and act differently, that there is a strong emphasis in environmental politics on democratic participation (Blowers (ed.), 1993). There is also an increasing interest in the assertion of rights arising from environmental considerations. This raises the question as to the kind of institutional capacity that would provide appropriate arenas and processes for debating and asserting our different ways of constructing our concerns about our relations with the natural world.

The environmental debate and spatial planning

Spatial and land use planning systems, which focus on what development happens where and on what terms, are unavoidably involved in the contemporary re-thinking of our relations with the natural world. But their established practices are also a source of resistance to the re-thinking. For this reason, new environmental policy systems are often developed, in uneasy tension with planning systems (Glasson *et al.*, 1994).

Proposals for land use change and development inherently impact on the natural world and how we value it, while spatial planners, as discussed earlier, are typically deeply infused with elements of a biospheric concern for environment, in Britain at least. It is therefore very difficult to separate questions of environmental policy from the practice of land use planning. Local development permitting practices routinely assess the impacts of a proposed project on local environmental qualities. Local development plans address the relations between development activity and natural environmental systems. Such local planning work is now required to mediate among competing claims, the terms of which have been transformed by the environmental debate. This means not only the introduction of new issues and priorities into local debate, for example, the promotion of biodiversity or the reduction of car-produced air pollution, but the infiltration of new languages and styles of argument, to challenge the legal-administrative style built up in previous decades (McAuslan, 1980). Land use planning systems are thus often presented as 'part of the problem'. This could lead to either the sidelining of land use planning systems in the management of local environmental change, or to their radical transformation. The British government has swung between resisting new EC policy measures for environmental impact assessment on the grounds that the planning system did the job well already, to introducing new parallel environmental regulatory practices (Glasson *et al.*, 1994). Responsibility for local environmental regulation now falls within the remit of both the planning system and the new Environmental Protection Agency, combining the previous National Rivers Authority and Her Majesty's Inspectorate of Pollution. Owens, discussing the challenge for the British land use planning system, has suggested that the new environmental debate could act as a transformatory 'trojan horse' as it permeates planning debate and practice (Owens, 1994). Yet, as discussed earlier, planning systems may already embody a strong tradition of environmental concern. Just as at the level of environmental policy in general, the debate tends to be captured by the dominant policy languages, so in the arena of local planning systems, the new conceptions may come to be reinterpreted in the language of the old.

What then do the new environmental debates bring to questions of the management of local environmental change? At one level, the consequence of closer attention to biospheric conservation recasts thinking about a whole range of material issues. It leads to new priorities for conservation, whether conceived as a stock of qualities or as critical biospheric capacities. It adds new criteria to considerations of the location of development and the terms on which development should take place. It emphasises the importance of considering the biospheric impacts of any proposal for changes to land uses and development and the ways adverse impacts could be mitigated. It suggests that policy should define critical natural capacity 'areas' within which particular standards and targets should be met. Planning policy should also promote environmentally-desirable development. This of course brings further conflict as some developments, such as local waste management plants and new forms of renewable energy development, may produce their own patterns of adverse local side effects (Hull, 1995). This may require the negotiation of compensatory measures for those adversely affected by these new developments.

These pressures encourage the recasting of planning thinking into a form which focuses explicitly on arguments about impacts, the impacts of development projects on different fields of concern. In the US, where local planning practice focuses on the rights of developers and the negotiation of limitations of these, complex practices have evolved around the negotiation of development exactions and the payment of impact fees, through which a wide range of environmental impacts are addressed (Cullingworth, 1993; Healey, Purdue and Ennis, 1995). Within Britain in the 1990s, encouraged by recent changes in national policy (DoE, 1991), similar practices have evolved to negotiate developers' contributions to mitigating the environmental impacts of their projects, through providing infrastructure, local community services and natural environmental assets (Whatmore and Boucher, 1993; Healey, Purdue and Ennis, 1995; Elson, 1986; Cowell, 1993).

However, these practices uncover considerable uncertainty as to how an impact is to be identified and the scale of its significance. Such bargaining represents an explicit approach to balancing and trading-off losses with compensation. It is justified by the principle that the producers of adverse impacts – the 'polluter' – should pay for the consequences of their projects. This should encourage developers to reduce the scale of their impacts, and hopefully reduce the 'demands' they make on biospheric capacities.

At the level of development regulation and guidance for the development of zones and neighbourhoods, the environmental agenda is currently being absorbed into issues to do with the orientation and design of buildings, to allow for solar heating, to reduce energy use in heating and to encourage internal waste recycling. There has also been much interest in reducing the segregation of uses in neighbourhoods, to enable energy-reducing synergies to be obtained. This has challenged the traditions of the segregation of land use zones, established in the post-war era to help protect residential neighbourhoods from industrial pollution in the form of smoke, noise and smell. The new planning vocabulary now emphasises the desirability of 'mixed uses' (CEC, 1990).

These criteria are now being consolidated in Britain into formal policies in the context of the preparation of a new round of development plan preparation. In many plans until very recently, the environmental agenda was approached by expanding the treatment of 'environment' as a topic, in parallel with other topics such as the economy and housing. Questions of pollution management and the location of renewable energy projects would be grouped together with policies for countryside protection, built environment conservation and urban design. By the start of the 1990s, a slow shift could be seen towards orienting the general strategy of the plans to reflect new ways of thinking about the environment. By the mid-1990s, this shift had gathered momentum, encouraged by revised government policy guidelines. A flood of plans has been produced with strategic statements referring to environmental sustainability. This re-orientation is translated into policies which restrict the location of development to areas serviceable by public transport, and which take a tougher attitude against peripheral development generally, in order to protect town centres. A new urban structure model of the 'compact city' is being asserted to challenge the decentralizing impetus encouraged in the 1980s. It harks back to the traditional model of the mid-twentieth century planners, of a contained city surrounded by its greenbelt (Breheny, 1992). Only a few plans have moved on to develop conceptions of capacity constraints, and the management of development to reduce the stresses on these capacities (Marshall, 1992; Healey and Shaw, 1994; Owens, 1994). In current British planning practice, however, there is a strong move to force the debates explicitly down the 'carrying capacity' path (C.Williams, 1993).

Despite these halting advances, the increasing emphasis in government policy and local planning statements on constraints and limits is beginning to cause concern among development interests. The hope embodied in the concept of *sustainable development* that environmental considerations and economic development priorities could co-exist to mutual benefit, looks increasingly unlikely, as policies reach operational specification.

But perhaps the most dramatic impact of the new concern with environmental issues is at the level of strategic spatial planning. This arises in part from the recognition of capacity constraints. As already noted, one factor behind the increased interest in strategic planning in the US has been the concern to 'manage' growth to protect critical thresholds in valued sensitive ecosystems (Innes, 1992; Nijkamp and Perrels, 1994). In Europe, however, and particularly in Britain, the environmental agenda has forced a reconsideration of the role of the car. The dominant theme in transport policy in Britain since the war had been towards accommodating the growing ownership and use of motor vehicles. Motorway systems were built to facilitate the conversion of travel from rail to road. Towns and villages were bypassed to speed up travel. The emphasis in evaluating such schemes was on efficiency gains in the form of time savings. While rail lines were closed because they were considered uneconomic to run, town centres were remodelled to accommodate the car, and neighbourhoods were designed to allow households to shelter their vehicles. When locations near good road access became attractive for business development and major retail complexes, planning policy which had sought to keep urban development contained and compact was obligingly relaxed by national government policy (Thornley, 1991). Public investment was justified in priveleging road building over rail through evaluation measures which hid the massive subsidies to road building while highlighting the subsidy towards rail (Whitelegg, 1993). This reflected in part the strong influence on government policy of the road-building construction firms. But it also reflected a cultural preoccupation with the car as a leisure item and status symbol. Many people *enjoy* their cars. What car you have becomes a status symbol within a status-ridden society. It liberates you from the constraints of neighbourhoods. It enables access to all kinds of leisure destinations, and it helps manage the complexities of household life, as discussed in Chapter 4. However, the new environmental concerns have revealed the car in a different light. It consumes a lot of energy. It produces congestion. It causes accidents and now it has emerged as the major cause of the serious air pollution of cities. Several cities have had to introduce some form of demand management on car use at times when air pollution is particularly severe. Even in Britain, with its more changeable and windy climate, air pollution is frequently at serious levels in many urban areas (Banister and Button (eds), 1993).

Faced with this reality, the British government has recently made a major rhetorical U-turn in its presentation of transport policy. There have been reductions in the road programme, while national planning policy directives now assert that peripheral retail development will be resisted and that all new development must be located near public transport routes. Exactly how this will work out is not clear as no funds are being provided to promote public transport. Cynics argue that the U-turn is as much a response to public expenditure crises and the political and financial cost of negotiating new road routes as it is driven by environmental considerations (Owens, 1995).

Nevertheless, this shift in transport policy signifies the end of one of the most alluring symbols of the modernist dream, the individualised transport technology item. The car is now so locked into popular culture that it is not at all clear how exhortation to limit its use will work out. The neo-liberal policy solution is to work through pricing policies, increasing costs both generally, and in particular vulnerable locations. But changing people's travel habits is much more than an exercise in economics. It involves cultural shifts, in ways of thinking about travel and ways of according social position and status. Pricing policies may merely exacerbate differences between access to status goods.

Within the planning community, the solution has been seen in terms of the spatial arrangement of urban areas. The challenge has been to analyse and develop principles of urban form which consume less energy, produce less waste and minimise car-borne pollution. There are now a number of studies which aim to explore which urban forms appear to be the least environmentally damaging. Some argue that cities should be compact – the traditional contained city of British planning policy. Others claim that there is no necessary reason why compact settlements would reduce travel distances or pollution levels. If people live and work in diverse, spatially extended relational webs, they may merely have to travel from one compact city to another. If cities are compact, they may also be congested and polluted (see Breheny, 1992).

These debates link rather uncertainly to conceptions of the critical natural capacity of particular urban regions (Nijkamp, Vleugel and Kreutzberger, 1993). They focus on natural biospheric relations and on managing demand within capacity limits. They combine with the pressures arising from local economic development concerns and new patterns of social life to find ways of reconceptualising localities in terms of spatial form and arrangement. The challenge is to develop concepts of urban spatial 'structure' which are underpinned by understanding of both the dynamics of the economic and social relations of contemporary urban life and by the specific relations which a way of living has with the particular natural systems in a place. But the most thoughtful contributions to this debate emphasise that there are no easy models. What urban spatial arrangement is appropriate in a place will depend not just on the nature of local biospheric systems, local economic dilemmas and local ways of living, but on how political communities in a place think about and value the various attributes of their place and lives. However much the environmental agenda leads to changes in conceptions, these are woven together with existing preoccupations and power relations. This is clearly evident in the way the environmental debate is being used to reassert the principle of 'compact cities' (Breheny, 1992). This shows clearly the way a new discourse is drawn back into the terms of an old one, in this case in Britain, that of the conservation of the countryside from urban sprawl.

The new environmental agenda thus brings into the field of local planning a flood of new issues to attend to, new claims for policy attention, new criteria to incorporate into existing justificatory practices, new conceptions of urban design and spatial organisation, new techniques of appraisal and evaluation, new policy languages and new modes of thought. In a curiously paradoxical way, the environmental debate is also acting as a channel for introducing a new economic language into planning practice, in the terms of impacts and how they are valued (Lichfield, 1992), while at the same time exposing, in new forms, conflicts between planning policies and economic activity. How these tensions are addressed depends then on how political communities deal with the issues 'in the round', interrelating their social, economic and environmental dimensions. As Owens (1994) stresses, this takes the debate beyond the language of stocks and capacities, to questions of value and culture, of morality and ethics. These issues, as noted earlier in this chapter, have long been embedded in planning tradition. The challenge for local environmental planning is to address them explicitly. To do this will mean challenging more vigorously the dominant British discourse, with its languages of economics and natural science, opening up to wider debates on *ethical land use* (Beatley, 1994).

The transformative power of the new environmentalism

The new environmentalism is now a wide-ranging popular movement, with significant political leverage in western societies. It has changed policy agendas and regulatory practices, altered business strategies and affected everyday behaviour, particularly among middle income groups. It is recasting the policies and practices of spatial planning, reviving traditional meanings of 'environment' and bringing in new conceptions, new stakeholders and new claims for policy attention. It is also fostering new practices – of audit, impact appraisal and negotiation over mitigation measures, and of consultation and participation. This 'transformative wave' illustrates well the power of ideas and arguments to mobilise forces to change ways of thinking and ways of acting.

Yet within this broad umbrella co-exist different and potentially conflicting strands of interpretation, producing different policy discourses. The institutionalist approach adopted in this book is most in sympathy with ecological ideas about the natural world which stress the interrelation of social and natural worlds, and which recognise the cultural embeddedness of conceptions of these relations. It also highlights the dangers of discursive domination. This is a critical issue at the present stage of the development of environmental policy. Will the new agenda transform old power relations embodied in the priveleged position of considerations of economic growth and the technologies of rational calculus in public policy? Or will these bastions of discursive power be able successfully to pursue strategies of accommodation to the new pressures without fundamentally changing the systems which consolidate their positions?

The strategies of 1970s green politics adopted a confrontational stance towards business and the state, suspicious of their motivation and ability to transform (Galtung, 1986). The Brundtland Commission turned the debate into more collaborative channels, arguing that an accommodation could be reached between economic interests and environmental concerns, if business could be persuaded to take on a wider moral remit to its social costs and its duties to others – both in other parts of the world and future generations. This offered the hope of a zero-plus game. Businesses were in any case already adapting to the new political climate, and the reality and potential of more robust regulatory policies. New market niches appeared in the production of environmentally-friendly products and technologies. This seems to confirm the power of ideas and new discourses to shape economic activity as well as public policy.

But beneath these accommodations, the old power relations are laying claim to the agenda. Governments everywhere, both local and central, are fearful of restraining the business sector too much, because of the vulnerability of national and local economies in a globalising economy. 'Technofix' solutions which mitigate the adverse consequences of economic activity are preferred over ones which reduce the level of activity, as the former have the potential to create jobs and profits, while the latter will reduce both. Public officials, groups of experts and powerful pressure groups capture control of policy-agenda setting and the definition of the terms of discourse from popular movements, encouraging techno-corporatist practices rather than inclusionary debate. Policy initiatives focus on national and international regulatory criteria, rather than on the specific interrelations which people and firms have with the natural worlds in which they exist. Moral and aesthetic issues are downplayed, and converted into the vocabulary of economic calculus. If people object, they are labelled as NIMBYs, pursuing resistance to any development, whereas they may rather be full of mistrust about the way government and business go about thinking about their concerns (Macnaghten *et al.*, 1995; Wolsink, 1994).

Counteracting these tendencies means opening up the environmental arena once again to popular involvement. This is a major thrust behind the Local Agenda 21 movement, set in motion at the Rio Conference in 1992, and pursued with considerable enthusiasm by local authorities and grassroots organisations in several European countries, notably Britain, Denmark and Sweden. Local Agenda 21 asks local communities to identify their key environmental problems and to set targets for addressing them (Patterson and Theobald, 1995). It is in the arenas set up for this activity that all kinds of experiments are developing in interactive agenda-building and collaborative policy development (Bell, 1996). Bubbling up through interactive encounters are a diversity of ideas about issues and possibilities, and the particular conditions of social and bisopheric life in local environments. These illustrate the importance of 'local knowledge' (see Chapter 2) in recognising locally significant environmental issues, and developing indicators for monitoring changes in important relationships. People have to become 'travellers in their own lands' to help accumulate the knowledge which will enable policy initiatives to pay attention to the finegrain of the particular relations of 'their' places (Latour, 1987). To convey this understanding into wider arenas they then have to connect to agenda-setting policy communities. This means becoming involved interactively in policy-making work. Given the potential for conflict between stakeholders in local environments, and the uneven power relations among stakeholders, a critical challenge for the integration of environmental, economic and social dimensions of managing change in local environments is to find ways of collaborative agenda-setting and policy development, to build policy approaches which are more inclusionary in the issues and stakes they encompass and more informed by locally relevant understanding. This will open up for debate the richness of conceptions of the environment, but it will also generate new cleavages and conflicts, between specific interests and between conceptions. The design of the institutional capacity for collaborative consensus-building practices in this context involves a creative effort in governance. It is precisely in the area of negotiating the relations between economic and environmental priorities and understandings that much of the innovation in consensus-building policy practices is taking place (for example, in the UK and Australia; see Innes *et al.*, 1994; Innes, 1995). These practices are discussed further in Chapter 8.

But collaborative consensus-building by itself is not enough to confront the power of traditional economic and political bastions, despite the leverage of popular environmentalism on economic and political systems. The environmental debate also raises questions about rights and duties. The power of discourse needs to be buttressed by the power of law, and the definition of robust rights and duties, to force issues important to all stakeholders, and ways of thinking about them, into the political and policy arena and bring potentially reluctant parties to the arena of collaboration. These questions of the design of policy systems are addressed in Chapter 9.

Part III

PROCESSES FOR COLLABORATIVE PLANNING

Introduction

Part II has elaborated an institutional approach to social, economic and environmental dynamics and has sought to highlight the implications both for understanding concerns with local environmental change, and the demands on governance for ways of addressing those matters of collective concern. Throughout, the complex social relational webs through which issues and interests are identified have been stressed, as well as their cultural diversity and differential spatial reach. Places and cultures are no longer coterminous. Different cultures may reach across many places, and particular places are likely to contain a mixture of cultural communities, more or less interconnected. This generates an enormous potential for conflict over the qualities of local environments. Such conflicts are not just between local groups of equal status, or over individual preferences and interests. They are infused with the power relations of the wider structuring forces which generate dominant economic orders, promote tendencies in lifestyle choices, and organise governance through state forms. Yet the quality of life, the natural environment and the economic health of places depends critically on local capacities for managing these conflicts. Further, what people do in particular places has wider consequences. So the challenge of managing co-existence in shared spaces reflects and expresses in acute form the wider challenge of the search for forms of governance appropriate to a world of global relations within which local action matters.

The focus of Part III is on this search, as pursued in relation to the management of local environments. It thus represents a shift from the analytical tasks of Part II to a normative agenda of institutional capacity building. It seeks to challenge the notion of governance as merely the formal institutions of government, and of government as primarily the provider of economic and welfare services, and protector of environmental qualities. In its place, an alternative notion of collaborative governance is developed, within which the formal institutions of government have a role in providing a hard infrastructure of a *structure of challenges*, to constrain and modify dominant centres of power, and a soft infrastructure of *relation-building* through which sufficient consensus building and mutual learning can occur to develop *social, intellectual and political capital* to promote co-ordination and the flow of knowledge and competence among the various social relations co-existing within places. A key challenge lies in the combination of the design of the hard infrastructure, and the inherent struggles which will take place as power relations are deliberately transformed, and the design of the soft infrastructure, which should be locally specific and collaborative. Sustainable institutional design results where both levels work well both with each other and in relation to their wider contexts.

Contemporary critiques of environmental planning systems, along with the machinery of government generally, suggest that this combination is not being achieved with any success in many parts of the western world. Planning regimes are decried as negative, rigidly rule-following, inefficient and subject to hidden influence (Schon, 1983; Reade, 1987). Government activities are criticised as ill-informed, oppressive, inefficient, unaccountable, insensitive to diversity. Governments are accused of being driven by the self-serving interests of politicians and officials, political parties and bureaucracies (Thornley, 1991; Dunleavy and O'Leary, 1987). Postmodern analysts present planning systems as a modernising 'relict' of an earlier era (Dear, 1995). Neo-liberals argue that our state forms are an unwanted inheritance of a centralist welfare state (Thornley, 1991). Structuralists see the state as an arm of capital, or as an institution of the technical and business classes (Castells, 1977).

Faced with such critiques, how can a governance capacity be revived which has the potential to address the challenges outlined in Part II, and generate a *public realm* within which *political communities* can develop new approaches? How can governance be transformed? Some argue that most of the current machinery of government can be dispensed with. This is argued by anarchists, communitarians and by neo-liberal philosophers. Anarchists and communitarians seek the disintegration of all except the self-management practices of small communities (Dryzek, 1990).

Such views tend either to ignore the complex ways in which we are interrelated these days, across time and space, or to abandon them in the search for alternative, more locally circumscribed, modes of life. Radical neo-liberals propose to 'roll back' the frontiers of the state, to release individual private initiative (Gamble, 1988). This neglects the extent to which individuals exist in social relations with others, and ignores the power relations which underpin capitalist economic processes. It also ignores the tendencies to market failure which have given rise in the past to state intervention in economic management. Rather than 'getting rid of government', the present critiques are more appropriately interpreted as asking questions about appropriate modes of governance, our arenas and forms of governance, who these privilege and who they marginalise; what they are effective in achieving and what they seem unable to cope with; and how to evolve modes of governance more appropriate to the ways we now think about economies, social life and nature.

The dilemmas of co-existence in shared spaces present starkly both the need for effective governance mechanisms, and the problems of devising them. As we have become aware of, and respectful of, the diversity of ways of living, of lifestyles and cultures, so we look for ways of providing space for choice and the assertion of difference. But this brings us into conflict at the finegrain of our spatial experience as well as in our broader concerns. A proposal for a childcare centre in an urban neighbourhood can be a helpful asset for working parents. It can also create traffic hazards as children are dropped off and picked up at busy times and can lead to cheerful but often irritatingly high-pitched noise for immediate neighbours. Protecting cultural heritage in the form of archaeological sites may mean that some poor farmers who have such sites in their fields, and can therefore no longer cultivate them, have even fewer options for survival than before. If we lose faith in our governance mechanisms, these conflicts will be resolved by the power of money and landownership. The result, as discussed in Chapter 4, may be short-term gain for those with resources, but often longer term destruction of what they themselves value, as well as what others value. It is also likely to lead to further polarisation of opportunity among the culturally diverse, to marginalisation of those whose differences are unacceptable to powerful groups, to active moves by the affluent to segregate themselves from the problems their actions create and to entrenching the language of distrust, struggle and opposition in people's ideas about collective organising strategies.

The same is true in the sphere of economic life. Economic activities take place in a dynamic world of globalising markets and organizational relations, within which companies are struggling intensely for competitive advantage. Without careful economic development policies, and measures to make companies comfortable in a place, firms may have a tendency to 'asset strip' their locales, moving on when a place has nothing further to offer, leaving behind the downsides, the adverse externalities of their operations. Drawing down benefits from companies into the social and economic life of a place in environmentally sensitive ways requires a capacity for locally-informed, place-based governance, as discussed in Chapter 5. Localities with intersecting social relations, rich in knowledge of production processes, business opportunities and the potential manoeuvres of the powerful seem to be able to achieve this task more effectively than those which are introverted, with conflictual and distrustful social relations and little knowledge flow between social groups.

The governance of economic life demands hard infrastructure as well, in terms of rules for regulating competition between firms and in relation to labour conditions, and resources to address questions of 'public goods', such as infrastructure, research and development investment, labour training, welfare and reproduction. Such measures, along with the arrangements for transferring profits from firms to pay for such public goods, may lead to actions across national or supranational space. It used to be argued that economic policy was a matter for national governments, while local governments were concerned with questions of local services and amenities (see, for example, Saunders, 1981). Chapter 5 has argued for the importance of a local role in economic management, particularly in relation to the soft infrastructure of institutional capacity. Others argue for the significance of supranational entities. The implication is that in our globalising economies, the governance challenge is to interrelate several *levels* or scales of economic governance.

This conclusion is obvious in the environmental sphere where the impacts on sensitive local ecosystems of pollution-generating localities in other parts of the globe is now well understood. Yet it could apply to all the tendencies discussed in Chapters 4, 5 and 6. It is in the environmental field in recent years that there has been a proliferation of hard infrastructure measures at national or international level, with the introduction of new wide-ranging environmental regulation measures. But these bear down upon the specific circumstances of localities. How may the diversity of claims for attention manifest within a locality be addressed with sensitivity to co-existence within a specific place while recognising that what happens in a place matters to other areas and other people? How can people in one place make a claim for policy attention in another?

This takes the challenge of developing new forms of governance into familiar debates about the *competences* of different *levels* of government. An institutional approach highlights other important dimensions of governance which focus on the forms and styles of social interaction in governance arenas. If we differ in the ways we know and value our conditions of life, if we speak languages which differ in their vocabulary, their metaphors and their points of reference, how do we develop styles of governance which suit us all? Is it inevitable that we are locked into power struggles within which the same groups always win the chance to dominate the rest of us? Government agencies in Britain and the US are under pressure to be more responsive to citizens, to have charters for 'customer care', to monitor perfomance by criteria which emphasise service to the 'consumer' of government (Mayo, 1994). But will not sensitivity to the stylistic demands of one group of citizens generate problems for another?

In the context of these questions, the aim of Part III is to:

- discuss current debates on the forms and styles of governance;
- explore the opportunities for more pluralistic, democratic forms of governance, and their characteristics;
- assess the challenge of processes of institutional design which could promote such forms in the context of the governance challenge of managing co-existence in shared places, such as local environmental planning.

Chapter 7 reviews the meaning of government and governance, before examining different forms of government and 'planning' as a style of governance. Chapter 8 examines the challenge of *strategic argumentation,* the processes through which political communities can articulate their common concerns about spaces and places in ways which are inclusionary, but which also can produce strategies which 'make a difference'. Chapter 9 explores the design of policy *regimes* for managing our local environmental concerns which will build in the legal and procedural safeguards needed for inclusionary argumentation while at the same time providing the authority for taking action in efficient and legitimate ways. This discussion is not intended as a recipe book for a new planning. Rather, it is provided to help people think about how to invent, and how to critique, local environmental management practices and possibilities. Part III thus shifts from an analytical mode of presentation to a normative one, presenting the case for collaborative planning as a style of governance and making suggestions as to how this could be realized.

7 Planning and Governance

Government and governance

This chapter reviews the dimensions of governance, and the different modes which governance can take. It explores in particular the nature of planning, as a style of governance characterised by a policy-driven, or *planning*, approach and how far this may co-exist with specific governance modes. It thus builds on the policy analysis approach to planning outlined in Chapter 2. It then confronts the critique of policy analysis as grounded in instrumental rationalism, serving technocratic and corporatist modes of governance, to argue for new directions in governance modes which are more sensitive to the 'consumers' of public policy rather than the government 'producers' of policy. These new directions make use of a policy-driven approach, but vary in their relative emphasis on 'hard' and 'soft' institutional infrastructures. The chapter concludes with an argument for a democratic pluralist mode of governance and a collaborative style of planning to help in realising it. This argument builds on both a normative concern with more people-sensitive modes of governance and a practical concern with the management of local environmental change in situations of multiple and often conflictual stakeholders, typical examples of 'shared-power worlds' (Bryson and Crosby, 1992). The approach to governance developed here expresses an institutionalist approach through its emphasis not merely on the interactive nature of governance processes but on the way social networks weave in and out of the formal institutions of government and develop governance mechanisms within themselves, and through the recognition that reasoning is a much wider activity than is captured in the model of technical-instrumental rationality and rational planning processes.

The systems of *governance* of a society or community refer to the processes through which collective affairs are managed. Governance involves the articulation of rules of behaviour with respect to the collective affairs of a political community; and of principles for allocating resources among community members. It is represented in measures for managing the defense of a society against attack, for economic promotion, as well as those for providing for the welfare of members of a society in times of youth, old age, sickness and other troubles. It legitimises initiatives taken 'on behalf' of a political community and speaks for the collective concerns of political communities in the language of collective interests and values, embodied in such terms as the 'common good' or the 'public interest'. *Political community* in this context means those who, by prior law, or common consent or by organizational membership, find themselves part of a collective entity. Political communities may be associations of those with a common interest, a community of acknowledged stakeholders. Such communities have no necessary territorial definition, for example, the World Wildlife Trust, Amnesty International or international sporting associations. They may also be territorial communities, defined by cultural associations with place or by the boundaries of political jurisdictions, such as all those living in a particular national boundary or local authority area. Governments typically operate through territorial communities, but the management of environmental change may draw many stakeholders from outside a territory. This is especially true of local government jurisdictions.

In modern societies, governance has traditionally been equated with what *governments* do, with the machinery of the 'state'. The growth of the modern state is one of the most characteristic features of modernity. Government as a separate sphere of social organisation is recognised in the distinctions often made between 'the state' and 'society', or the 'public sector' and the 'private sector'. Neo-liberal political philosophers and neoclassical economists commonly make this latter distinction, arguing that the state, as the public sector, should deal in those matters, and only those matters, which the 'private' economy has difficulty in addressing (Low, 1991). An older distinction, going back to Aristotle and the world of Greek democratic community, distinguishes the *public realm* from the world of the private household

(Young, 1990). In this sense, the public realm means the arenas for discussion of collective affairs, although this ignores the collective affairs discussed within the household. In our more complex societies, some analysts separate out the economy, social life and government. Drawing on Marxist political economy, Urry (1980) describes society in terms of three overlapping spheres – the economy, civil society and the state. Debate in this political economy tradition has focused on whether the relations of civil society and the state are driven by the dynamics of the economy, or whether the state can act autonomously (Pickvance, 1995). In everyday life in western societies, our metaphors and arguments commonly present government as an autonomous structuring power, over which we have limited influence, but which yet shapes our worlds.

Such distinctions suggest that governance is something apart from, outside, the world of economic activity and social life. Yet theory and empirical evidence deny this. Neoclassical economists argue that government comes into existence only as a result of the failures of economic systems. Marxist political economists argue that the state is either a creature of capital, or the product of class struggle between capital and labour. Habermas talks of systems of governance, like those of the economy, 'colonising' our daily lives, our 'lifeworlds' (see Chapter 2). An institutionalist analysis emphasises the complex interactions between the activities of formal government bodies, economic activity and social life, interlinked through social networks and cultural assumptions and practices which cut across formal organisations. Thus ideas from a business or social arena are drawn into the development of policy ideas and help to frame assumptions about government practices, and vice versa. Further, firms may change the way they behave in response to government initiatives and people may change what they do as a result of what governments do. For example, the introduction of new forms of government incentive may lead to the reorganisation and creation of companies to capture the opportunities they generate. Thus, in Britain in the 1980s, some housebuilding firms created urban renewal sections targetted at grant-winning projects, and Enterprize Zone regimes led to the creation of development traders who specialised in developing in these areas (Kennedy-Skipton, 1994; Healey, 1994a).

Not only do formal mechanisms of government, in Giddensian fashion, contribute to shaping economic and social life. The activity of governance also pervades our social relations. Firms are 'managed' by boards, chief executives and management teams. Households and families manage themselves, drawing on gender and generation collaboration, or on principles of patriarchy, or the efforts of women in keeping the social group together. Styles of governance are learned in firms, in households and in other social arenas, such as trades unions, church organisations, sports clubs or pressure groups.

Thus governance activity is diffused through the multiplicity of social relations we have, and may take many forms. It is a matter of specific geography and history how responsibilities are distributed between formally-recognised government agencies and these other arenas of governance. One of the characteristics of our present times is the questioning of this division of responsibility. Neo-liberal political philosophers aim to 'roll-back' the state, and reduce the role of formal government. Such strategies 'offload' what have previously been government responsibilities onto the business sector, the voluntary sector and onto households. Reflecting this shift, the language of privatisation and deregulation is accompanied by the promotion of 'partnership' and 'empowerment' between the public and private sectors, and by exhortation to private companies to perform a social role, for example, in promoting art in the community, or providing environmental benefits (Bailey, 1995). Meanwhile, local communities are encouraged to take on the management of such facilities as their local open spaces, and tenants are expected to manage their own housing blocks (Mayo, 1994). Such initiatives, in Britain at least, are proceeding in parallel with measures to make government agencies themselves more responsive to the concerns of businesses and citizens, and to require them to be more accountable to the people who, in a democratic society, they are supposed to serve.

This suggests that the degree of 'autonomy' of formal government is not fixed, but is negotiated over time through the active webs of relations which link those in government agencies to firms and to households, and through the discourses which are used to evaluate and legitimate what governments do. Demands that government be more open and accountable sometimes arise where government traditions have become out of step with the way business and citizens are conducting their lives. Thus many now argue that the practices and styles of formal government in many countries reflect a 'modernist' conception of a social order, in which the state 'provides for' a stable expanding economy and a society of nuclear households. David Harvey (1989a) argues that such a 'managerial' approach was appropriate for a 'fordist' economy. The flexible, dynamic economic networks of our present times, he suggests, meet their response in the adoption by governments of a more 'entrepreneurial' style (see also Fainstein, 1994). Others argue that government must shift from a role and style appropriate to the welfare or 'provider state', to that of a 'strategic enabler', framing and promoting the activities of business and citizens (Stoker and Young, 1993). This implies a substantial effort in institutional re-design, shifting the hard infrastructure of institutional arrangements, legal rules and resource flows, to enable a soft infrastucture of institutional capacity building to take place among firms and among citizens. People are being asked, in effect, to invent their own governance institutions.

But demands for openness and accountability also arise from the perception by some that others have undue influence behind the scenes. The role of powerful property interests in shaping government policy at both national and local levels has frequently been recorded. In Britain in the early 1980s, Rydin (1986) showed how construction and property interests were close to the ear of the Secretary of State for the Environment. Marriott's account of city centre redevelopment in the 1960s in Britain showed how private deals were done between councillors, officers and developers (Marriott 1967). Similarly, Logan and Molotch (1987) and Stone (1989) show how business interests can infuse local governments in the US. Land and property stakeholders often dominate in these situations.

Such comfortable co-existence may prevail for a long time unnoticed and unquestioned, especially where politicians and developer interests keep in mind the wider interests of businesses and the community. After all, a community needs some kind of development capacity. However, unchecked, developer pressure may lead governments to equate the general development of a community with the interests of property developers. The general problem of governance that these examples illustrate is that regulatory mechanisms set up to constrain market activities are prone to 'capture' by the industries they regulate.

In these days of greater environmental awareness, however, popular pressure to limit business influence may become a powerful force. In such situations, governments may accept that greater openness and accountability may help to re-establish trust, that is to repair the faith of citizens that politicians and officials behave in a fair and legitimate way in the 'common good' rather than a particular interest. A major impetus behind the principles of the rational planning process (see Chapter 1) was to find a government management style which would help to clean up informal partisan practices in US local government (Meyerson and Banfield, 1955; Friedmann, 1973). Contemporary interest in collaborative consensus-building policy arenas to address environmental concerns is driven by the challenge of developing policies openly in contexts where there are many conflicting interests, often with little initial trust among themselves or in government agencies (Innes *et al.*, 1994).

To conclude, governance is not the sole preserve of governments. We are all involved in some way, and have experience of managing collective affairs. This experience, though largely neglected by those writing on politics and planning, provides a resource through which new forms of governance can be invented. Governments, however, have distinct remits and particular organizational arrangements and ways of working, or *routines* and *styles*. How these mesh in with the other social relations of a society varies in time and place. In western societies, particularly in Europe, in the post-war period, states have organised a whole range of economic management and welfare programmes, producing the 'welfare state' in various forms (Mishra, 1990; Esping-Andersen, 1990). By the 1980s, many of these programmes had lost touch with the changing needs and governance capabilities of the citizens and firms they were intended to serve. It is in this context that there is pressure for a renegotiation of the remit of formal government activity and for a reconsideration of the ways government agencies work. As a government activity undertaking regulatory work in highly contested contexts, spatial and land use planning agencies are at the sharp end of many of these pressures.

Politics, policy and planning

So far, governance has been discussed as a general process, the management of collective affairs. But any governance effort embraces both policy development and the delivery of programmes; on the one hand, the articulation of the purposes of governance and the making of strategic decisions about directions and key actions, and and on the other, the organisation of programmes to deliver what has been agreed upon. *Policy* and *planning* are terms used to describe particular styles of governance activity, and may also focus attention on their content. Terms such as *politics, administration* and *management* are used to describe governance activity. Each of these terms is loaded with meanings, and around each there are major academic disciplines (political science, public administration and management) and traditions of debate. There is much overlap between the concerns of these disciplines, with each other, and with the traditions of planning thought, particularly the *policy analysis* stream outlined in Chapter 1. There is also an empirical overlap, as in practice each dimension flows into the other.

The meaning of 'politics'

There are two major senses in which the term *politics* is used. The first refers to relations of power, wherever exercised. The second refers to deliberate efforts to gain influence and exercise power in the public realm, the arenas for the public management of collective affairs, that is beyond the household and the firm. In its first sense, the discussion of politics connects the political relations of everyday life to the political structures of societies. Foucault, for example, dissects the micropolitics of social behaviour in prisons and hospitals (Rabinow, 1984). Feminist campaigners highlight the gender discriminations of daily life, arguing that the 'personal' is 'political' (Young, 1990). Giddens emphasises the way our daily lives are 'structured' by relations of power, including those embodied in political systems. An institutionalist approach emphasises that our activities take place within, and are constituted by, the structures created by our predecessors. These generate patterns of resource flow, of behavioural rules and cultural systems of meaning which embody particular relations of power. Through these resources, rules and ideas, we come up against the relations of power. Through our daily actions, we reconstitute them, and alter them, accidentally and deliberately. Lukes (1974) describes these power relations as the 'deep structures' which underpin the flow of activities we undertake (see Chapter 2). In another famous metaphor, Bacharach and Baratz (1970) referred to politics as 'the mobilisation of bias', which happens invisibly as we act. The implication of this meaning of politics is that it is everywhere, not merely in the arenas of governance or specific government activity. It also means that, within any government agency, politics is not just what politicians do. It inheres within the arenas, routines and styles of agency life. Recent accounts of planners at work provide vivid examples of how planning expertise is deployed in the micropolitics of local planning practices (Forester, 1989, 1992a; Krumholz and Forester, 1992; Thomas and Healey, 1991; Hoch, 1992).

But the term 'politics' is also used to refer to the activity of governance, and specifically to the ways in which government activity is controlled. In this sense, politics may be defined as deliberate efforts in social mobilisation, in order to gain control over the mechanisms for the management of collective affairs. It involves taking control over the flows of resources which pass through government systems, over the power to define formal rules, in law and government procedure, and over the agendas of governments. It involves the practices through which people get elected to government positions, and the machinery of political parties. It also refers to the politics of influence which cluster around governments, either in the behind-the-scenes way discussed in the previous section, or in more open and formalised arrangements. In post-war Germany, government programmes in the arena of social and economic policy have typically been developed through a tripartite discussion between the representatives of business, of labour and of government. This arrangement is the classic model of 'corporatism' (Schmitter, 1974). In the Netherlands and Denmark, a broader-based partnership between government agencies and interest groups produces modes of governance which have been referred to as 'co-sociational' (Jessop and Nielsen, 1991; Goldsmith, 1993; Needham, Koenders and Kruijt, 1993; Faludi and Van der Valk, 1994).

In the more adversarial traditions of British politics, corporatist modes of governance have not flourished (Goldsmith, 1993).

However, echoes of it can be found in some policy fields, for example the management of agriculture or of the locational policies of the minerals industry (Marsden *et al.*, 1993; Healey *et al.*, 1988). In the planning field in the 1980s, the discussion of housing land allocation in Britain began to take on this form, as government turned to the Housebuilders Federation and the Council for the Protection of Rural England to help find a balance between the interests of residential developers and of environmental conservation, but these two organisations could never adequately represent the views of either the housebuilding industry or all amenity and environmental groups, and stable arrangements have proved difficult to develop. This illustrates how, in the field of local environmental planning, 'corporatist' modes encounter difficulties, as interests in local environments are typically disparate, and difficult to construct into consolidated interest 'camps'.

Politics then is a pervasive activity. It focuses attention on who controls what and how, and on who gets what. Formal governments may concentrate political power and are a powerful structure constraining the lifeworlds of everyday life and the activities of the economy itself. The machinery of government can become increasingly separated from the dynamics of social change in the wider society, so enabling government activity to 'carry on regardless'. Meanwhile, those who enjoy the struggle for power may become absorbed in it for its own sake. This can lead to tendencies for dictatorial or patronage regimes. A vigorous pluralistic politics helps to counteract these tendencies, but may lead to short-term bargaining and the promotion of single-issue programmes. A key issue for contemporary societies is therefore how to transform the machinery of formal government and politics to enable a sustainable and supportive interaction between governance activity, everyday life, the business world and the biosphere.

The role of policy

The development of policy-making across all areas of government activity emerged this century as a mechanism to make government both more effective in delivering on its objectives and more accountable, providing political communities with principles by which to judge the performance of their governments. Through the articulation of policy principles in some form, the 'logic of issues' may be moved away from the 'logic of power games', separating the 'problem' from the 'players' (Fisher and Ury, 1981). The challenge in our times is to maintain that separation, in order to limit 'I win–You lose' situations, while drawing upon practical consciousness, people's experiential understanding.

The word *policy* carries many meanings. In some languages, there is no distinction between policy and politics (this is true, for example, of French, Spanish and Italian). In the Anglo-American tradition, the term 'policy' is commonly used to refer to an explicit statement of a governance objective, with the implication that the policy articulated will be used in some way as a guide to what the governance entity will do. A policy thus 'frames' subsequent action. But policy can also be used in a broader sense. In an interesting discussion of the meaning of 'social policy', Townsend (1975) argued that every society has a social policy, in this broader sense of an approach to managing the welfare of its citizens. But what this is may not be made explicit. It may exist as an implicit approach, embedded in cultural practices, rather than formally articulated in policy statements. Thus every society could be said to have a *land policy*, a way of distributing rights to get access to, to use and to benefit from land (Darin-Drabkin, 1977).

There has also been recognition of the implicit nature of policy in the debate in the policy analysis literature on the relation between policy and action (see Chapter 1). Barrett and Fudge (1981a) argue that policy intentions are often not formally articulated, but rather that they emerge during the flow of governance activity. As people in agencies deploy rules and manipulate resource flows, they interpret and invent policies through their actions. Barrett and Fudge argued that policy as practised was thus a bottom-up process. From time to time, such informal policies would be explicitly acknowledged and converted into policy statements. Much spatial plan-making work in Britain arises from such attempts to formalize practices existing in policy terms (Healey, 1983; Healey, Ennis and Purdue, 1992).

Barrett and Fudge were heavily influenced by the structure of the British state, with its strong centralism and its hierarchical traditions. They sought to challenge the top-down hierarchical view of policy which had dominated much of the policy literature. Based on research on policy implementation in a number of fields of policy, they emphasised a more interactive relationship between policy as expressed by political leaders and in strategic planning statements, and what those 'implementing' policies actually do. They looked to social exchange theory for concepts to describe this interaction, and particularly the work of Theodor Lowi (Barrett and Fudge, 1981b). Such continual interaction, between attempts to 'frame' the actions of others and the way these framing intentions are then interpreted by others, is captured and placed in a broader context in the Giddensian idea of structuration (see Chapter 2).

Barrett and Fudge assumed that the purposes of government politicians and officials were not merely self-interested survival or ad hoc responsiveness. They envisaged officials seeking ways of responding appropriately to real problems manifest in specific situations. The explicit concern with policy presupposes a governance activity which is directed at achieving some democratically acceptable public purpose, rather than particular private purposes, or the domination of the powerful. A *policy-driven* approach to governance activity requires that policy objectives and strategies are articulated, and linked to programmes of action, judged by output and outcome criteria linked to the objectives. The rational planning process outlined in Chapter 1 provides a particularly powerful expression of how this might be done. A policy-driven approach helps to render the exercise of governance power in a society legitimate. Explicit policies become the reasons given by those exercising power on behalf of collectivities when asked why they did something. They become the basis for decision rules (Faludi, 1987), and/or feed into processes of public argumentation about policies and actions. Policies thus help to make governments accountable. They may in addition be a valuable tool for managing government activities in efficient and effective ways. Debates within the planning culture on planning processes have developed in this context, in an attempt to devise ways of developing policies which have qualities of accountability and effectiveness.

In this sense, policies are not only a mechanism to distance what governments do from merely a naked power play. They are also tools for influencing how governments organise themselves. It is here that the terms *administration* and *management* come in. In our complex and formally democratic societies, organizational arrangements develop to follow through programmes which 'politicians' decide upon. These presume some formal separation of the political arenas in which policies are debated and agreed and an administrative arena which delivers these policies. These arrangements are an amalgam of organizational structures, which formally specify competences and reporting reponsibilities, and procedures, operating practices, and cultures, which shape ways of thinking about how to do the job, and about the technique and ethics of government work. They become the operating *routines* of governance, with their accompanying modes of behaviour, or expressive *styles*.

In the great bastions of government bureaucracy which have evolved during the twentieth century, these organizational arrangements typically divide activities into major functional departments (for example, education, social welfare, agricultural support, public works). They have traditionally had a hierarchical form, with junior officials answerable through senior officials to politicians or political appointees. They frequently work through policies translated into procedural and legal rules. In countries which have their governance styles rooted in the Napoleonic Code, it is common to separate the work of policy, as part of the arena of politics, from that of administration, as part of the arena of legal interpretation of formal rules. In such contexts, the work of urban and regional planners may be confined to developing the policies. Legal technicians may then administer the resultant policy rules. The legal land use zoning ordinance is a typical example of such a separation. In theory, in such situations, planning experts prepare master plans. These are then converted into land use ordinances giving landowners rights to develop according to the ordinance. The monitoring of the ordinance is a task for administrators, not experts. In reality, there is usually a much more interactive relationship between politicians, administrators and applicants (Barlow, 1995; Benfield, 1994; Healey, Khakee, Motte and Needham, 1996).

Such rule-bound systems reflect one approach to making the actions of governments legitimate, that is, ensuring that such actions follow politically-agreed principles. It is this model of bureaucracy that Max Weber encapsulated in his influential discussion of the organization of the modern state (Weber, 1970). The rule-bound bureaucracy was attractive as a mechanism to organise government programme delivery because it displaced earlier structures where officials carried out government tasks in return for a 'cut' of the tax takings. This fostered patronage relations between officials and citizens, and encouraged clientelistic modes of governance. This was appropriate for revenue-raising functions, but not for the expanding activities of the state in providing services. The rule-bound bureaucracy was aimed at transforming the state into a providing and regulating role, rather than merely a tax-collecting role, squeezing out the opportunities for patronage and private gain. The problem with this hierarchical, rule-bound approach is its inflexibility (see Chapter 1). This problem is very visible in local environmental management today, when changes to the local environment come in very variable shapes and sizes. As with the approach to urban planning which assumed a spatial plan could be precisely specified in advance, it is very difficult to develop rules for all contingencies. The result is either that rules are followed irrespective of particular conditions. This is likely to lead to criticisms of inefficiency, ineffectiveness, or irrelevance. Or rules will be circumvented or ignored. This can lead to charges of manipulation or corruption.

It is here that the approach of management-by-objectives (MBO) has proved so attractive, as discussed in Chapter 1. Rather than being translated into formal rules and codes, policies become key tools of a management style which assumes individual agents are able to interpret the meaning of a policy in relation to the circumstances of an individual case. Policies become principles which are drawn into an argument about decision criteria, not fixed into *a priori* rules. This approach provides for flexibility, and draws upon the learning capacity of government officials. It also assumes that officials operate ethically. Such a conception parallels in many ways the long-established practices of British administration, which allow broad discretion in policy interpretation to officials, on the assumption that their judgement and ethics will produce 'good government' (Jowell and Oliver (eds), 1985). This requires officials skilled in policy judgements. The distinctive discretionary form of the British planning system reflects this approach (Healey, 1988). But such a policy-driven approach may well encounter problems in political cultures which are more populist and open to the influence of competing power bases, and in which the barriers between government and governance are more fluid. As British society moves away from its traditions of 'deferential democracy' in which government was trusted to act competently for the 'common good' (Beer, 1982), so the exercise of administrative discretion is increasingly coming into question. Such extensive discretion also raises conceptual problems. If officials are making decisions which have the potential to affect the structures within which they operate, if policy is being invented in action, if powerful interests look for partnership with officials to influence policy and if the politics of pressure group influence pervades every level and dimension of government organization, how can the actions of officials remain accountable? Do not officials then become either 'little dictators' or creatures of the power of particular interests? A policy-driven approach to governance may therefore work well with a form of administration which makes use of skilled official judgement. But without careful checks and balances, in a more pluralistic and 'shared-power' world, the legitimacy of a discretionary approach will be called into question. These issues are discussed further in Chapter 9.

The adoption of a policy-driven approach thus may be part of an effort to drive government activity according to policy principles. It may co-exist comfortably with other tendencies in governance practices for such a policy-driven approach. It could be said that the major advance in democratic forms of governance in western societies this century has been the evolution of policy-driven governance discourses and practices. However, as many planners know only too well, this presupposes styles and cultures of politics and administration of a particular kind. Policy-driven approaches do not co-exist easily with some modes of governance, as Meyerson and Banfield (1955) showed in their famous example of competing approaches to allocating public housing sites in Chicago.

Planning, understood in the general sense of the policy analysis tradition, is a style of governance within a policy-driven approach. It could be equated with that approach, but it is helpful to add two further qualities, the taking of a long-term and strategic look at the direction of governance activity, and the attempt to interrelate different spheres of that activity, that is, different policy fields. Local environmental planning is therefore quite clearly a part of governance and a particular style of policy-driven governance. Clearly, also, the introduction of planning processes into governance has the capacity to challenge the forms of governance, the distribution of power within government agencies, and the power relations of governance activity. Such processes will flourish better in some governance cultures than others. It may become compartmentalised, for example, the way in which in Britain, national government policy tends to treat local environmental planning as a discrete function of government dealing with 'land use matters', separate from other functions (Bruton and Nicholson, 1987). Or it may be reduced to a narrow rule-following activity, or corrupted to the pursuits of powerful interests. Which of these outcomes arise will depend on the mode of governance in which local environmental planning is inserted.

Forms and styles of governance

To recapitulate, the adoption of a policy-driven, planning style of governance process makes a number of assumptions. It expects firstly that governance activity will be guided by explicit policies; secondly, that these policies will have some leverage on the regulative and allocative work of governments; and thirdly, that policies will be derived from available knowledge. It is not inherent in the style that such knowledge will be limited to rational-technical reasoning, or that the relation between policy and action should take a hierarchical, top-down form, although both have been widespread in actual cases and in theory. However, a policy-driven, planning style of governance is not likely to promote inclusionary practices unless it occurs within a sympathetic governance culture. Planning is thus more than the translation of knowledge into action, as proposed by John Friedmann (1987). It involves a style of governance which emphasises knowledgeable reasoning and argumentation. The challenge for a style of planning which recognizes the democratic demands of intercultural communication outlined in Chapter 2 is to transform these demands into inclusionary styles of argumentation, within which different forms of knowing, different forms of reasoning and different values and systems of meaning are interrelated. Translated into the field of the management of local environmental change, such a planning approach would involve developing 'conversations' between stakeholders from different social worlds and cultures, to help arrive at principles for local environmental management. Such principles would then provide the basis for providing 'good reasons' for often difficult decisions between conflicting interests and claims for policy attention.

In effect, a planning approach to a field of governance involves the adoption of a particular way of thinking, an organizational *style*, and the development of a distinctive expressive, communicative culture, through which activities are conducted. Within what *forms* of governance could such a style arise or be given opportunity? Since at least the days of classical Greece, western societies have discussed appropriate forms of democratic governance. These debates have a new vigour in our present times, as the need to renew our inheritance of government structures and processes is recognised. Categorization of democratic forms helps in the process of describing what exists and exploring how these might be changed. Such models of governance forms are always gross simplifications of actual governance systems, which evolve uniquely, contingently and dynamically. Nevertheless, they are a helpful tool to enable exploration of the conditions which might favour the evolution of a democratic, policy-driven planning culture in our governance forms and those which might inhibit it.

Four models are widely employed in describing existing western governance systems. These are presented briefly, focusing specifically on the form of governance, as embodied in principles of representation and legitimacy (Who represents a political community? To whom must their actions be legitimated?), and on the style of governance, as reflected in working practices of regulation, allocation and justification. The purpose of the review is to identify which forms of governance tend to be favourable to planning approaches, understood in a general sense, and which have most democratic potential, in terms of contemporary ideas of inclusionary discursive democracy. The four models are: representative democracy; pluralist democracy; corporatism; and clientelism.

Representative democracy

The model of representative democracy is familiar to many westerners through our school textbooks. We are taught an idealised model of a democratic state, in which governments are created on behalf of, and at the service of, the people as electors. We (that is, most adults) elect our representatives, the politicians, who oversee the work of officials in the departments of government. The task of politicians, guided by their officials, both administrators and experts, is to articulate the 'public interest' on any issue, and to develop government action to achieve that interest. The officials are answerable to the politicians, and the politicians are answerable to the people through the ballot box. Governance is focused on the institutions of formal government. Politicians are responsible for articulating the 'public interest' in any issue. The good decision is one which best achieves this 'public interest'. This model could work well in a relatively homogeneous society, with limited cultural diversity. It fits with European post-war ideas about a modern managed economy and a welfare state.

The representative model encourages governance styles which emphasise either the legal-administrative rule-bound behaviour which Max Weber described, or the more flexible discretionary judgement of officials of the British system. Both allow the work of governance to be carried out at arm's length from the play of politics. The model encourages the development of hierarchically-structured bureaucracies, focused around technical and administrative expertise, in which officials justify their actions and decisions upwards to their seniors and the politicians to whom these are accountable, rather than outwards to 'people'. Such hierarchical accountability may be tempered by the prospect of legal challenge, with the legitimacy of government action in general being monitored by the courts. This model provides fertile ground for a form of policy planning which emphasises technical and legal reasoning, in relation to policy objectives. The form of many land use plans in the US and the UK reflects such an approach (Kaiser and Goldschalk, 1993; Healey, 1983, 1993).

This model is now widely challenged. These challenges do not affect the basic premise, that governments in democratic societies should be elected by universal franchise. The criticisms relate to the forms which such elected governance systems may then take and the supplementary ways in which government can be rendered more effective and more accountable. A central problem for the model is that its practice is not like the theory, and that politicians and officials are subject to all kinds of influences in all areas of governance work. This criticism implies that practice has shifted towards another model. A more fundamental conceptual criticism is that politicians cannot aggregate up all our interests in any meaningful way on every issue. Our interests are too diverse. Therefore there have to be mechanisms for sharing the task of policy formulation and the carrying out of government programmes with citizens and businesses. Equally, officials cannot 'know enough' about issues and our concerns about them to advise politicians sufficiently. The interpenetration of outsiders and insiders in politics and government has many advantages, although in the representative model, this interaction is hidden and unaccountable. Politicians and officials need to open out to the resources of knowledge and understanding within a political community in order to make good judgements and undertake competent reasoning. Growing interest in 'public participation' in local spatial planning since the 1960s is evidence of attempts to overcome this weakness in the representative model. But such public involvement challenges the basic premises of the model, as many politicians were quick to recognise. Involving the public in articulating 'the public interest' challenges the politician's responsibility for this task and the role of representatives (Hoggett, 1995).

Pluralist democracy

The significance of interest diversity is recognised in the model of pluralist democracy. This model was acknowledged in popular discourse in the United States in the post-war period, and is now used more frequently to describe governance systems in the European context. It presupposes a society composed of many different groups with different interests, all competing to define the agenda for the actions of governments. Politicians get elected through the ballot box, but their task is less to articulate the public interest on behalf of society than to arbitrate between the interests of the different groups. In this context, there is no necessary role for policies to guide government action. The style of such a system combines a 'politics of voice' with the language of legal discourse. It produces a politics of competing claims, grounded in what legal precedent determines to be legitimate. It encourages groups to articulate their concerns in adversarial forms as fixed interests and preferences. Such practices are widely recognisable in the treatment of environmental issues since the introduction of environment protection legislation in various forms. There are strong tendencies towards this form in many land use planning systems (Brindley, Rydin and Stoker, 1989; Healey *et al.*, 1988).

Such adversarial positions do not make for smooth planning processes. In the US, the introduction of strategic planning systems has arisen in a few states to try to reduce the scale of conflict over individual issues (DeGrove, 1984; Innes, 1992). This was also the impetus behind the introduction of strategic planning mechanisms in Switzerland (Ringli, 1996), and in the spatial planning field in the early 1990s (Healey, 1993). Strategic planning exercises sought to transfer the locus of pluralist argumentation from the arena of project permits, to the construction of policy frameworks within which the principles for making project decisions could be articulated, that is, through a plan. This involves a shift to developing policy reasoning in advance of a regulatory decision, rather than probing it in costly legal arenas after a decision has been made. This shifts the emphasis from pluralist competition and argument over projects to consensus-building practices over strategy, which will be discussed later.

Paul Davidoff had a different idea (see Chapter 1). He argued that each interest group should prepare its own plan, reflecting its particular interests. This would produce, he argued, a rich democratic debate, as groups argued about the relative merits of different plans. Davidoff imagined a situation where planning work was undertaken for specific interest groups by sympathetic consultants. He does not explain how a final plan is articulated and agreed upon. This idea, which Davidoff, a lawyer-planner, called *advocacy planning*, attracted a great deal of attention in the United States in the late 1960s–early 1970s because it seemed to offer a way of challenging the state-driven urban redevelopment projects which were rolling across many US cities. Advocacy planners encountered powerful resistance from state planners, as illustrated by the story quoted in Chapter 3. Instead, a rather different 'advocacy practice' developed, around competing *claims*. Interest groups hired consultants and lawyers to promote and protect their claims, in negotiation over projects, in policy and plan preparation exercises. A great deal of the work of land use planning systems these days is undertaken in this kind of climate. In such contexts, planning becomes a practice of mediating between competing interests. This is clearly a vigorous process of argumentation, but cast in an adversarial and contestational form.

The problem, whether groups are arguing over projects or over plans, is that the argumentation is set up as a competition, a bargaining situation in which outcomes are zero-sum games of the 'I win–you lose' variety. Participants come into the bargaining arena with articulated positions which they seek to defend. This then makes it difficult to open up discussion to explore new possibilities, still less to learn about cultural differences in the construction of meanings and values (Forester, 1992b). Such processes in effect come to generate a NIMBY-style politics, in which groups retreat to saying 'no' to anything government or other groups propose, in order to safeguard their position. Government agencies in their turn cease bothering to consult people on the assumption that they will respond negatively to any proposals (Bryson, Crosby and Carroll, 1991; Wolsink, 1994).

Such bargaining practices also raise questions about who gets involved and how agreement is reached. In effect, they are a form of active 'mutual adjustment', to use Charles Lindblom's term (1965). In pluralist processes, the good decision is the one upon which everyone can agree, but the terrain of agreement is arrived at through elimination of all matters on which participants cannot agree. It does not involve the institutional effort of building up new ways of mutual understanding to generate a wider basis upon which to agree. In governance cultures with a pluralist form, planning processes either become absorbed into mediation processes, or planners become involved in the competition, arguing for particular qualities of local environments, or particular values and interests. This of course raises major problems of ethics and legitimacy.

Corporatism

While the model of pluralist democracy seems to describe the governance cultures within which many planners do their work only too well, it has been criticised for its assumption that all groups are relatively equal in the competitive game. Far from being an egalitarian 'politics of voice', governments, as already noted, may in effect be the creatures of a few powerful interests. Some political analysts refer to this situation as a neo-élite version of democracy (Dunleavy and O'Leary, 1987; Harding, 1995). Good examples of this situation in the the field of the management of local environmental change may be found in the accounts of 'spatial alliances' and 'growth coalitions' which build up in urban regions, as a partnership between business interests, often linked to landowner and developer interests, and local governments (Harding, 1995; Stoker, 1995). At national government level, the classic model is a stable routnised practice of collaboration between government, major business organisations and the trades unions in determining and managing economic and social policy. The type example of these arrangements developed in post-war West Germany, and came to be known as corporatism (Schmitter, 1974; Esping-Anderson, 1990). It is generally argued that such a model, to be found elsewhere in Europe, and most notably in the Netherlands, never developed fully in Britain, although there are examples in particular policy fields, as noted in Part II. The corporatist model assumes a 'shared-power' world, as does the pluralist one, but the power is shared among a few, powerful interest groups, articulated to national level organizations. In contrast to the pluralist model, but in common with representative democracy, this approach thus has an 'apex' structure. The 'public interest' is recognised as primarily the interests of the major businesses, moderated by their recognition of the need to pay attention to the social and environmental concerns of labour, if only for the purposes of maintaining their legitimacy. The apex organisations in the formal corporatist model do not necessarily recognise either the concerns of all businesses, with the small business sector often misunderstood or ignored, or the everyday life concerns of all citizens, with the concerns of organised labour having priority over other considerations.

The corporatist model has many advantages. It can develop and deliver a stable consensus. It can co-ordinate various dimensions of government policy, and enables long-term horizons to override the ebb and flow of political majorities. It allows 'mutual learning' among the partners, and has thus some capacity for development and flexibility. It avoids the kind of adversarial competitive politics which have developed in the US, the UK and Australia. The good decision is the one which best achieves the public interest as defined by the corporate alliance. This is the form of government which Marx expressed in his view of the state as a mechanism for managing the common affairs of the bourgeoisie in the interests of maintaining the conditions for healthy capital accumulation (Castells, 1977).

This model reflects a reality often experienced at the local level, as noted above, even where the nation state is not so corporatist. Stable organizational routines may develop around consultation practices, which allow certain interests a priveleged 'first cut' on local planning issues before the more visible wrangling among competing interests gets going (see Figure 7.1). This may evolve into the kind of stable governance arrangements characterised as *urban regimes* (Stone, 1989; Lauria and Whelan, 1995; Stoker, 1995).

In this governance form, the expressive communicative style of governance is more likely to be driven by well-informed policy considerations than in the representative model. The major interest groups represented in the apex-organisation will demand good quality information to justify and monitor actions. Within

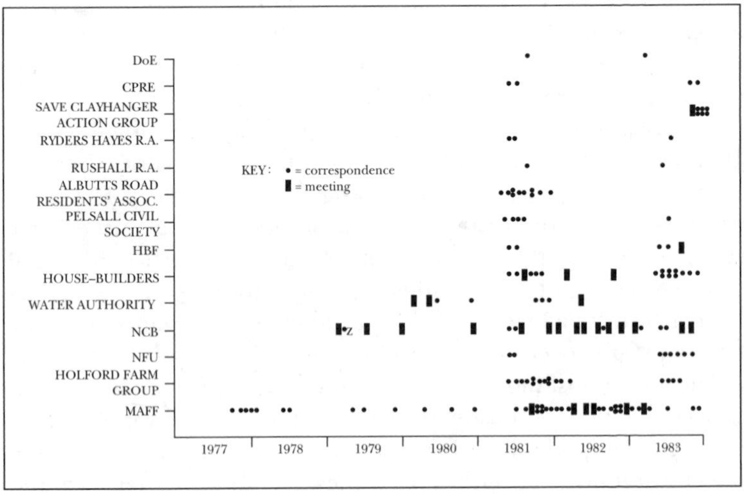

Figure 7.1 Influences on local planning policy over time: the Aldridge–Brownhills local plan
Source: Healey *et al.* (1988) p. 111.

the consensus structure, agreement can be reached on the type of knowledge to provide the information base for policy development and monitoring work. Typically, this has favoured the scientific, engineering and economic modes of thought of the 'managerial' disciplines. For this reason, this mode is sometimes referred to as a techno-corporatist form (Fischer, 1990). The concern of the 'corporatist alliance' is with effective management to pursue the policy objectives of the consensus. Good quality technical information combined with clear policies which are effectively and efficiently followed is an asset in such a model, parallelling the strategic management practices of businesses. The corporate consensus gives stable time horizons for public policy across electoral periods.

It is this tendency in governance forms which promoted much of the interest in policy 'science' and planning processes in the 1960s. Generalist policy planners and other experts, particularly economists and technologists, have typically flourished in such contexts. But as a mode of governance it is now strongly challenged. Firstly, it has a narrow social base. These days this is being exposed as the environmental movement brings in new issues and national organisations, while economic re-structuring undermines the power base of the traditonal business and labour organisations. Social change meanwhile, and notably the increasing power of the women's voice in national politics, challenges the privileged position of the business manager and the male manufacturing worker. Secondly, the emphasis on scientific knowledge and instrumental rationalism is increasingly considered inappropriate as the primary route to knowledge about society (see Chapter 2). Thirdly, the range of values incorporated in the consensus may become too limited in relation to the values of the society as a whole. A narrow corporatist consensus can thus be challenged as both unrepresentative and unable to learn, innovate, and adapt to new conditions.

Clearly, policy-driven governance flourishes in a corporatist context, and it is particularly likely to foster a planning approach, given positive interests in co-ordination of government programmes in time and space, and the ability to take long-term time horizons. Where the corporate interests are concerned with social well-being and environmental quality, the evidence from Northern Europe suggests that significant advances in quality of life and environmental quality can be achieved. But planning processes flourish at the expense of a narrowed agenda. This creates particular problems in the arena of local environmental planning. Firstly, such corporate consensuses may visibly neglect many of the critical dimensions of local environmental conditions. In centralised nation-states, such as the UK, they tend to be sectorally constituted around functional divisions of the economy rather than territorial divisions, treating concerns with space and place as peripheral matters. Secondly, the interest mix in local arenas may be at odds with that of a corporate alliance. These tensions are often reflected in conflicts between governance entities at different levels.

There can be no doubt of the continuing attraction of this model of governance to business interests. Such forms are likely to arise in situations where strong business interests seek to control governance processes, unless moderated by other forces and challenged by other forms of governance. In Britain in the mid-1990s, there was much evidence of business interests in urban regions seeking to build up new regional alliances with government agencies to try to create a stable structure for developing and promoting the economic assets of regions and maximising the chances of capturing European Union funding (Tickell and Dicken, 1993; Davoudi, Healey and Hull, 1996). The terminology of collaborative governance and consensus-building is particularly attractive to such alliance-building efforts. This activity, however, highlights the importance of assessing when such efforts are likely to spread power among the stakeholders in urban region change, and extend the range of knowledge forms and systems of meaning which are drawn into discussion, and when in contrast they are likely to narrow them. It is the narrowing tendencies which indicate a drift to corporatist modes of governance.

Clientelism

Clientelism is an ever-present tendency in governance systems. It involves an interactive relationship between politicians and government officials, through the social networks which politicians and officials have. It in essence substitutes social networks – of family, friendship, fiefdom and business – for governance structures for allocating and distributing resources. It does this in hidden ways, which are not open to democratic scrutiny. Clientelistic practices seem to arise where the role of governance is to distribute resources acquired through taxation, or through some regional or transnational redistribution programme. In this context, elected politicians and officials become critical gatekeepers in managing the direction of the flow of resources. They become patrons with bands of clients, clustering round the 'pork-barrel' or the 'gravy train'. In return for a vote and other favours, patrons flow out resources to their clients, in a system of reciprocal relations of obligation. In this system, the good decision is that which best sustains such patronage relations. Local governance in Southern Italy has long provided an archetypal model of such a situation. (Eisenstadt and Lamarchand (eds), 1981; Goldsmith, 1993). Favours may include not merely access to government funds and contracts. They may involve favourable decisions on land use and environmental regulation, or the tolerance of 'illegal' building, that is, building without permits. Much of urban Southern Italy has been constructed in this way.

There are many examples of similar practices elsewhere in the world. They are often associated with societies with relatively weak economies, in the international sense, and a top-heavy machinery of post-colonial government, as in much of Africa (Clapham, 1985). Here the state may in effect be 'parasitic' on the society. Elsewhere, the clientelistic mechanism may work quite well to distribute available resources to poorer groups, so long as there are many patrons around which different 'clients' can cluster. Examples of such situations can be found in squatter development processes (Healey and Gilbert, 1985), and are reported from British local authorities in the 1930s which developed social welfare distribution systems during the depression (Ward, 1984).

Clearly, such governance forms are inimical to planning processes, as they depend on a personal patron–client relation, rather than achieving general policy objectives. In many countries, such practices are looked on as corrupt. It is assumed that safeguards to ensure proper political and adminstrative practice prevent such forms and styles evolving. Introducing policy-driven routines and styles of governance has sometimes been driven by a desire to challenge and eliminate these tendencies as in the case of the Chicago housing allocation process in the 1950s noted earlier (Meyerson and Banfield, 1955).

There is much evidence to suggest that the possibility of such practices remains as a potential in most governance systems. Politicians like to benefit their political supporters. Officials may come under pressure to bend rules to favour the friends of politicians and disadvantage their enemies. Individuals with particular interests may lobby vigorously for 'special attention' in relation to their development project. Some companies cluster around government agencies with grants to distribute, getting to know officials and lobbying politicians. Local politicians may favour their friends and supporters when making permitting decisions. In Britain, the vigorous encouragement of partnership arrangements, and the involvement of business interests on local Training and Enterprise Councils, is potentially generating fertile grounds for clientelism (Peck and Emmerich, 1994). The discretionary planning system in Britain is always vulnerable to clientelism, as there is no formal mechanism to challenge the grant of a planning permission, in contrast to the rights of applicants to challenge a refusal. The probity of officials and civil servants, the ethic of public service among officials, the principles of administrative procedure, as well a policy-driven governance culture are claimed to be adequate safeguards against clientelistic tendencies. What is lacking is an adequate structure of rights and duties, a major deficiency for the British state, with its unwritten constitution. In the context of the efforts to make government more responsive and collaborative with business and citizens, however, it should not be forgotten that clientelism has long been a way of linking government and citizen in a direct way. Without careful checks and balances, responsiveness can become patronage. The design of appropriate checks and balances is discussed in Chapter 9.

Evolving forms of governance

The above discussion illustrates that policy-driven styles of governance and planning approaches are only likely to flourish in particular modes of governance, a recognition that writers on planning systems have long been aware of (Braybrooke and Lindblom, 1963; Dyckman, 1961; Bolan, 1969; Etzioni, 1968; Christenson, 1985). Often planners and planning systems are working against the grain of local political. Planning, as a policy-driven, co-ordinative, knowledge-rich and future-oriented approach to governance processes, associates most comfortably with the models of representative democracy and corporatism. These provide both a stable consensus around which policy programmes can develop and a way of developing a 'unitary' conception of the 'public interest' with which to develop policy directions. These are also, however, the models most associated with the apparatus of the modernist, managerial state by post-modern critiques (see Chapter 2). They tend to operate in apex, or hierarchical ways. They encourage a separation of policy development and delivery from the arenas of political argumentation. They involve a narrow range of interests in the processes of governance, either through the representation of elected politicians or a partnership with business. They seem to separate the activity of governance from the flow of economic and social life. They therefore seem out of tune with contemporary tendencies for more open relations between government, economic activity and social life, for more horizontal or networked governance linkages, and for a spreading of the power relations of governance to encompass more of the diverse interests in our societies.

The model of competitive pluralist democracy seems to achieve this, but in a way which emphasises short-term political bargains. Such an approach has difficulty in addressing ways of shaping the structuring dynamics which are changing the very conditions within which interests are formed and bargains struck. It lacks the capacity for a 'wide-angle strategic lens', to use Etzioni's metaphor (Etzioni, 1968). It also leaves out those interests for whom there is no powerful political voice. It thus tends to marginalise those less able to articulate their views in a particular political community. Clientelistic practices share these problems. Further, their focus is entirely on distribution. Governance in these contexts has little interest in how resources can be developed or the local quality of life improved. Clientelistic governance lacks a developmental agenda and is thus deeply conservative. Its patronage structure also both reflects and reinforces the existing power relations of political communities.

The search for new governance forms, as discussed earlier, seeks ways of opening out government to a more broadly-based effort in governance, that is to a more responsive and collaborative relationship with the worlds of economic and social life. Active roles for governance, in social and economic development and environmental management, remains important for all the reasons discussed in Part II. Effective governance is needed to engage in explicit efforts at generating and maintaining the structural framing of our activities. Given the diverse interests and cultural points of reference in our differentiated societies, a governance effort which remains legitimate cannot afford too much narrowing, either with respect to stakeholder involvement or to forms of knowledge and systems of meaning. The challenge is therefore to find more inclusionary ways of collaborating and consensus-building. This focuses attention on both the soft infrastructure of governance style and the hard infrastructure of rights, resources and competences.

Three trends in governance forms indicate ways in which these objectives might be achieved. Each are policy-driven, as explicit policy articulation provides a mechanism for legitimating changes in how things are done or how resources are distributed. They also aim to be knowledge-rich, and to consider the future. All therefore are likely to make some use of planning processes. But they vary in their approach to the use of knowledge, to involvement of members of political communities and in their forms of reasoning. The three trends are towards a criteria-driven approach, an entrepreneurial consensus, and inclusionary argumentation (Healey, 1994b).

The criteria-driven approach

This is evolving within contemporary attempts to realise a neoliberal approach to the necessary limitation of market and social behaviour in contemporary societies. The objective is to devolve as much of the delivery of collective activities, from research and development to rubbish collection, to private or semi-private agencies, and to constrain these through a mixture of regulatory structures and financial incentives. The 'public interest' justifying such regulation is translated into regulatory criteria and performance targets designed to encourage the efficient achievement of policy objectives by a fragmented, market-like, agency structure. The approach derives from neoclassical economics and public choice theory (Dunleavy and O'Leary, 1987). As with the model of representative democracy, it assumes that governments get elected and have the legitimacy then to make policies. As with the corporatist model, it draws heavily on the expertise of economics, science and technology. Its objective, however, is to design government programmes so that they work through the ongoing flow of economic and social life, and to manage the delivery of government programmes to ensure that they meet the expectations of those they are intended to benefit in ways which use resources efficiently. A good decision is one which achieves agreed government objectives as efficiently and as accountably as possible.

Citizens and business are conceived as driven by instrumental rationality and by individual preferences. They will therefore respond to market signals, that is, to pricing policies. Thus people and businesses can be persuaded to train their workforce better, engage in research and development, conserve resources and protect environmental assets by pricing policies which make other actions more costly. Local environments can be construed as a collection of assets with both market and policy values. These policy values are then reflected in regulatory restraints or tax rebate incentives, encouraging a trade in policy opportunities. For example, 'markets' in *transferred development rights* have been encouraged in a number of US cities (Cullingworth, 1993). In a similar way, attempts are now being made to control traffic congestion and pollution levels in central cities by road pricing, which combines smart card technology with market signals. The advantage of this approach is that, apart from start-up costs, and the work involved in determining appropriate pricing structures, such strategies do not require special agencies through which to deliver government programmes.

Where it remains necessary to engage in substantial subsidy or direct provision, the preferred form is through the development of a *contract culture.* This applies both whether a function is formally contracted out to a private agency, or whether it remains within the public sector. The principles, as these have developed in Britain, are that funds are made available in return for both the specification of a precise corporate plan and of performance criteria through which these objectives are to be achieved. This approach has been developed in the 1990s in British urban policy (in the City Challenge and SRB schemes), where local authorities must participate in a competition to get the resources in the first place, and must then deliver annual performances which meet defined output targets (Wolman *et al.*, 1994). In the local environmental planning field, experiments are being made with providing performance indicators, both for outputs (what an authority has done) and outcomes (what conditions in an area are like). These outcome indicators can be treated as 'benchmarks' against which performance can be judged. The most developed example of this approach has been evolved in the state of Oregon, in the US (Oregon Progress Board, 1994).

This performance-driven approach reproduces in a much more rigorous way earlier ideas of management-by-objectives. The intention is to give agencies the flexibility to deploy the subsidy provided, within the constraint of the need to meet the performance criteria. The measures used are of course significant controlling devices, and their specification is likely to lead to a complex *politics of criteria* which has the potential to distort the strategic policy objectives (see Innes, 1990, 1995). Governments seeking responsiveness to the concerns of clients may demand performance criteria to reflect this, as in the adoption of 'Citizens' Charters' and measures to monitor their achievement. However, indicators take on a life of their own, structuring situations in terms of delivery on performance criteria, rather than on the objectives the criteria are supposed to express. British urban policy in the 1990s illustrates this phenomena well (Oatley, 1995)

This approach has enormous leverage on public policy formulation at the present time, linked to neo-liberal political philsophy and economic technique. It also offers great attractions as a way of breaking away from the bureaucratic bastions inherited from the past. It suggests all sorts of useful ways of achieving public policy objectives which deserve to be given careful consideration. But its legitimacy, efficiency and effectiveness are called into question on a number of counts. Firstly, it represents a very narrow approach to the construction of people's interests and how they behave. A central thrust of this book is that instrumental rationality is insufficient to address how we reason and come to identify 'what is at stake' for us and for others in our societies. Policies based on such assumptions may therefore fail. Secondly, it draws people into the implementation of policy, not its formulation. It therefore maintains the power of a centralising elite, and a particular construction of policy priorities. It represents an often not-so-benevolent paternalism in a new form. Thirdly, it constructs policy arguments in the language of monetary values and performance indicators. This is a highly culturally-specific vocabulary which is not likely to be widely shared in the political communities for which such policies are designed. It thus ignores the institutional conditions under which knowledge and preferences are arrived at. Finally, it assumes the dominance of competitive behaviour, creating problems for any effort in co-ordination and consensus-building, or the generation of relations of trust through which knowledge and skills can flow through the various social networks in an urban region. Such approaches thus have a significant potential to disadvantage and marginalise not merely many who cannot jump to the criteria. They also have little potential to build the kind of institutional capacity which contemporary urban regions require. They focus on the hard infrastructure of formal rules without considering the mechanisms through which the soft infrastructure of institutional capacity-building comes about, and deliberately avoid consideration of how interactive practices develop, while often exhorting 'partnership'. Thus the criteria-driven approach, intended to ensure that taxpayers' money is spent more efficiently and in ways which are more responsive to the demands of business and citizens, rapidly becomes profoundly undemocratic and ineffective.

Entrepreneurial consensus

This idea builds on the reality of local alliances with developmental agendas and can be considered a form of local corporatism. This model underlies many of the partnership-building activities which have also been promoted in British and American urban policy in recent years. These exist in considerable tension with the criteria-driven approach. The model deliberately fosters interactive practices. It is a direct response to the significance of urban region institutional capacity in providing the framework to support local economic innovation, as discussed in Chapter 5. It represents an effort in local consensus-building among 'key' regional and local players, a deliberate effort in horizontal network-building. The objectives of such consensuses are the promotion of the region, understood as a collection of economic relations, and often in terms of its environmental and social relations too (see the examples in Chapter 3). Where a formal urban region level of government already exists, this provides a ready made arena for such activity. But where this does not exist, as in many American states, or in England, arenas have to be constructed (Innes *et al.*, 1994; Davoudi, Healey and Hull, 1996). This effort in informal institution-building may have advantages as new people and new ideas are brought together. A key attribute of many contemporary efforts in such alliance-building is their openness to more than merely economic interests, as all players have an awareness of the way their activities impact on the qualities of places, both socially and environmentally. This consciousness encourages more accountability to whatever are the expressed concerns of a local political community. Alliances of this nature may have a very significant role in setting the strategic agendas for local environmental management efforts, and represent overt efforts in strategic urban regional planning.

Such alliances are significant in the articulation of local policies and strategies. Much of the contemporary local effort in strategic place-making in Britain is working through governance forms which take on such characteristics. In recognition of the fragmenting tendencies in contemporary urban regions, such alliances tend to recognise the importance of collaborative consensus-building among key urban region players, to overcome the conflictual interest bargaining of much traditional pluralist local politics (Bailey, Barker and MacDonald, 1995). Those involved from the business world are often familiar with consensus-building practices and ways of encouraging mutual learning through the management cultures of their firms, or through the management courses they have attended. Such new alliances typify efforts to make the activity of government more coherent, more relevant to the needs of the locality, and more explicitly linked to the relational webs. They open up the opportunity for new styles of collaborative consensus building, to replace adversarial politics and competitive interest conflict. Through consensus building, co-ordination of different governance efforts could be achieved, with benefits for the efficiency and effectiveness of urban region governance.

The challenge for such alliances lies in their ability to become both knowledge-rich and interculturally-sensitive. Such groupings tend to draw upon the knowledge of local business and political elites. The informal nature of such alliances contribute new ideas to the local arena, but there is no mechanism to encourage attention to the diversity of social networks within a place, and how these may be affected by policy ideas. As a result, such alliances may not endure or be challenged by coalitions from different social bases, or may maintain power but exercise it in narrow, exclusionary ways. The problem with such alliances lies in their informality. They could become merely channels for the reconstitution of local corporatist elites, colonising the institutions of government for their benefit. The good decision could thus become that which most promoted the interests of this elite. This approach focuses on the soft infrastucture of relation-building without attention to the hard infrastructure of rights, duties and competences.

Inclusionary argumentation

This model seeks to pull the relation-building of local entrepreneurial alliances beyond these tendencies to corporatism. It develops a style which could realize the ideas of participatory discursive democracy in a practical way. It too emphasises collaborative consensus-building, but underpinned by an explicit inclusionary intention. A key attribute of a good decision would be that it is taken in cognisance of the concerns of all members of a political community and that these members have the opportunity to express their views, and to challenge the decisions made on their behalf, not just in the ballot box, but through rights and opportunities to challenge policies as they are developed and as they become guides for subsequent action. As with the model of pluralist democracy, it is assumed that all members of a territorial political community have a right to make a claim for policy attention. It also has the capacity to recognize others who have a stake in what happens in a place. Such procedures could lead to a 'politics of challenging' dominated by adversarial arguments in legal courts. There is a strong tendency in this direction in US local environmental planning. In all governance systems, courts are needed to arbitrate where differences cannot be argued away. The model of participatory discursive democracy proposes that claims for attention are redeemed not in adversarial argument over specific rights, but in forms of collaborative argumentation about what issues are, the different ways they may be understood, what constitute problems, what possibilities for acting on them there may be, how these may affect the lives and cultures of all members of political communities and how choices may impact on different members. The giving of rights to be heard goes with the responsibility to listen, to give respect, and to learn, through procedures which foster respectful mutual learning about the concerns of others, and which draw on the knowledgeability of all members of a political community. The approach thus combines attention to both the soft infrastucture of the style of relation-building and the hard infrastructure of rights and duties.

This model is further developed in Chapters 8 and 9. In its style, it emphasises processes of collaborative argumentation within which those who make decisions about governance matters, that is, matters of collective concern within a political community, should expect to give good reasons for their decisions, grounded, following Habermas, in the 'best available attempts' at inclusionary argumentation. This means paying attention to the range of ways people have of knowing and valuing things and the cultural underpinnings of knowledge and values. It allows technical knowledge, drawn from various sources, to be woven together, through discussion, with practical knowledge. It allows questions of material costs and benefits to be considered together with questions of moral value and emotive appreciation. It encourages interlinking policy issues in ways which make sense to political communities rather than merely to government organisation. A good decision would be one derived from inclusionary argumentation, made in the expectation that good reasons, based in inclusionary processes of collaborative discussion, could be given for it if challenged.

This approach seeks to widen out governance effort to include all those with a stake in a locality in both strategy formation and policy delivery. To many critics, it seems to lead to a massive amount of time consumed in consensus-building and argumentation. The costs of 'democracy' are then often set against the need for quick strategic action, to take a key economic opportunity or to safeguard an environmental asset. It is also suggested that people do not have the time to be continually engaged in governance. Issues cannot be contested all the time (Latour, 1987). This is to misunderstand the approach. It is often the case that full consultation on an issue is not possible. Political communities may wish to delegate areas of decision-making to smaller groups – of community leaders, or officials, or experts. Where the approach differs from the others discussed in this section is in the ways such delegated action is undertaken. It demands a culture of argumentation based on policy reasoning which pays attention to the diversity of people's concerns, their ways of knowing and of valuing. This sensitivity to diversity is not maintained merely by the values of the central participants in governance. If this were so, then it would be all too easy to revert to a practice of corporatism, or of competitive pluralist conflict. What makes it different is the structure of rights to challenge and the language of reasoning which evolves around the exercise of such rights. This in turn could change governance practices such that people would trust their governance machinery sufficiently that challenges were the exception rather than the norm.

The transformation of governance

Each of these new ideas for governance forms takes a different emphasis. The criteria-driven approach stresses the hard infrastructure of the form of *policy measures*. The model of entrepreneurial consensus concentrates on the soft infrastructure, the processes of *consensus-building*. The participatory approach combines both hard and soft infrastructure, emphasising the *style of reasoning* and the construction of *rights* with respect to process. All assume a formal democratic form for governance, in which politicians are elected by citizens. All accept that this by itself is insufficient to enable a legitimate relation between government activity and economic and social life. All seek ways of opening up government processes to enable a more continuous interaction between government, business and citizens. They differ, however, in how this is done. The criteria-driven approach converts citizens' interests into technical criteria with which the performance of government agencies are to be monitored. The other two approaches respond to demands for active involvement by business and citizens. The first builds consensus through ad hoc alliances among key players. The second seeks a more systematic approach to including members of political communities, and offers a style of reasoning which brings into play the range of ways of knowing and valuing within a political community and among stakeholders.

In any particular instance, of course, the form and style of governance will represent a mixture of tendencies. As Claus Offe (1977) argued, governance activity is always caught in the tensions of an impossible demand, that it should meet everyone's objectives accountably and legitimately. He described how government agencies tried different styles in succession in a 'restless search' to find a stable approach which would be accepted as legitimate by all parties. He did not imagine that a stable approach could ever be found. Yet in some times and places, governance activity has developed a surprising degree of stability and legitimacy. German corporatism and Dutch co-sociational arrangements appear to have achieved this enduring quality, producing, in the Dutch case, a long-standing stable environment for the elaboration of 'planning doctrine' (Faludi and Van der Valk, 1994).

This emphasises that modes of governance and their associated routines and styles are the product of local contingencies, of the cultural traditions of particular places and political communities, and on the dynamics of change which are re-shaping these traditions. For anyone concerned with transforming governance cultures and innovating new styles, learning to read the specific 'politics of place' is a critical skill. This involves contextualising specific practices, in terms of both their local contingencies and broader structuring dynamics. This is particularly necessary for those involved in planning processes within governance. A sensitive grasp of specific governance forms and styles may help explain why some aspects of planning work which are seen as important elsewhere are difficult to introduce (for example, open strategic debate on policy issues). It may also help identify windows of opportunity to introduce procedures and activities in the planning arena which had been difficult before. 'Reading local political culture' means going beyond the surface of both formal politics and informal power games, into the embedded cultural practices which structure routines and styles, and flow knowledge and value around the political networks. However, this local embedding is not a 'bedrock'. Rather, it is a shifting sand, subtly moving in response to internal and external forces. Those promoting institutional change need some capability to 'read' the directions of the movement of the sand flows if institutional redesigns are to 'take hold'.

This means that analysts of governance and planning systems should avoid simple generalisations about what style of planning will arise in particular circumstances. A neat 'functional fit' between political and economic conditions, forms of governance and styles of planning should not be expected. The actual practices of institutional forms grow out of specific conditions. They are not 'implanted' into situations, though formal structures are often imposed from outside. Yet it is possible to identify commonalities in modes, routines and styles. The models used in this chapter have tried to capture these commonalities. Particular tendencies inhere in each of the models, with respect to knowledge, values and power. As Fischer (1990) argues, there is a pervasive struggle in the terrain of governance at the present time between pluralistic democratic tendencies, which seek to acknowledge a wide range of stakeholders, forms of knowledge and value bases, and techno-corporate ones, which seek to keep control over the management of our societies, using the tools of technical analysis and management, or the knowledge and interests of key corporate interests. This may be interpreted as the contemporary form of Offe's 'restless search'. In this struggle, the politics of criteria and of entrepreneurial consensus confront the politics of inclusionary argumentation in an encounter masked by a common vocabulary of 'empowerment', 'consensus building', 'stakeholders', 'consumer responsiveness' and 'collaboration'. Identifying how the tendencies in governance forms are working out through this struggle is a key task of critical political analysis.

Planning, as a policy-driven approach to the practice of governance which is both knowledge-rich and inclusionary, has a part in all the evolving governance forms. In the criteria-driven approach, it becomes a form of urban and regional economics, focused on the development of methodologies for policy evaluation. This is evident in the 'evaluation culture' sweeping through many governance agencies in Britain in the 1990s. In the entrepreneurial consensus, its role is to supply the research and information needs of the strategic alliance. In the model of inclusionary argumentation, it provides expertise in the management of collaborative argumentation processes. All of these styles of planning may evolve in governance efforts at managing local environments. However, the experience of working with a multiplicity of interests and claims for policy attention, a day-to-day experience for many local spatial and land use planners, provides a considerable resource upon which to develop the understanding needed for inclusionary argumentation, if fully recognised and appreciated. Yet we still know little about the practices which would realise such a style of governance. In the following chapters, I explore the processes of collaborative planning and inclusionary argumentation, and the hard infrastructure of instutional design which would support such processes. Together, these provide a specification of an institutional approach to collaborative planning.

8 Strategies, Processes and Plans

Planning as generating strategic conviction

The institutional design of governance forms, and of policy-driven and planning routines and styles, is a dynamic endeavour which evolves in interaction with local contingencies and external forces, in order to address the agendas of those with the power to shape the design. The resultant structures and processes generate an institutional capacity which may enhance or inhibit the ability stakeholders with concerns about local environmental change of the kind outlined in Part II. In Part II, it was argued that, to pursue their social, economic and environmental agendas in the social contexts of contemporary urban regions, there are shared interests in finding forms of governance which enable discussion among these disparate stakeholders and their networks. This leads to an interest among many stakeholders in the design of institutional processes which will facilitate collaboration, mutual learning and consensus-building. Consensus-building thrives on openness and trust. Expanding networks of collaboration and trust provide a resource of *social and intellectual capital* (Innes *et al.*, 1994; Ostrom, 1990), through which economic knowledge can flow around localities. Such social capital also encourages more people and more firms to get involved in governance activity, enriching the knowledgeability and value sensitivity of the public realm. This chapter explores the challenge of the design of processes of collaborative planning, the soft infrastructure of inclusionary argumentation, and the way this can contribute to building social and intellectual capital.

Planning approaches, with their emphasis on knowledgeability, on interrelationships between activities in places, and on the relation between short- and long-term actions and effects, have much to offer collaborative governance. But traditionally, they have been associated with technocratic 'representative' governance, where experts are separated from interested parties, or corporatist practices, where only a few powerful interests are involved in the collaboration. This produces too narrow a base of social and intellectual capital for the challenges most urban regions face. The challenge for planning is to develop new practices. These need a breadth which admits of diverse ways of knowing and being, and which have the capacity to reflect on, and call attention to, what lies behind the 'politics of interests' and the 'politics of voice' (see Chapter 2). They need a capacity to move beyond a broad-based 'scoping' of issues to the invention and consolidation of organising ideas and strategies. They require an ability to reflect on the 'membership' of consensus-building activities, on who is involved, who should be involved and who may be left out. Effective institutional processes for collaboration can build consensus not only around what the problems are, but about strategies and directions. Strategies provide simplifying concepts. They organise thinking about issues. They indicate what are priorities and why. They provide points of reference which people call upon in certain situations. In this way, they have the capacity to frame the social relations over which they have influence, to become 'structures', to carry power. This chapter is about how such framing work takes place.

Strategy making and strategy 'acknowledging' in the flow of action is one of the most demanding and powerful characteristics of a style of governance which adopts a planning approach. The articulation of strategies requires those involved to take a major leap in reflexive activity, to stand back from their particular concerns, to review their situation, to re-think problems and challenges, to work out opportunities and constraints, to think through courses of action which might be better than current practices and to commit themselves to changing things. Such changes are more than fine-tuning. They involve re-shaping the frames of reference in which issues are discussed and decisions are taken (Forester, 1996; Schneecloth and Shibley, 1995). This requires participants to shift the systems of meaning about a set of problems which they have used in the past. In Kuhnian terms, strategy-making is a process of deliberative paradigm change. It aims to change cultural conceptions, systems of understanding and systems of meaning. It is more than just about producing collective decisions. It is about shifting and re-shaping *convictions*. Such re-framing efforts aim to influence the allocation of resources within a governance sphere. They may also lead to changes in legal rules and administrative procedures governing a class of actions. The most powerful strategies achieve their impact by entering the consciousness of the political and organizational culture of a place. Once embedded in the thoughtworlds of the 'key players', co-ordination and implementation are achieved as part of the flow of routine rather than through deliberate mobilisation and struggle. Thus planning concepts can become culturally-embedded 'doctrines', such as the British greenbelt or the Dutch Randstadt (see Chapter 2).

Part II identified why, at the present time, stakeholders in urban regions may feel the need for such 'cultural change' projects. The most evident pressures arise from the interests of those firms and agencies concerned about the health and dynamics of urban region economies. They are deeply and unavoidably involved in forces of territorial economic transformation. Explicit strategy-making offers a way of capturing a degree of understanding and control over these forces. Local alliances in many urban regions in western economies seek ways of 'holding down' the dynamics of change to benefit their own interests and their region, 'pinning down' globalising economic opportunities to benefit their place. Those concerned with biospheric environmental quality raise difficult questions both about the economic development strategies being pursued in localities, and about the threat which existing ways of living and doing business, and the spatial organisation of places, pose to the maintenance of environmental asset stocks and carrying capacities for future generations. Those anxious about community development, about increasing social polarisation and social tension seek ways of making better links between economic opportunities, environmental conditions and the quality of social life.

These searchings for new ways of doing things not only represent a demand for better policies to solve today's problems rather than yesterday's. They also express a seeking out for ways of re-formulating how problems have been thought about. The traditional vocabulary of party ideologies, the customary division of public policy into economic and social functions and sectors, the language of redistribution, the articulation of general principles in the form of policy criteria such as 'the polluter pays' or 'value for money', seem inadequate to the task of making the links between the various dimensions of these new concerns about urban regions. The challenge raised in Part II of this book demands a re-thinking which could lead to a more rounded and interrelated view of urban region change, a way of making links among the fragments of the relational webs which co-exist in an urban region.

But the discussion in Part II also makes clear the scale and complexity of the challenge of efforts in strategy-making in the context of contemporary urban regions. How is 'cultural change' in people's thinking about the urban regions they live in or do business in to happen when there is such a diversity of webs of relations co-existing in a place? How is it possible to represent this diversity in the effort in strategy-making? How do people get to share enough understanding about what the issues are and about how to discuss them to enable a collective effort in strategy-making to proceed?

It is often claimed that the task of strategy-making is inherently too complex, requiring too much specialised knowledge, to be tackled in broadly-based interactive ways within political communities. The literature on informal institutional design stresses the importance of homogeneity in interests and in cultures, and of clear boundaries as to who 'belongs' in an organising community, if such institutions are to survive over time (Ostrom, 1990). But the stakeholders in local environmental change are clearly diverse, and conflicting. Further, local environments and urban regions are very much 'open systems' not closed ones, and it is extremely difficult to fix membership boundaries. A simple interpretation of these findings suggests that in complex, open-system, heterogeneous situations, either the effort in strategy-making should be abandoned and left to the market, or the state should step in and hand over the process to expert policy analysts and key political and economic elites who can form an 'apex' group, acting for their political communities.

But, as discussed in Chapter 7, there is today little respect or tolerance for such managerial paternalism. Is the technocratic state really the only answer? Could it not be possible to develop non-paternalist forms of representation, which could reflect the diversity of stakeholders' knowledge and values? In any case, if strategies are to be legitimate, they need to be broadly-based, both with respect to what strategies offer and how they are made. This raises questions about what 'broadly-based' can mean. A corporatist approach is broader than policy-making within the walls of the state bureaucracy, but it does not reach beyond powerful apex groups. A pluralist conception of social order would seek out the plurality of interest groups in an area. An institutionalist approach focuses on the range of social nodes and networks in a place and their actual and potential links, that is, on relation-building work. Through these relations, trust and knowledge are generated and circulated, to provide a foundation of social and intellectual capital upon which collaboration can build. Broadly-based strategy-making efforts are thus deliberate attempts at institutional capacity building by the forging of new networks and the infusing of ideas into the array of relational webs which layer over an urban region. The resultant strategies should then have the potential to be richly informed, drawing on a multiplicity of understandings and values. They may also end up being more effective too, as more people are directly involved in actively seeking to change their own 'culture' with respect to how to share spaces and make places, that is, in transformative work. An institutionalist analysis would suggest that the broader the base and depth of involvement in strategy-making and the richer the links among the relational webs involved, the greater the 'ownership' of the new strategic understandings is likely to be, and the more strategic directions, once invented, are likely to endure (Innes *et al.*, 1994).

So the challenge for urban region strategy-making is to find ways of collaborating across the webs of relations with a 'stake' in an urban region's future, to develop new ways of thinking about how to share place and space which can endure over time. To respond to this challenge clearly demands a considerable effort of collective political will. Building up that will, mobilising concern for urban region futures around the hope of collaborative strategy-making, is always an important precursor to effective strategy-making. Without propitious moments, strategic planning exercises are likely to fade into empty rituals or the re-affirmation of the status quo. Chapter 9 discusses the hard infrastructure of institutional rules which could encourage such moments. Yet there is plenty of evidence that strategies, once made and given legitimacy, not only endure but enter popular consciousness. The strategic idea becomes, to use Faludi's term, a pervasive *planning doctrine* (Faludi and Van der Valk, 1994).

It is here that the ideas developing around the concepts of *strategic consensus-building* through *inclusionary argumentation* introduced in Chapter 2 offer rich possibilities. To quote Jürgen Habermas:

> Argumentation is not a decision procedure resulting in collective decisions but a problem-solving procedure that generates convictions (Habermas, 1993, p. 158)

How can such ideas be developed to facilitate processes which help policy communities articulate their common concerns about spaces and places in ways which are inclusionary and create strategies which 'make a difference', which are owned and used subsequently by the participating members?

Strategy-making as politics and technique

The task and technique of strategy-making is the heartland of planning culture (see Chapter 1). It is here that the co-ordinative and future-oriented qualities of planning as a style of governance are most visible. The making of plans which translated strategies into operational principles and regulatory rules to guide development was the core activity of economic planning, with its focus on five-year plans, and of physical development planning, with its interest in urban masterplans. The policy analysis tradition also focused on strategy, introducing rational goal-directed techniques for analysis and evaluation which would allow the selection of the 'best' or 'most satisfactory' alternative from among an array of possible strategies. These ideas flowered in the widespread interest in regional strategy in Europe in the 1960s. They were challenged by those who thought in more pluralist terms and by the reality of pluralistic, politicised practices. Debate on local environmental change shifted in Britain and elsewhere, from co-ordinated strategy to issue politics, and conflicts over projects. The qualities of places and how they might develop got lost in these struggles (see Healey, Khakee, Motte and Needham, 1996).

The evolving forms of governance discussed in Chapter 7 all emphasise strategy development. In the criteria-driven approach, strategies are issue-based, and rapidly translated into performance criteria and targets. In entrepreneurial consensus, strategy-making is about the production of a co-ordinating and marketing 'vision'. The idea of inclusionary argumentation demands instead a broadly-based social technology of strategy-production. The focus is on the processes through which participants come together, build understanding and trust among themselves, and develop ownership of the strategy, rather than the specific production of decision-criteria or an attractive image. The objective of the social technologies proposed below is to help release community capacity to invent processes through which to collaborate and build consensuses which are useful to those involved and which have the potential to endure.

The policy analysis tradition of planning in particular (see Chapter 1) provides rich resources of critical debate for thinking about social technologies for strategy-making and acknowledging. The key points from the debates will be summarised very briefly in the form of a contrast between two approaches, the rationalist analytical means–ends technologies of the 1960s, and recent work in interactive strategy-making. The first has been pervasive in planning thought and in policy-making practice. For this reason alone, it is important to understand its assumptions and principles, as it deeply infuses both expert and popular conceptions of how strategies are made. It also contains many ideas and principles which provide valuable insights for the task of inclusionary strategy-making efforts. But it is limited by its assumptions of instrumental rationality and objective science, and needs to be recast in the context of knowledge as socially produced.

The rational process approach to strategy-making

The rational planning process sought to develop a scientific technology for strategy-making in complex, interconnected, public policy contexts. It assumed that strategies could be derived from social goals by analytical routines based on empirical inquiry and deductive logic. Goals express the ends of strategies, analysis works out the most appropriate means. Following the principles of scientific objectivity and instrumental rationality from which the process model derived, it sought to separate the discussion of objective 'facts' from the discussion of values. This encouraged a separation of the activity of technical analysis, the province of experts, from that of setting values, the province of politicians representing the 'public interest', as in the political model of representative democracy. In a classic statement of the approach, Davidoff and Reiner (1962) identify 'necessary components of the planning act' as:

1. The achievement of ends.
2. The exercise of choice (as between means to achieve the ends).
3. Orientation to the future.
4. Orientation to action, to bringing about the desired results.
5. Comprehensiveness, relating to coverage of the components of a system. (pp. 17–18)

The 'necessary and sufficient steps' for a planning process are therefore, they claim, *value formulation, means identification* and *effectuation*. In this early statement, two critical innovations of the rational process are highlighted – the explicit treatment of values, and the emphasis on how policies could be translated into action.

Almost immediately, the approach was subjected to critique (Lee, 1973). Part of this critique derived from those who shared a commitment to instrumental rationality, while recognising the limits to knowledge. They differed, however, in their understanding of the political context of policymaking. Charles Lindblom mounted a sustained but creative attack on the rational model, arguing firstly that, in a pluralist polity, agreement on goals was unlikely (Braybrooke and Lindblom, 1963; Lindblom, 1959). Secondly, politicians in such contexts were rarely prepared to subcontract the articulation of possible courses of action to technical teams. Thirdly, public policy was less an effort in moving to new imagined futures. Rather, it involved moving out from existing positions by small incremental steps. With this in mind, Lindblom advocated an 'incrementalist' decision technology which involved successive comparisons with present conditions, rather than the articulation of means to achieve new positions. Other commentators explored the variability of contexts and its implications for the likelihood that rationalist or incrementalist policy processes would be adopted (Bolan, 1969; Christensen, 1985; Etzioni, 1968). This led to the conclusion that policy process models, and the alternatives developed by critics, should be treated as a battery of techniques, to be applied differentially, according to the characteristics of contexts. This is encapsulated in Hudson's idea of the SITAR (synthetic (rationalist), incremental, transactive, advocacy and radical) to describe planning theories about process forms (Hudson, 1979). It is an idea which begins to move towards the recognition of the local specificity and contingency of choices about process forms.

More vigorous critiques came from other directions. These were underpinned by either a general critique of the model of representative democracy (see Chapter 7), or by a challenge to the epistemology of instrumental rationality and positivist social science (see Chapters 1 and 2). Some commentators confirm the essential conservatism of the methodology, though from a practical rather than a theoretical-ideological standpoint. Black (1990), in an interesting reflection on a major exercise in the rational planning of Chicago's transportation system in the 1960s, identifies a major failure of anticipation:

> The staff often talked about the future, but it was a future that extrapolated the past and maintained the status quo. .. [Although air pollution was causing trouble in Los Angeles], no one expected air pollution ever to be a problem in Chicago. No one anticipated such developments as the environmental movement or the energy crisis. Little attention was given to the transportation problems of the poor, minorities, the elderly and the handicapped. (Black, 1990, pp. 35–6)

This failure of vision, Black argues, arose because the methods encouraged analysts to describe trends and then extrapolate them in order to arrive at conceptions of social and economic futures. This may be appropriate in very stable situations, but is little help in grasping the dynamics of complex and contradictory changes, and hence in institutional design for dynamic contexts.

The epistemological critique challenged the separation of fact and value which the model required, the objectivity of scientific understanding and the dominance of instrumental rationality, as discussed in Chapter 2. Paul Davidoff himself came to modify his original model substantially. Yet it is worth stressing the innovations which the rational planning model brought to the discussion of policy processes (see Friedmann, 1987; Sager, 1994). It emphasised:

1. The complex interconnections among the activities policy sought to influence. This recognition continues in contemporary institutional concern with the interconnections between webs of relations.
2. Conscious specification of the form of the process of arriving at strategic proposals. As Urlan Wannop notes in his account of the Coventry-Solihull-Warwickshire Sub-regional study of the late 1960s which he led, 'our declared intention [was] to reveal our processes at all times' (1985, p. 206).
3. The effectiveness of policy making activity, rather than the efficiency of the process (Webber, 1978). As Faludi (1987) has since stressed, it provides a consequentialist methodology, focusing on whether policy proposals have the means to achieve desired outcomes.
4. Explicit recognition of the value dimension of problem-definition and choice of strategies, rather than leaving values hidden within professional or political assumptions.
5. The deployment of available knowledge about situations in a systematic way, rather than relying on unreflective anecdote, implicit intuitions and unstructured judgement.
6. An explicit and systematic approach to testing out, and evaluating policy ideas.

There are many aspects of the model that any alternative ideas about policy processes would do well to safeguard. Yet the problems with the model are fundamental and primarily relate to its assumptions about ontology and epistemology, that is, approaches to identity and to ways of knowing. As Mel Webber (1978) argues, the model represents a technocratic concept of social engineering, in which planning is conceived as if it were an objective science. Webber recognised that, because values are involved as well as facts, and because values are located in people's consciousness, not floating around in the ether to be discovered by objective science, some way of bringing people into policy processes needs to be found. This brings politics and values inside the policy process. Webber also stresses the diversity of people's interests and preferences, and seeks a permissive planning which works with the differences among people. In the end though, he maintains an individualist conception of identity, conceiving of people reacting rationally in the light of their preferences. In contrast, as discussed in Chapter 2, a Habermasian perspective emphasises how people's conceptions of their preferences are communicatively and intersubjectively constructed. Further, and in the light of Giddens' conception of the active interrelation of structuring forces and individual agency (see Chapter 2), it is not possible to assume that the context of a planning process provides a defined 'action space' within which technical work can proceed. The rational planning process imagines technical teams serving representative politicians. These teams undertake analytical and evaluative work in their offices. This leads to ideas for tools with which to manage the environment 'out there'. This environment is brought into planning work in a controlled way through the collection and manipulation of data. No attention is given to the way the 'outside world' is brought into the planning office through the experience of team members. An institutionalist view, in contrast, recognises that firms, agencies and households are made up of people, who bring their own professional and socio-cultural frames of reference to particular tasks. And in both the processes of planning and the practices of implementing policy ideas, strategic planning exercises not only manage trends in urban systems. They contribute to changing their form. Thus the 'inside' is in continual and multifaceted interaction with the 'outside' (see Latour, 1987).

It was the political and organizational challenges to the rational model which attracted most attention in the 1970s and 1980s. These emphasised who got involved and who was in control of the process. It is only recently that the philosophical challenges have come to the fore, as the critique of instrumental rationality has gathered force. This has fostered the development of ideas about the forms and methodologies of *interactive* strategic policy processes, which work through *interpretive* policy routines rather than deductive and scientific logic (Innes, 1995).

Interactive approaches to strategy-making

The shift to an interactive perspective on the activity of strategy-making recognises that strategies and policies are not the outcome of objective, technical processes, but are actively produced in social contexts. The institutionalist perspective has grown out of this assumption. This recognition has, however, grown slowly and has taken different directions. There are precursors of these ideas in some of the rationalist writings. Cowling and Steeley (1973), in their account of the British experience in subregional planning, note the use of what they refer to as the 'consensus method' as a way of bringing together the different sectors of analysis. The participants in this consensus effort were viewed as representatives of government departments and researchers. Webber (1978) describes planning as a 'cognitive style' rather than a scientific field. The planner, he claims, should be a 'facilitator of debate' rather than a 'substantive expert' (p. 162), and he argues that planning should become a process of 'open argumentation' (p. 162). Breheny and Hooper (1985) note emerging ideas of policy processes in which the planner is a participant rather than being in charge.

Interactive approaches have thus been slowly building up momentum in the discussion of strategy-making, reflecting the increasing acknowledgment of a pluralist governance reality (see Chapter 7). As they have evolved, there has been a shift from a preoccupation with the mechanics of co-ordination towards an emphasis on the social construction of the appreciation of problems and the articulation of strategies. It is this last recognition which is central to the institutionalist position. To illustrate the shift from a rationalist and technological conception of interaction to a social-constructivist one, three contributions will be discussed: the strategic choice approach of John Friend and others; the ideas of social learning and framing associated with organizational development ideas; and, in the planning field, the work of Donald Schon and John Bryson's conception of strategy-making in a 'shared-power' world.

A technology for strategic choice

Friend drew on work with Jessop at the Institute for Operations Research (IOR) in London in the 1960s to develop ideas for the selection of strategic options. They drew on Emery and Trist's conception of the way organizations interacted with their environments (Emery and Trist, 1969). As in the rationalist conception, policymaking occurred in a definable 'action space', which separated the activity from the world around it. Relations with the 'environment' outside had therefore to be deliberately constructed. The key problem for strategy-making was presented as the resolution of uncertainty. This was multidimensional. A critical analytic exercise was the exploration and mapping of interconnections in the problem-definition process. In a series of studies (Friend and Jessop, 1969; Friend *et al.*, 1974; Friend and Hickling, 1987), Friend and his colleagues developed a technology for analysing uncertainty and mapping interconnected decision areas (AIDA) (see Figure 8.1).

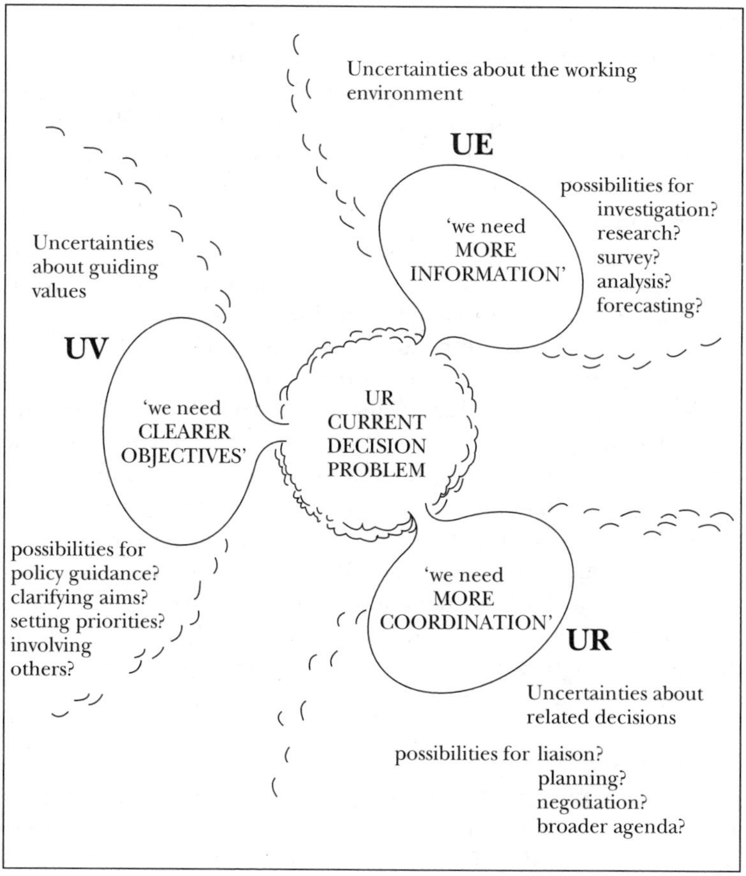

Figure 8.1 Three types of uncertainty in decision-making
Source: Friend and Hickling (1987) p. 11

These ideas were pursued in a major empirical study of policy co-ordination in the West Midlands of England (Friend, Power and Yewlett, 1974). This work decisively challenged much of the British literature on policymaking in public administration which had until then emphasised formal legal and procedural rules. It revealed how co-ordination was actively achieved across organisational boundaries not by formal procedures of consultation, but by the construction of informal networks among key players in the various agencies with a stake in a policymaking exercise. This empirical demonstration of the significance of policy networks led Friend and his colleagues to propose a technology for intercorporate networking which emphasised the interactive work which was involved. These inter-agency policy networks were presented as interrelating with their environments. The drive to co-ordinate arose from efforts to resolve uncertainty about values, about the wider environment and about related areas of choice in the policy-making process.

Friend and his various collaborators aimed to provide a managerial technology for network building. But they gave very little attention to the power relations of the intercorporate networking process, or to the ethical issues of network building generated by the individual and informal construction of policy networks bypassing the hierarchical accountability arrangements of individual public agencies (Healey, 1979). Yet the focus on policy networks resonated with the reality of practice. By the late 1970s, political scientists in Europe were beginning to describe central–local government relations in terms of policy networks (Rhodes, 1992). Although in their later work, there is much more emphasis on how to facilitate group discussion and how to involve stakeholders (Friend and Hickling, 1987), it remains in the mould of a technocratic managerial technology.

Social learning

The radical transformation introduced by the social learning tradition is the recognition that the knowledge developed in group work is not 'out there' waiting to be discovered, but is actively being produced through social interaction and social learning. People make knowledge, in relation to their purposes (Latour, 1987; Shotter, 1993). They develop theories about how things are in the course of, and relation to, action. This recognition represents a decisive ontological and epistemological shift from the rationalist conception of knowledge in policy processes, as discussed in Chapter 2. The ideas and techniques of social learning have been extensively developed in the human relations school of management (Clegg, 1990), and have leaked out into wider use, for example in the mediation of environmental conflicts, or in group therapy practices. However, in explaining the social dynamics of group processes, contributors to this strand of ideas look to social psychology rather than sociology, emphasising agency but neglecting structure. Rather than recognising the potential for structural divisions and cultural conflicts to lie behind tensions and disagreements in small groups, there is an assumption that a consensus on values and information exists, to be discovered by group members (see, for example, Rein and Schon, 1993).

John Friedmann, in a valuable summary of the approach, claims that radical proponents of planning in the past have emphasised group learning processes, from Lewis Mumford to Mao Tse Tung (Friedmann, 1987). More significant within recent planning theory has been the work of Donald Schon. The core propositions of this work may be summarised as follows (see Friedmann, 1987; Schon, 1983; Rein and Schon, 1993):

1. People learn through doing; they develop theories in action. It would help the learning processes if people were more conscious of this learning-in-action, if they became 'reflexive'.
2. There are two dimensions to such learning; the first, or single-loop learning, involves working out how to perform a task better within given parameters; the second involves learning about the parameters and thereby changing the conditions under which tasks are performed. Schon's model of the *reflective practitioner* emphasises double-loop learning.
3. Such double-loop learning can take place in social situations, through dialogue, through which people can collectively explore and learn about issues and each other's attitudes to them. Such group dialogue can be assisted by techniques of group dialogue facilitation.

4. Problems and objectives, facts and values, emerge through such group processes; they are not waiting 'out there' to be discovered by scientific inquiry.
5. Group discussion processes which reach double-loop learning can re-set parameters for subsequent action, and in this way engage in setting the 'frame' for action. This *framing* work can be equated with deliberative strategy-making.

John Friedmann, in his critique of this approach, stresses the importance of the shift to a social constructivist position. The approach is also in line with Wittgensteinian philosophy, with its emphasis on the construction of knowledge in relation to human purposes (Wittgenstein, 1968). The perception that knowledge and understanding are produced through social interactive processes decisively shifts the understanding of strategy-making work from analytical and managerial technologies to social ones. But the approach is still caught within an individualist and objectivist conception of the external world. Schon's reflective practioner learns about facts and value through interaction with external world, through experimentation and reflection (Schon, 1983). People correct errors in their perception of the world; they don't actively construct it (Friedmann, 1987). Further, there is a strong assumption of underlying consensus and equality among group members. There is little discussion of how such group processes would work outside self-selected groups, where some equality among members may be presumed, or company management, where power relations are reasonably clear and taken-for-granted, if typically highly unequal. Rein and Schon (1993) acknowledge, in their discussion of framing, that it is not clear how group efforts in framing would work in the public sphere, with many stakeholders and complex power relations.

Social technologies for a shared-power world

The extension of interactive strategy-making from the arena of company management practices into the public sphere is the focus of John Bryson's work. He moves beyond sociopsychological explanation into a sociological understanding of power relations, and, drawing on Giddens, the interaction of structure and agency. Underpinning and enriching his approach is an institutional view which enables him to set mutual learning processes in the context of strategymaking as the active work of structuring or framing social relations. In a major consolidation of their work, Bryson and Crosby (1992) present the activity of strategy-making as an effort in deliberative innovation. It is conducted in a world of unequal power relations, but one where power is dispersed among a plurality of organizations and interests. The challenge for strategic policymaking is therefore how to make strategies in a 'shared-power' world. They draw on Lukes' three dimensions of power (see Chapter 2) to emphasise that power is much more than that manifest in the overt interplay of interests. It is also embedded in systems for defining acceptable rules of behaviour, in flows of resources and in the ideas and frames of reference people use. They use Giddens' ideas of structuration to emphasise this point. The effort of strategic policymaking is aimed at innovating through changing structures, through reworking the deeper power relations below the interplay of interests.

They conceive of the cycle of policy change metaphorically as a drama of strategy-making, with the strategy being conceptualized as a story about what should be done. The 'drama' proceeds through three types of setting, *forums, arenas* and *courts.* Participants in the drama are key decisionmakers and opinion leaders. For Bryson and Crosby, 'leaders' are the key initiators and managers of the policy innovation process. They champion solutions and promote processes. The critical interactions are among the leaders and key players, and between these and all the stakeholders in a policy issue.

This interactive, strategic work of storymaking proceeds through three phases, though not necessarily in sequence. The phases are linked to the settings. In *Forums,* the emphasis is on the 'creation and communication of meaning'. In *Arenas,* the emphasis is on the development and implementation of policy. In *Courts,* residual work of arbitration takes place. Figure 8.2 illustrates Bryson and Crosby's conception of the process, developed in relation to a combination of Giddensian structuration and Lukes' three dimensions of power.

The work of forum construction involves 'forging an agreement to act' among the key players, with 'leaders' playing a critical role in bringing the parties together. At this stage, attention needs to be given to how the process will proceed and particularly the 'design and use of the settings' (Bryson and Crosby, 1992, p. 131).

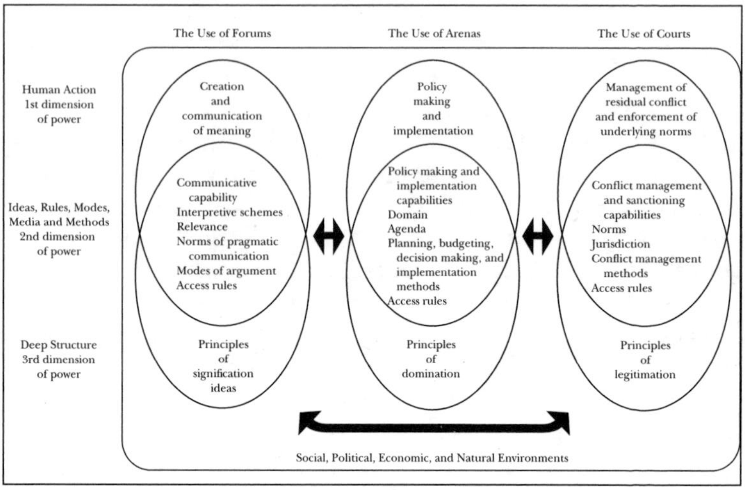

Figure 8.2 The triple three-dimensional view of power
Source: Bryson and Crosby (1992) p. 91

This includes an initial work of analysis to identify the stakeholders – that is, all those with a 'stake' in an issue or area. The concept of stakeholder acts as a net to 'capture' both the articulate and the silent, the powerful and the powerless, those within a territorial political community, and those beyond its boundaries (Figure 8.3 provides an example).

It is in the forum setting that particular attention should be given to building up networks and coalitions around an issue agenda. Then various techniques can be used to 'search' the issue area to arrive at some common understanding of what the issue is about, about what is a problem and what might be solutions. Bryson and Crosby emphasise the importance of holding off from developing solutions until a rich sense of the issue has been arrived at and 'owned' by all those involved. In these discussion processes, they stress the significance of open discussion, within which the various players can make claims and arguments, and explore each other's arguments. 'Analysis' is therefore an interpretive activity, trying to bring out the 'worldviews' that lie behind the way participants articulate issues, problems and the solutions they offer.

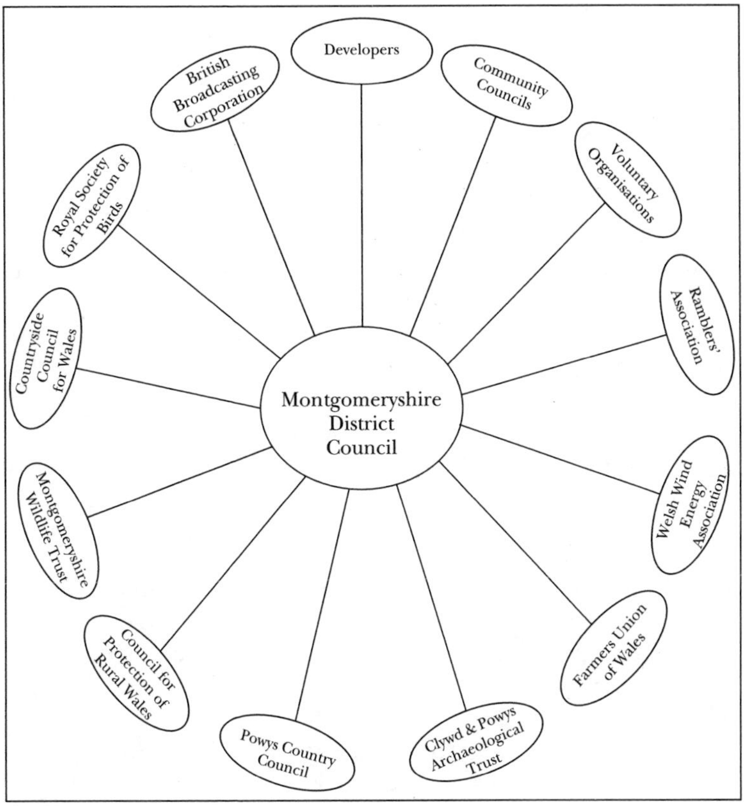

Figure 8.3 A stakeholder map: active stakeholders in renewable energy policy design in a Welsh District
Source: Hull (1995) p. 291

Bryson and Crosby provide a rich interpretive conception of strategic policy processes in a world of multiple players, grounded in social theories which emphasise how power relations infuse our assumptions and routine practices as well as our overt conflicts of interest, and in an appreciation of the way social structures are produced by the actions of agency. Strategy-making is thus an effort in transforming structures and changing power relations. Their concern is with ways of doing this collaboratively and interpretively, working through and building up policy networks and alliances as the work proceeds. They present a process whereby considerations of fact ('What is happening?') and value ('What do we care about?') are intermeshed, as the various participants bring into discussion their own understandings of the worlds in which they live and of the problems and aspirations they have with respect to the agenda of issues in discussion. In this way, the 'outside' is brought 'inside' the process. They recognise the fluidity of the way claims about issues are made, and the significance of holding back from arriving at policy ideas, 'solutions', before discursive exploration has opened up the issues and ways of conceiving them. They emphasise that, in this process, experts are far from being 'in charge'. Instead they are at the service of the process and its leaders. They push even further than the social learning approach towards a conception of policy-making processes as a dynamic social effort of institutional shaping.

This approach resonates with the ideas of institutionalist social theory, with its recognition of social relations as intersecting networks, complexly structured by power relations operating on several levels at once. It offers a great deal for the project of inclusionary strategy-making with respect to the way local communities work out how to share spaces and make places. But yet there are missing ingredients for an inclusionary intercultural collaborative effort in spatial strategy making. Bryson and Crosby implicitly assume the context of a competitive and entrepreneurial culture, almost a 'monoculture', in which strategy leaders and innovators set out not only to make a collaborative strategy, but to get their strategy to 'win'. This takes them very close to managerial manipulation. They recognise the complex ethics of the interpretive work of the interactive processes they favour, but say little about what it means to be ethical, or about the norms to guide the collaborative processes they describe. Despite the recognition of multilayered power relations, and a deep commitment to a humanitarian and democratic society, there is little reference to either the substantive or normative challenges facing policymakers. The approach outlined could work very well as a service to the leaders of the corporatist strategic alliances, in the corporatist and entrepreneurial consensus forms of governance outlined in Chapter 7. But is 'sharing power' really about helping community leaders to get back some control, through collaboration, of the flow of events in urban regions. Is it sufficient for the ambitions of inclusionary, participative democracy? Is it sufficient for situations where the social relations and existing government activities within urban regions are both fragmented and deeply infused with relations of dominance? Will the approach work in conditions where there are many parties who want to get involved, yet who initially know each other little and trust each other less? Bryson and Crosby focus on mutual learning but have less to say on how the power relations of interaction work out, and little appreciation of the potential communicative difficulties which face many stakeholders in getting involved with governance processes dominated by well-educated elites.

Strategy-making through inclusionary argumentation

The institutionalist approach developed in this book drives Bryson and Crosby's ideas into a wider context. The fundamental viewpoint is that of a socially constructed reality, in which, following Giddens, agents act inventively in situations constrained by structuring forces. Knowledge and understanding are produced through collaborative social learning processes, not by the manipulation of abstract techniques by autonomous individuals. The approach is based on the following general propositions.

Firstly, collaboration, that is power-sharing, occurs in a multicultural world, in social relations where individuals construct their own identities through potentially multiple webs of relations. Through these multilayered culturally-embedded, intersubjective processes, people acquire frames of reference and systems of meaning. This contrasts with Schon's conception of a deep structure of consensus. The present approach assumes a deep structure of dissensus, riven with current and historical relations of dominance and oppression (Young, 1990). Social learning processes which engage in consensus-building thus have to build up trust and confidence *across* these fractures and chasms, to create new relations of collaboration and trust, and shift power bases. The approach thus focuses on transformative work, and the mobilisation of power through communicative work. Essentially, the argument, following Habermas (1984) and Forester (1989, 1993), is that power struggle which engages in social learning strategies will be more effective in producing real shifts in power and removing the hegemonic communicative distortions through which powerful groups have maintained their position in the past, than the grand battles of the ideological titans.

Secondly, it emphasises the importance of paying attention to practical consciousness and local knowledge, as well as the systemised scientific and technical knowledge made available by expert groups. Local knowledge has its own reasoning processes, in which conclusions are drawn from premises, but the line of reasoning may not be made explicit and one group's premises may be quite different to another. There is no priveleged, correct 'rationality' (Latour, 1987). Further, in many cultural communities, technical reasoning, moral attitudes and emotive feelings are all woven together. What are problems, what are seen as solutions, people's values and concerns, will crop up in a variety of forms in collaborative contexts. If the distortions of the powerful are to be avoided, all these potential forms of reasoning have to be learned about and given respect in the collaborative exercise, in order to discover the range of claims for policy attention, and the forms in which they are cast and can be redeemed. Without acknowledgement of the cultural embedding of reasoning processes, Schon's double-loop learning becomes an exercise in the more effective domination of the powerful.

Thirdly, consensus on problems, policies and how to follow them through is not something to be uncovered through collaborative dialogue. It has to be actively created across the fractures of the social relations of relevant stakeholders. This requires careful attention to the communicative contexts in which dialogue takes place, to the routines and styles of dialogue, since these too carry power; the power to encourage and include the participation of all stakeholders, and the power to discriminate and exclude (see Chapter 2). Consensus-building work can build trust, understanding and new relations of power among participants, generating social, intellectual and political capital which can endure beyond the particular collaborative effort (Innes 1994; Innes *et al.*, 1994).

Fourthly, such work builds institutional capacity, not merely through the impact on the participants, but through the way the institutional capital created flows through the social relational webs of participants. Consensus-building work thus involves a reflective interaction between the local knowledges to which the participants have access through their social networks and the development of understandings and valuings within the consensus-building arena. It is this capacity which provides the possibility for inclusionary collaborative strategy-making efforts in urban regions, where there are many stakeholders and consequently many cultural worlds to interact with. Policy ideas adopted in collaborative consensus-building work have leverage because they enter the 'local knowledge' of the social relations of participants. Consensus-building thus has the capacity both to create new cultural communities, and to filter into and sometimes transform, the local knowledge of the participants' relational worlds. The result is not merely the generation of new ways of knowing, new modes of acting and new policy discourses. Consensus-building practices have transformative potential, changing the frameworks for thinking, and potentially changing the content and modes of use of rules, and the way resources flow, the key dimensions through which structure and agency interact in Giddens' formulation of structuration theory. They thus have the potential to transform institutional capacity and relations of power. Consensus-building practices are a powerful form of social mobilisation.

Finally, this transformative effort is a field of struggle, in which those who have power may easily control access, routines and style. It is in this context that Habermas' communicative ethics performs a vital role, in providing a vocabulary to critique dialogical practices and to highlight communicative 'distortions' (see Chapter 2). Habermas' concerns are deeply normative. He seeks a re-construction of the public realm, and searches for ways in which we can hold public discussion and organise our public affairs without being dominated by the interests and languages of the powerful (Habermas, 1984, 1987, 1993). He draws on the conditions for a 'conversation between equals' to derive principles for evaluating public debate which can be brought into play in the process of public dialogue. Following in the tradition of critical theory, he argues that the way forward is to maintain a constant critique of dialogical practices. Both the relations of dialogue and the process of claim-making can be evaluated through a communicative ethics, in terms of their comprehensibility, integrity, legitimacy and truth (Habermas, 1984). Habermas derives these principles from a notion of an ideal speech situation – a dialogue between people who are in every respect equal in power and understanding. Habermas of course does not imagine that such a situation could exist. He believes, however, that every communicative act presupposes a capacity to understand, that the speakers and hearers routinely judge each other's sincerity, that people listen to each other differently depending on their standing in relation to an issue ('Are they likely to know anything about it?'), and whether it seems to 'make sense', to 'ring true'. These criteria do not describe a dialogical state to be reached. Rather they represent the evaluative criteria that inhere within the process of communication itself. Speakers and listeners, he suggests, routinely use such critieria to judge their exchanges and to learn from them. Therefore, they can be used to critique public dialogues, as a way of identifying and challenging the one-sided conversation and the power embodied in "thought" systems. They provide probing tools in our struggles to 'make sense together whilst living differently', as Forester puts it (1989). They encourage a practice of respectful 'speaking and listening', to encourage processes of 'mutual learning' through the dialogical process. In this way, political communities can build consensus which is particular to specific times and places, and has meaning in particular contexts, yet may also stretch out, through the knowledge and understandings built up in the various relational webs available to them, to a wider world whose concerns may be known of, though direct conversation cannot be achieved.

Through such processes of situated learning, political communities in one place can draw on the many relational channels which connect them to other places, as well as their knowledge about the different cultural communities which co-exist in a locality, to build an understanding of their situation, the possibilities available to them, and the actions which could help improve the circumstances of those with a 'stake' in a place. This effort generates sytems of rules and flows of resources, and creates cultural resources, which then 'structure' our daily lives. In such reflective conversations, members of political communities can attempt the task of intercultural communication. A communicative ethics would require that members are prepared to 'listen' for difference, not merely in interests, but in values and cultural references. Through such efforts, we may create the possibility for multi-cultural consensus-building, ways of thinking and strategies for action within which to make sense of our diversity while according it respect.

Through reflective dialogue, Habermas argues, through *monitoring* the mechanisms we create to manage ourselves, we can arrive at the richest conceptions of both what is 'true' and what is 'right' that we can collectively imagine and agree upon, using all our resources of reasoning and all our cultural awarenesses.

Strategy-making exercises, in this perspective, are thus deliberate efforts in collaborative social mobilisation, the objective of which is to transform policy discourse, and maybe also policy processes, rules and resource flows. It involves interactive work through communicative practices through which participants learn from each other not merely about facts, interests and preferences, but about what participants care about and why. This involves recognition not merely of the information communicated, but reflection on the way people say things, the images they use, the communicative routines they adopt, emotional responses as well as rational-technical ones, moral arguments as well as empirical ones. Communicative practices are social routines or 'rituals' (Forester, 1996) which require a minimum degree of interest and of trust between the parties to proceed. Those from different social networks and cultural worlds bring different traditions and experiences of such routines.

Strategy-making may occur in many different institutional settings, which affect who gets access to the activity and its routines. These reflect the power relations of the strategy-making instance. 'Successful' strategy-making efforts produce strategies and policies which convince stakeholders of the value of a new direction and its implications, through the creation of a new discourse or story about a set of issues. Such discourses innovate by re-framing issues and enabling new types of action to be thought about. Thereby, they have the potential to change the structuring of social relations in some respect – that is, they carry power.

Those strategy-making activities which aim to be inclusionary can be distinguished not merely by the deliberate attempt to search out the universe of those affected by, or with a stake in, a policy, and to give voice to, and to listen to and learn from them all during the strategy invention process. They may be identified by the recognition of the diversity of ways of knowing, forms of reasoning and routines of communicating and organising. Where the range of those thereby involved is great and the diversity of their relational cultures wide, this will involve communicative practices which can both 'listen for difference' while 'making sense together' (Forester, 1989). It will involve reflecting on the 'worldviews' which lie behind what is asserted in the various settings through which a policymaking exercise flows.

Questions for the institutional design of strategy-making activity

Strategy-making activity which 'makes a difference' and transforms what happens thus involves social processes through which new shared convictions are generated. The challenge of the design of specific strategic-making efforts, that is, of the soft infrastructure of specific instances, is to set in motion processes through which to review and reflect upon existing ideas and organising routines, and to generate new ones which are widely owned among the relevant stakeholders. To be effective in achieving such social ownership, new ideas and organising routines need to grow out of the specific concerns of stakeholders. They must be capable of becoming embedded in their local knowledges. They must develop with the grain of local contingencies. Yet to carry transformative power, they must have the capacity to challenge existing conceptions and re-frame ways of thinking, ways of valuing and ways of doing things. In addition, the new ideas must be able to flow around through the social networks of the stakeholders, altering cultural conceptions. Strategy-making is thus a delicate balancing act, between what is and what could be. If too little is changed, the effort merely reproduces the status quo. If the activity goes too far, it may reach beyond social and political acceptability to the stakeholders, and float away into irrelevance. If the delicate balance is achieved, however, the strategy-making effort can carry substantial and enduring power. Because of this powerful potential, strategy-making efforts in the public arena need to be linked to an ethics which keep under review the way that power is exercised and encompass an inclusionary moral sense.

The invention of such processes cannot be captured in an *a priori* process model, such as propounded in the rational planning process tradition. Any model is the product of local invention. But such invention can be aided through questions which help to review the existing 'soft infrastructure' of organising ideas and routines, a kind of institutional audit of 'how we do things here just now', and to open up inquiries which can lead to re-thinking what could happen.

Four such questions are explored below: stakeholders and arenas; routines of organizing and styles of discussion; making policy discourses; maintaining consensus (Healey, 1996a).

Getting started: Initiators, stakeholders and arenas

A strategy-making exercise always starts 'from somewhere' among some people and in a specific arena. Initiators have a critical responsibility for the first stages of opening up the strategy-making process. A key task is to explore who has a 'stake' in an issue, and where discussion might take place. The arenas of political, administrative and legal systems create formal 'places' through which policy principles have to pass to achieve administrative or legal legitimacy. They allocate rights to be represented and heard in these arenas. For those initiating institutional design processes for collaborative strategy-making activity, these formal arenas are attractive because they reduce the ethical dilemmas they face. Formal political structures embody principles of ethical conduct. But it may well be that these arenas are currently dominated by particular ways of thinking and ways of organising which have inhibited stakeholder voices and constrained the development of new ideas. They may be, at least initially, part of the problem, rather than the starting point for the solution. Much of the literature on strategy-making and on institutional innovation argues that most effective transformations start off in informal contexts (Innes *et al.*, 1994; Ostrom, 1990). The impetus for spatial strategy formation arises from particular institutional situations. Some stakeholders become concerned about how things are going on, and set about mobilising a social and political impetus to do something about it. Or an outside agency requires the production of a strategy as part of bids for funding. To move beyond a feeling that 'something needs to be done' to getting support for an organizational effort, there needs to be a 'moment of opportunity', a 'crack' in the power relations, a situation of contradiction and conflict, which encourages people to recognize that they need to reflect on what they are doing, that they need to work with different people, that they need to evolve different processes. For example, local councillors in North West England in the early 1990s realized the value of collaborating with each other and the business community in the context of European Union regional development funding (see the example in Chapter 3).

One of the critical resources at this stage is the capacity to 'read the cracks', to see the opportunities for 'doing things differently', and to be able to widen a crack into a real potential for change. Bryson and Crosby (1992) assign a key role to 'leaders' in recognizing moments of opportunity and mobilising networks around the idea of an effort in strategy-making. But such activators need not necessarily be in formal leadership positions. Innes *et al.* (1994) note that initiators came from different institutional positions. They may arise in all kinds of institutional settings and relationships, and are merely those with the capacity to see and articulate to others a strategic possibility. Behind this skill lies the capacity for an acute sense of the relation between the structural dynamics of local economic, social and political relations and how these are manifest in what particular people in a place are bothered about. Accounts of planners talking about their work provide rich evidence of this capacity at work (for example in Krumholz and Forester, 1992; Crawley, 1991; Mier, 1995; Kitchen, 1991).

The next step is the decision on the arenas within which the next round of discussion can take place. The initiators have to mobilise interest and engagement. This means thinking about who to get involved, where to meet and how to conduct discussion. These choices are critical, both in terms of the likely future support for, and ownership of, whatever emerges, and for whether the resultant mobilisation effort is of a corporatist or inclusionary nature.

A strategy-making exercise which ends up in a corporatist form may merely include a few self-selected key players, with perhaps others who actively push their way in through a clever 'politics of voice'. The informal regional alliance-building among business and government taking place in Britain in the 1990s has such characteristics (Tickell and Dicken, 1993; Davoudi, Healey and Hull, 1996). This is a sign of a corporatist process in the making. The inclusionary alternative seeks to identify who could have a 'stake' in the exercise. There is no objective way of identifying the 'universe' of stakeholders, still less of getting access to them. The politics of voice and reliance on existing organised groupings leaves out those who are silent in public arenas, and those who may have a stake but do not really realise it. Another possibility is a kind of permanent snowballing technique, through which those who come into contact with the strategy-making exercise are reminded to keep looking for others. A third is the stakeholder mapping discussed earlier in this chapter. This technique seeks to identify the kind of stake people may have in a strategy-making exercise, from being residents of neighbourhoods to the interests of global investors, or national heritage considerations, or the nesting needs of migrating birds. It generates a conception of a *stakeholder community*, with both territorial and functional reasons for membership. Such stakeholder analysis needs to be conducted in an explicit, dynamic and revisable way, as stakeholders may change over time in their concerns. Given the range of potential stakeholders, it is always possible that those involved in the strategy-making exercise will become aware of new stakeholders as they go along. Inclusionary strategy-making exercises need to be open to admit 'new members' as work proceeds, and even after agreement about strategy has been reached.

The ethical challenge at this stage is that a start on a democratic discussion gets made before the members of the relevant stakeholder community have had a chance to work out what kind of arenas they would prefer or who the stakeholders are. This situation is a common experience, for instance, in the City Challenge and Single Regeneration Budget bidding processes in British urban policy (Oatley, 1995). As a result, some people 'carry responsibility' for 'initial moves'. Two ideas may help to distinguish those 'first moves' which have inclusionary democratic potential and those which may entrench the dominance of a few powerful people. The first refers to an 'inclusionary ethic'. This emphasizes a moral duty to ask, as arenas are being set up, who are members of the stakeholder community? how are they to get access to the arena in such a way that their 'points of view' can be appreciated as well as their voices heard? and how can they have a stake in the process throughout.

The second idea recognizes that the 'where' of strategic discussion may shift about, and use different arenas at different times. Not only may it be helpful to encourage discussion in several 'institutional places' at the early stages of a strategic planning exercise (such as Council Chambers, business clubs, community halls, schools, radio phone-ins). The arenas may change in nature as discussion proceeds. As Bryson and Crosby (1992) stress, initially discussion needs to be open and fluid, focused on the construction of meaning. Then, as new discourses are invented and consolidated, it may be necessary to move to more formal arenas, within which legitimacy is given to the principles which have been developed and agreed. This recognizes that, over time, discussion moves from discursive 'opening out' to consolidation around particular ideas and consequential actions and values – from Bryson and Crosby's forums to arenas. But the danger is that such discursive closure loses touch with the rich manifestation of concerns raised earlier on. The important quality of an inclusionary approach is that the style and ethics of the discussion *setting* enable awareness of the stakeholder range to be sustained throughout the process and also maintain opportunity for the assertion of all stakeholder claims for attention

Routines and styles of discussion

Once at least some initial decisions have been made about the settings for strategy-making, attention is needed to what gets discussed and how. An inclusionary effort in rethinking spatial strategy is much more than merely identifying 'what is going on' and 'what the issues are'. It involves 'opening out' issues, to explore what they mean to different people, and whether they are really about what they seem to be or something else. It requires a sort of mental 'unhooking' from previous assumptions and practices, to try to see issues in new ways, even if only to recognize that some of our old ways are quite useful in new worlds. It also means recognizing the often deep divisions among stakeholders, and the cultural, economic and political bases for these. This is a critical and delicate operation. It can easily be undertaken in ways which reinforce stereotypes, which narrow agendas and which alienate many interested parties. But undertaken with inclusionary commitment, it can have enormous power in helping people learn about each others' concerns, about problems and possibilities, in ways which reach out across our cultural differences. While there is now a considerable body of practical advice on how to engage in such discourse within the context of small groups, the challenge of collaborative discussion about urban region futures is more complex. Not only are the cultural differences among members of the relevant political communities likely to be large, with the consequence that the potential for misunderstanding is substantial. The issues themselves often involve making difficult chains of connection between what bothers people, what causes this, and what could be done about it.

Three aspects of this dimension are of particular interest. The first concerns its *style*. The possibility of inclusionary argumentation is barely satisfied merely by ensuring everyone has 'voice' or a 'route to voice'. 'Voices' may be ignored or misheard. People may often find it difficult to speak in alien surroundings (Allen, 1992; Hillier, 1993; Davoudi and Healey, 1995; Healey and Hillier, 1995; Wood *et al.*, 1995; Macnaghten *et al.*, 1995). Different cultural communities have different, and often 'taken-for-granted', routines and styles for collaborative activities. These may well reflect how people prepare themselves, how rooms are arranged, how communicative routines are set up (who speaks when and how), how discussion is concluded, remembered and called up at a later time. John Forester refers to these as the *rituals* of policy discussion. The problem for strategic spatial planning exercises is that different participants may have different expectations of such routines, learned from local politics, from company management, from the practices of labour unions, from household collaboration, or from community organization initiatives. An inclusionary approach will therefore mean actively discussing and choosing a style of discussion, and recognizing that not everyone will be comfortable in it to begin with. The growth of 'facilitators' in environmental mediation and community development, as in the management field, is an illustration of the importance of this work (Susskind and Cruikshank, 1987).

The second aspect concerns its *language*. Participants may try hard to give each other respect and to follow routines which give space for everyone. But they may still 'talk past' each other through using different ways of expressing things. These differences are not merely a matter of metaphors and imagery. Such images may have a particular meaning for those in one cultural frame of reference but be quite strange to another. Ironical and ambiguous expression from a speaker may be richly appreciated by some and completely missed by others. Such differences apply also to the way statements are made. Some people are familiar with the language of consequences, grounded in economic reasoning or scientific evidence. Others are more accustomed to the language of belief or the political assertion of rights. Others again may be more comfortable with the expression of fears and dangers (Healey and Hillier, 1995). The challenge for strategic argumentation is to accept them all, but to recognize that translation between them is a complex, delicate and powerful task (Latour, 1987). Even then, there are limits to intercultural communication (Geertz, 1983).

The third aspect concerns *representation,* how the members of the stakeholder community are 'called up' as discussion proceeds. Depending on how decisions about discussion arenas have been made, strategic discussion may take place in meeting rooms, in a mixture of meeting rooms and working groups, through videoconferencing or whatever ways participants can think of for spreading involvement. But participants have to do much more than just 'representing the stakeholders'. However energetically the opportunity to 'give voice' is pursued in a community, some will be more actively involved than others, and a few will play key roles in shaping discussion, sorting out arguments and developing a strategic discourse. This does not mean that the others are inevitably marginalized. Any analysis of a conversation will typically reveal that more people are present than are actually speaking. It may also show that some people are present but not able to find expression. Studies in textual deconstruction illustrate how we construct, through our talk and our non-verbal language, definitions of ourselves and others, of me, you; of we/us, you and them (for example, Allen, 1992; Silverman, 1993; Liggett and Perry (eds), 1995). Further, we 'call upon' other people in conversation, to legitimate a view, or to ground a point. (Planning staff do this routinely, as they discuss regulatory requirements with those seeking development permits (Healey, 1992b).) If these processes of defining who 'we' are, and of 'calling up' non-present others are going on routinely in everyday conversation, can they not be used in discussions about matters of strategic spatial concern? This suggests that a key quality of inclusionary strategic argumentation is the capacity to keep under explicit review the various ways the members of a political community describe both themselves, and the 'others' of significance to them, as they engage in discussion, combined with the ability to maintain active respect and appreciation for those members who for one reason or another are 'not present'. In any strategic discussion on urban region futures, it will always be the case that 'those present' will outnumber those 'not present'. The inclusionary challenge is to prevent those 'not present' from being 'absent' from the discussion.

Making policy discourses

If the arenas for strategic spatial planning take the inclusionary forms proposed here, pursued through the open style suggested, the result can be that a huge array of issues are brought up for attention. A visual and verbal record of what goes on in such interactions would show an 'argumentative jumble' of statements about facts, about values, about claims for attention, about fears, about consequences and apocalyptic disasters (Throgmorton, 1992; Grant, 1994; Healey and Hillier, 1995). But these are more than just statements. They indicate how speakers feel about matters, who they most relate to and who they are trying to get to listen. As John Forester (1996) argues, how a point is made or a story is told tells people about how the speaker conceives of things, about the power relations they perceive around them, about the languages they use. As many people recognise in the ordinary flow of communicative relations with others, these multiple dimensions of the communicative act have a crucial importance in building up trust and understanding, and 'feeling towards' ways of thinking in the work of collaborative 'making' (Shotter, 1993).

In conventional strategic planning exercises, such material is translated into and filtered through the technical language used by planning analysts and the administrators of planning systems. This will almost immediately reduce a person's speech into a 'point', to join other 'points' in a structured analytical framework through which the planners seek to 'make sense' of what is going on. The argumentative jumble is translated into the familiar 'analysis' work of spatial planning. As far as most stakeholders are concerned, it then becomes an impenetrable 'black box' of 'taken-for-granted' knowledge (Latour, 1987).

In a process of inclusionary argumentation, such 'analytical work' needs to be much richer and more widely shared. Participants need to be encouraged to probe the meaning of the different points raised and to test out in discussion their implications for the concerns of other people. As discussion 'opens out' and 'works through' the issues raised, participants learn about what the issues are and about each other's ways of thinking and acting. 'Analysis' is thus not an abstract technical process but an active social enterprise in mutual sorting through the arguments and learning about possibilities. This 'sorting out' process is not just about exploring and working out what are problems and why, and how conditions may be changed. It is more than developing an analysis of urban and regional change. It involves working out what people value in moral and aesthetic terms as well as in a material sense, and how values are affected. It requires attention to rights, to the legitimacy of the multiplicity of claims for policy attention.

In many strategic planning exercises, wide-ranging consultation takes place in defined stages, before or after strategies have been articulated. This is particularly so where strategic planning has been formalised into procedures for preparing particular kinds of plans, such as the British structure and local plans, or the French *schèmas directeurs*. Politicians or experts 'invent' the strategic ideas. In the past, this was acknowledged in referring, for example, to Abercrombie's plan for London. Later, it was said that plans were produced 'by planners for planners'. Formal consultation procedures would be used to test out the robustness of the policies. Many still argue that it is impossible to go into consultation processes without something to 'consult on'.

This raises a challenge for the collaborative, discursive processes described here. How can a strategy 'emerge' from such open processes? It requires a capacity to reach some agreement across differences as to what the issues are, the purposes of action and the way the consequences, the costs and benefits of action, should be assessed. But it also represents a feat of 'collective imagining' of possible courses of action and what these could achieve. Making a strategy according to these new ideas involves a collaborative effort in selecting from among possibilities, and 'sharpening up' the selected strategies so that they 'make sense', both operationally in relation to resource allocation and regulatory power, and in terms of general understanding. The first is necessary to meet criteria of effectiveness, the second of legitimacy.

One way of thinking of this task of inclusionary spatial strategy-making is as a collaborative task in creating a new *policy discourse.* Here the term discourse is understood sociologically rather than linguistically (Silverman, 1993; see also Hajer, 1995), as a system of meaning embodied in a strategy for action and expressed in concepts, metaphors and a storyline. The system of meaning begins its evolution as the 'argumentative jumble' is scrutinised. As ideas about possible action come forward, new ways of thinking about the issues raised in argumentation are likely to emerge. The processes of 'sorting through' ideas and 'discourse creation' are thus interactive. This might suggest that they can proceed in parallel, and in practice this often happens. However, a strategy-making process which aims to 'open out' discussion to enable new ways of looking at issues to emerge needs to avoid consolidation of the options for action too early in the process, before people know each other and the issues. Otherwise, debate can quickly regress to adversarial argument about entrenched positions. Further, policy discourses can become very powerful, imposing organizing concepts and a vocabulary of images and terms through which issues are discussed.

The way policy discourses develop is well-described in recent studies of environmental issues. In a valuable review of approaches to the analysis of policy discourses, Hajer (1995) highlights the importance of the new understandings, or concepts, which provide the *discursive key* which 'turns' the discussion from one conception to another. He argues that this phenomenon can be put to normative use in the process of strategy development, shifting the 'storyline' of policy debate from one account to another. It performs the critical transformative work which allows an issue to be re-framed. Hajer analyses how particular ways of understanding the phenomenon of acid rain were the key which changed British national policy on air quality regulation. The model of a European City in Lyons (see Chapter 3), or on Atlantic City in Lisbon (see Vasconcelos and Reis, 1996) provided similar examples from spatial planning policy. Once the transformation has been achieved, these new metaphors and storylines carry the strategic idea, often through many reinterpretations, into the social worlds of the stakeholders who have been influenced by it.

Strategically perceptive planners and politicians may be very conscious of their role in creating new discourses. The defining quality of an inclusionary strategic discourse is that, within its storyline, there are parts for most people, and there is acknowledgement, where relevant, that some suffer more and some benefit more as the story proceeds. Any story has its regrets and little tragedies, the things that cannot be done, the people who were neglected. In the rational planning mode, these were ignored in the emphasis to build a coherent, scientifically-justified, preference-maximising strategy. An inclusionary approach demands explicit attention to them (Forester, 1993), to what cannot be achieved, what the costs of this may be and for whom, as well as what can be done. For an inclusionary approach to strategic spatial planning, the work of discourse creation is therefore both the most important and the most dangerous part of the process. Once a policy discourse has gained attention, it carries forward with it a distinctive storyline, about what is and should be, about what are seen as good or bad arguments and about appropriate modes of argument and claims for policy attention. It gives meaning and significance to issues, problems and actions, and focuses the setting of priorities for action. Once momentum has been achieved, policy discourses spread out and may come to influence a wide sphere of social action, sometimes achieving 'hegemonic' status. It is this persuasive power of discourse embedded in existing practices, and pursued by the powerful, which an inclusionary discursive form of strategic argumentation seeks to challenge, yet at the same time to acknowledge and use.

The formation of policy discourses carries dangers, therefore, because a policy discourse is a selective simplification of the issues in discussion and because it gains momentum by exaggeration. A strong discourse provides legitimate reasons for ignoring some evidence, some values and some claims for policy attention. A cautious policy-making exercise might seek to avoid the production of such organising conceptions. But this would be to reduce its power to influence events. The challenge for an inclusionary approach to strategic spatial planning is to experiment with, and test out, strategic ideas in initially tentative ways, to 'open out' possibilities for both evaluation and invention of better alternatives, before allowing a 'preferred' discourse to emerge, and 'crowd out' the alternative. As Bryson and Crosby (1992) note, the timing of 'problem definition' in a policy-making process is a difficult issue. This suggests that a discursive process needs to be designed which explicitly explores different 'storylines' about possible actions and offers up different 'discursive keys' for critical attention, maintaining a critical attitude until there is broad support for a new strategic discourse. Having thus generated a knowledgeable consensus around a particular storyline, the task of consolidating the discourse and developing its implications can then proceed. The discourse community can be said by this time to have collaboratively chosen a strategy, over which they are then likely to have some sense of 'ownership'. A new 'cultural community' has been formed around the strategy.

Maintaining the consensus

If the culture-building process of strategy-making has been rich enough and inclusive enough, the strategy should have become widely shared and owned by the participants and the stakeholders to whom they are linked. It will express a robust consensus. But such agreement will always disadvantage some, and may well be put under pressure as circumstances change, new stakeholders appear, and new fractures appear among them. It is here that the hard infrastructure of institutional design plays such an important part, providing formalised rules and resources which may foster maintenance of agreements, or undermine them (see Chapter 9). As part of the soft infrastructure, however, stakeholder communities which engage in strategy-making exercises need to consider how agreement will be formalised and maintained, and how the strategic ideas and processes will be monitored and maintained over time.

To formalise an agreement, some process is needed to record the agreement reached, and some means of appeal is then required if stakeholders feel they have been unfairly treated or if some feel that others are breaking the agreement (Ostrom, 1990). Existing political or legal institutions may well provide appropriate processes. As Bryson and Crosby (1992) argue, some form of court provides the locus for such arbitration. Such courts, in judicial or semi-judical form, have an important role in most spatial planning systems. But they are more than merely a legal backstop to be used when the collaborative process reaches limits. An inclusionary form of argumentation needs to agree at the start how such disagreements will be addressed and keep the agreed processes under critical review throughout. It also needs to pay attention to the terms in which challenges to processes and decisions are to be discussed. Formal courts tend to have their own styles and processes, which often appear very alien to lay people. It may be that the preoccupation of established legal systems such as the British with 'fairness' and 'reasonableness' is a valuable resource for arbitrating on local environmental disputes. But if not, some alternative principles need to be adopted as a matter of policy. Effective consensus-building thus builds on clear understanding, early on in the process, of rights to challenge the consensus, and the terms on which such challenges can be addressed.

The 'right to challenge' which should underpin the consensus-building effort can become a 'duty to challenge' as the selected strategy begins to have effects. It can become a formalised way of monitoring the strategy's effective implementation and continued relevance. The importance of this duty arises from the power of strategic discourse once it has gained acceptance, and from the potential to re-interpret a strategy selectively as it is called upon in subsequent situations. Strategies affect the dynamics of social relations through contributing to the way people 'frame' how they think about how to act, and through generating constraints or barriers to action in one form or another. To have effects, a spatial strategy needs to frame the work of those involved in regulating spatial change. It also needs to influence the way public action in investment and regulation is justified. It should provide a store of reasoning and arguments to draw upon when exploring and justifying what has been done. But this 'framing' role involves continual reinterpretation of the meaning of the strategy and selective emphasis on its different elements. A rich strategic debate which includes relevant stakeholders may have the benefit that, with greater general understanding of what a strategy means and the reasons for it, the interpretative distortion will be minimised, as Habermas argues (see Chapter 7). A powerful discourse, energetically 'diffused', has the capacity to change what people think and what they do, and to maintain these changes. But inevitably over time there will be some interpretative drift. Further, conditions may change and new bases of power may evolve to confront and undermine the strategy. A spatial strategy should, after all, aim to enable those co-existing in shared spaces to evolve their activities flexibly, not to control and direct what they do.

For all these reasons, a strategic policy discourse needs to be subjected to continual reflexive critique. In rationalist methodology, this was understood as 'monitoring'. However, such monitoring has tended to focus on changes in the context of urban regions and their implications for strategy, and on whether specified policy objectives were being achieved (Reade, 1987). Such techniques derive from the criteria-driven approach outlined in Chapter 7, not that of inclusionary consensus-building. A reflexive critique of a strategic policy discourse needs to attend to these matters but also to keep an eye on whether a strategy still 'makes sense', whether its storyline still rings true, whether it still provides parts for most members of a political community, whether a new storyline has emerged over time, and whether this is as inclusionary as the old. One way to do this is to require some form of regular review. But this is likely to leave the work of review in the hands of particular stakeholders who may have a strong interest in a particular interpretation of the strategy. It would work better if regular review were combined with formal specifications of duties to review, and with rights to challenge the performance of these duties. This takes the institutional design into questions of the hard infrastructure of rules about rights to be discussed in Chapter 9.

From radical idealism to 'common sense'

The above indicates the approach to spatial strategy-making efforts which arises from an institutionalist understanding of the social dynamics of urban region change and governance and a communicative ethics of interactive consensus-building. Through such processes, social, intellectual and political capital may be developed among the stakeholders in a particular place which generates an institutional capacity to 'add value' to the activities of many networks, whether in terms of the management of daily life, of business activity, of biospheric sustainability or cultural co-existence. It does this by providing better solutions to problems of collective concern among many stakeholders, and by creating trust and understanding through which knowledge can flow, and act as a resource for subsequent collaboration.

As an approach, in some respects it re-visits aspects of the well-known rational planning process. It involves review of issues (survey), sorting through findings (analysis), exploring impacts in relation to values (evaluation), inventing and developing new ideas (choice of strategy), and continuous review (monitoring). But these activities are approached in a very different way. They are undertaken interactively, often in parallel rather than sequentially. They deal explicitly in the everyday language of practical life, and recognise the multiple communicative tasks accomplished in social interatcion. Technical language is treated as but one among many languages. As a result, the approach extends the reasoning process beyond instrumental rationality, to allow debate on moral and emotive dimensions. Technical analysis is replaced by a 'feeling towards' what meanings could be (Shotter, 1993). The epistemology of positivism and deductive/inductive logic of the natural sciences and of economics is put in context and combined with other ways of knowing and valuing through a hermeneutic attitude, which aims to explore how people's interests and claims for policy attention are both actively constituted and framed by socio-cultural systems of meaning and acting. Such strategy-making activities involve active discursive work by the parties involved.

As an approach to spatial strategy-making, it does not set out to provide a set of procedures for strategy-making activities to follow. Its objective is more to offer a set of questions to help political communities invent their own processes. Realising it in any particular circumstances would involve shaping it pragmatically to the social relations and political possibilities of particular situations. The result will inevitably be a locally-specific process. Some situations will be more favourable to the evolution of such an approach than others, reflecting the dynamics of particular cultures and histories, and the way political systems are evolving (see Chapter 7). But if its invention is informed by an inclusionary communicative ethic, its form should allow both voice and influence to be more evenly distributed among those with a stake in issues than is common in most strategic planning exercises these days.

Many will see this approach as too radical and too idealistic for our present times. Fearful of environmental risks and of economic decline, we may turn to old hierarchical and technical habits, hoping these will deliver safety and security at least, if not democracy and an open society. In some countries, notably Britain with its recent sustained experiment in neo-liberal public policy, it seems difficult to imagine building a collaborative, open society, given its traditions of class power, adversarial politics, hierarchical centralised government and individualist conceptions of interests. But already there are experiments in alternatives which show the possibilities (see Bell, 1996). Elsewhere, in Northern Europe, for example, collaborative policy-making and an inclusionary ethic is more deeply embedded in local cultures.

This raises the question of the structural conditions which foster collaborative consensus-building and which enable the invention of locally-contingent processes of spatial strategy-making which have the capacity to build up social, intellectual and political capital among the full range of urban region stakeholders. This moves the discussion into the hard infrastructure of institutional design, and of structures of rules and resource flows.

9 Systemic Institutional Design for Collaborative Planning

Systemic framing and framing the instance

The previous chapter has described an approach to the design of instances of collaborative inclusionary argumentation through which new understandings and new ways of framing policy and action could be developed. These have the potential to generate storylines and key actions which could help those involved sort out their dilemmas as regards co-existence in shared spaces. The approach provides a way of realising a policy-driven approach to governance, grounded in the resources of formal knowledge and empathetic understanding available to those with a stake in issues, within which the culturally-bound and value-laden dimensions of people's concerns about their local environments can be brought into discussion. It generates policy ideas, systems of meaning and social relations which provide a store of 'capital' to be drawn on in the future. It helps to build the institutional capacity of places to enable a proactive, developmental response to the conditions and relations of an urban region. The ideas and understandings generated help to frame the way people think about their subsequent actions. Through such framing work, subsequent actions are shaped in new ways. This leads to co-ordination without the need for formal co-ordination procedures. Strategies thus 'become active' through this shaping effect, as culturally-shared efforts in making futures. Thus the relation between policy and action is a framing, enabling one, rather than a linear one. Framing ideas replace the blueprints of the 'command and control' models of planning systems, and the linear ends-means policy sequences of the rational process model (see Chapter 1), as the driving force of a broadly-based co-ordinated transformation of knowledge and values into actions.

In these processes of collaborative strategy-making, participants engage in collective efforts in institutional design. Through it, they change themselves and their contexts. They build new systems of meaning, new cultures, new organising routines and styles and new social networks. These reflect and add to the loose relational networks of contemporary economic and social life. Such processes are powerful co-ordinative tools. Co-ordination happens through shared meanings, rather than the 'partisan mutual adjustment' of autonomous, self-centred, rationally calculating individuals. Collaborative strategy-making processes build up institutional designs from the 'grass-roots' of the real concerns of specific stakeholders as these interact with each other in specific situations in place and time. This produces an institutional infrastructure which is as near as possible to the lifeworlds of the stakeholders.

It could be argued that there is no need of further formal institutional arrangements to foster such processes. Institutions should be designed by those who will use them, according to their purposes. This argument appeals to those seeking to escape from too much governance, whether neo-liberal free-marketeers or communitarian anarchists (see Chapter 7). This position is attractive too to those arguing for a communicative, participatory democracy. For example, John Dryzek argues, in the development of his ideas for *discursive democracy,* that:

> overly precise specification of model institutions involves [for the critical theorists drawing on communicative discursive practices] skating on thin ice. Far better, perhaps, to leave any such specification to the individuals involved. (Dryzek, 1990, p. 41)

Yet there is much evidence that relying on the soft infrastructure of individual instances of framing processes is not enough. Elinor Ostrom, in her detailed account of the self-management of *common pool resources,* emphasises that how well these grass-roots arrangements work depends on external institutional factors as well as a range of internal ones (Ostrom, 1990). John Friedmann, in his discussion of the proliferation of intermediate, third sector agencies in the third world, stresses that state systems of some kind are needed to maximise the synergy of these agencies and to avoid competitive destruction (Friedmann, 1992). Judith Innes and colleagues argue in their report on consensus-building practices in California that informal processes of discursive collaboration have to attend to the political, administrative and legal processes which give legitimacy to the arenas of discussion and their conclusions (Innes *et al.*, 1994).

The task of institutional design thus has two interacting levels. The first, discussed in Chapter 8, concerns the work that stakeholder communities undertake as they build social, intellectual and political capital in the course of developing strategies to address their collective concerns in the management of local environmental change. The second concerns the design of the political, administrative and legal systems which structure the context of local instances. This is the terrain of *systemic institutional design*. The difference is captured in the metaphor of the soft infrastructure of social collaboration and invention and the hard infrastructure of social structuring. If the work of collaborative strategy-making involves the design of a journey, the formal arrangements of governance provide a backcloth of opportunities and constraints, the routes, the modes of travel, the rules of access to them, the resources for navigation. As Giddens (1984) and Latour (1987) insist, systemic institutional designs are just as much the products of social invention as are the particular instances of strategy-making work. But their design raises challenging issues. The rule structures, resource allocation procedures and the policy ideas embedded within systemic institutional designs 'carry power' to the individual instances, which may distort as much as support what stakeholders seek to do. For example, in the spatial planning field, the lack of constitutional rights for third parties in British land use planning tips the balance of power towards property interests, unless there is a vigorous political mobilisation to prevent this (Healey *et al.*, 1988). In continental Europe, the way land use principles get expressed in zoning rules means that new strategies become technically illegal until translated into formal zoning ordinances (Davies *et al.*, 1989).

The challenge is made even more difficult if the objective is to facilitate and foster locally-based processes of collaborative strategy-making which are both inclusionary as regards stakeholders, and forward-looking and transformative as regards their perspective. How may abstract systems be designed, or at least modified, so that they support stakeholders and their collaborative efforts, rather than forcing them into moulds where they feel oppressed and impeded? Specifically, what are the key parameters of system design in relation to the collective management of co-existence in shared spaces, which involves governance in proactive developmental work, in delivering services and in regulatory functions?

This chapter will argue that systemic institutional design is important because it carries substantial power to frame the specific instances of governance activity. These systemic designs are not autonomous, isolated from the wider relations of governance. They are enmeshed in networks of relations which contribute to their articulation and realisation (see Chapter 7). The task of institutional design at the level of appropriate institutional frameworks which could have the capacity to encourage collaborative, inclusionary consensus-building is therefore the design of appropriate systems or regimes. It involves the transformation and re-making of 'abstract systems' (see Chapter 2) which will perform useful shaping, structuring and framing work, rather than inhibiting the development of collaborative consensus-building.

The systemic institutional design of a particular policy field, such as the management of local environmental change, will always vary according to the particular phenomenon in question and social values about it. But beyond these specific substantive considerations, the design of public policy in any field embodies important purposes related to the quality of the public realm and the nature of citizenship in a political community. In western democratic societies, a strong post-Enlightenment principle has been that the formal institutions of government, which concentrate vast amounts of power within their practices, should be accountable to the citizenry at large. So the struggle for change in the formal institutions of government, for example, for 'one man, one vote', and then 'one person, one vote' and 'equality in the eyes of the law', that is for equal rights as human beings, versus the power of abstract systems, has been basic to any conception of a democratic system in the modern period. As the nineteenth century evolved, it became clear that equal voting rights were not enough and ideas of social justice based on the fairness of distribution of state benefits and outcomes were developed. Without a reasonable share of economic and political resources – that is, power – many people have little chance to participate in what modern society has to offer. The social and environmental development of recent years, and especially the need to safeguard social diversity and biospheric relations have revived interest in issues of rights, duties and the meaning of citizenship (Young, 1990). Thus the challenge of the systemic design of governance institutions requires consideration of both how to address substantive issues effectively and how to foster the legitimacy of and trust in formal systems of governance, and thereby recover a positive view of citizenship and engagement in the public realm. As a conclusion to this book, this chapter reviews five key parameters of systemic institutional design which deserve consideration in the design of the hard infrastructure of spatial planning systems.

The parameters of systemic institutional design for participative, democratic governance

In discussing the institutional, communicative approach in this book, in the context of a normative commitment to pluralistic participation in collaborative planning processes, a range of attributes which the systemic design of governance processes should satisfy has been put forward.

1. It should recognise the range and variety of stakeholders concerned with changes to local and urban region environments, their social networks, the diversity of their cultural points of reference and their systems of meaning, and the complex power relations which may exist within and between them (Part II).
2. It should acknowledge that much of the work of governance occurs outside the formal agencies of government and should seek to spread power from government outside the agencies of the state but without creating new bastions of unequal power (Chapter 7).
3. It should open up opportunities for informal invention and for local initiatives. It should enable and facilitate, encouraging diversity in routines and styles of organising, rather than imposing single ordering principles on the dynamics

of social and economic life. It should cultivate a 'framing' relation rather than a linear connection between policy principles and the flow of action (Chapter 8).

4. It should foster the inclusion of all members of political communities while acknowledging their cultural diversity, and should recognise that this involves complex issues of power relations, ways of thinking and ways of organising (Chapters 2 and 8).
5. It should be continually and openly accountable, making available to relevant political communities the arguments, the information, the consideration of stakeholders' concerns, the images and metaphors which lie behind decisions, and should include requirements for critical review and challenge (Chapter 8).

These principles provide criteria with which to engage in a critique of established practices and contribute to the multifaceted processes of change through which policy systems (in non-revolutionary situations) are transformed from one form to another. However, they remain at a very general level. There is a vast literature in the social sciences, in policy science and political philosophy which provides ideas on the dimensions of public policy. This cannot be reviewed here, but some key points will be drawn out to support the selection of parameters with which this section concludes.

Dimensions of policy systems: contributions from public administration, political economy and political philosophy

The public policy literature has traditionally emphasised the organisation of government competencies and policy tools and measures. More recently, this conception has given way to the recognition that the wider society enters into governance processes in all kinds of ways. A particular focus of attention has been on the social relations through which governance activities are accomplished. This has led to a new emphasis on the development of policy networks, coalitions and alliances linking different parts of government institutions together and connecting government to the wider society (Rhodes, 1992) (see Chapter 8). It has tended to focus on agency, with less to say on the influence of structure.

The literature on urban and regional political economy has always emphasised the close structural nexus between the economy and the state, but has been concerned at a general level with how state forms reflect changes in economic forms. The urban politics literature explores this in relation to the finegrain of the development of spatial alliances and growth coalitions (Lauria and Whelan, 1995; Stone, 1989; Harding, 1995; Stoker, 1995). It tends to emphasise the soft infrastructure of institutional invention and realisation, and to locate this in the dynamics of economic and social structure. It has less to say about how systemic institutional characteristics, such as the nature of a political constitution, frame the practices described.

These limitations have recently been overcome in research on governance understood as the *social regulation* of civil society and the economy. There are two different strands to this discussion, that on regulatory regimes (see Francis, 1993) and that on modes of regulation (Boyer, 1991; Jessop, 1991). Both regime theory and regulation theory emphasise a key dimension of contemporary governance – the need to create institutional arrangements which enmesh formal government structures and processes within the wider relational webs of economic and social life. Francis's discussion of regulatory regimes argues for an analytical focus on governance competencies, on tools and mechanisms for regulation and the forms through which regulation takes place. Regulationists recognise the significance of 'cultural habits and norms' at the core of modes of regulation, but provides little specification of the dimensions of the design of regulatory relations which might support the more participatory forms of governance to which advocates of this approach tend to be normatively committed (Goodwin *et al.*, 1993; Tickell and Peck, 1992; Painter, 1995).

Another literature within political philosophy is committed to exploring theories of participatory democracy. This provides more ideas about the parameters of policy systems. Three contributions help in the search for the parameters of systemic institutional design. David Held (1987), whose concern is the transformation of the British polity, emphasises rights, duties and the meaning of equality in governance. He stresses the importance of a formal constitution, a bill of rights, the re-formulation of two chambers of government, the introduction of systems of proportional representation to replace single majority voting, open information, accountability of government, and the state's role in economic development and improving the quality of working conditions. He identifies five key areas for the development of his model, which give a further indication of significant dimensions of institutional design. These are: the specification of rights and obligations with respect to participation in governance; the boundaries of the public sphere and what should be left as the private concern of people in firms, households and voluntary associations; what 'equal conditions' could mean with respect to membership of a society and hence its governance; how to address diversity and difference; and what limits to liberty are tolerable for the sake of the overall policy, *the political community*. He has little to say about the processes through which governance activity could take place, apart from providing an institutional framework which enables 'experimentation'. His approach retains a strong role for *government*.

John Dryzek (1990) develops a model of participative *discursive democracy*. He would like to dispense with the state altogether and only reluctantly turns to the question of systemic institutional design. He seeks to promote free associations of people in discursively-established political communities, continually engaged in critical reflection on the purposes and consequences of their governance policies and practices. He emphasises the importance of the resources for democratic participation – of money, time and information; and the social construction of rules of procedure, and their 'redeemability' through discourse involving all parties. His approach is a refreshing alternative to Held's strong, if democratically participative, state. But there are clear problems with this ideal. Firstly, participative, inclusionary critical reflection could easily decay into the practices of a small coterie of people who see themselves as embodying the community's collective interest but without formal mechanisms to hold them to account. Secondly, without formalised 'reminders', political communities could neglect the interests which other political communities have in what they do. Thirdly, in the European context, with its traditions of strong states, formal measures for change are needed to confront the existing formal organisation and procedure of government. Thus, as argued earlier, it is neither good pragmatic politics nor likely to secure the conditions for the practices of Dryzek's *discursive design* to advocate such a limited role for the state.

A third discussion can be found in the work of the planning theorist, John Friedmann. He has for many years advocated a model of territorial development which emphasises local autonomy and interactive, non-rationalist modes of governance (Friedmann, 1973; Friedmann and Weaver, 1979; Friedmann, 1987, 1992). He has developed this model over the years into a political project of social mobilisation to transform governance and achieve social conditions which are both more just and more sustainable than current practices. A key element of this project is the 'recovery of political community' (Friedmann, 1987). Within this model, in contrast to Dryzek, he emphasises that people belong to many political communities, from the village to supranational groupings. States and formal institutions of governance arise to deal with common concerns and to defend political communities from outside powers, and notably the corporate economy.

The problem in western societies is that the structures of the state, intended to serve communities and to protect them from structural power, have become autonomous from political communities and thus a source of oppressive power, paralleling the continued expansion and domination of the corporate economy. In this view Friedman shares Held's interpretations. The political challenge, he argues, is for the agency of civil society to take back control from these bastions of modernist power. He emphasises that this will require new relations of governance, rooted in the practices of everyday life. The project of radical social mobilisation is, then, to re-make political life in the image, not of instrumentally rational bureaucracy, nor competitively rational markets, but mirroring the organisational forms and dialogic processes of 'everyday life'.

In discussing the political forms of such an enterprise, the significant dimensions of institutional design emerge as rights (of access, of challenge to the exercise of power), resources (of time, space, knowledge, skill, relational links, social capacities), policy principles or criteria (which encourage critical thinking, which stress quality), and distribution of competencies (among levels of territorial life, which cultivate self-reliance) (Friedmann, 1987; Friedmann, 1992).

Proposed parameters

The literature discussed above rarely focuses directly on questions of systemic institutional design or the specifics of formal systems for managing collective co-existence in shared spaces. There are several reasons for this. Firstly, many writers wish it could be possible for governance to be 'invented' as needed out of the logic of individual collaborative instances. They fear that designing structures could lead to yet more ways of unequally embedding the power of a few to dominate the many. Secondly, they recognise that situations are so different, in their cultures, histories and geographies, that general principles may be inappropriate. This suggests that institutional design which endures should be locally developed and invented. Thirdly, there is a considerable intellectual division between those who come to the question of forms of governance for participatory democracy from the analysis of urban and regional political economy and those who are interested in participative political practices. The former tend to stress the power of the state and the corporate economy. The latter are more concerned with the level of agency, and with the way power is conveyed in communicative processes.

Yet systemic institutional design matters. We cannot dispense with the formal organisations and legal processes of the state altogether. Resources need to be distributed in some way. Some collective tasks need to be undertaken, such as organising national defence, or bargaining with supranational levels of government. Some collective goods are better provided by a government machinery which can accumulate resources and deploy them over a long time scale. Some political communities need to be persuaded to take on board the values of groups their actions affect; for example, the social consequences of policies for the conservation of resources, which tend to make things harder for poorer people. But, if a participatory political culture is to develop, and reclaim the public realm, then the machinery of government must be surrounded by requirements which encourage inclusionary responsiveness to the diverse ways of living, ways of doing business and systems of meaning of the relevant political communities. In the European context, this means that government forms need to be encouraged to break out of their hierarchical and rationalist traditions. They also need to escape from the strait-jacket of the instrumental rationality of management and the rule-following procedural language of administration. One way to do this is by the mobilisation of ideas about democratic inclusionary practice. This will create a force for change. But that force then needs to be translated into structures, procedures and rules.

There are no models of how this could be done which will guarantee that the outcome will be particular political practices. These practices, as emphasised in Chapter 7, will be moulded by the meanings given them within the social relations within which they are realised. Any innovation, however much imposed from the outside, will become locally embedded. This means that there are no standard answers to the specification of the systemic institutional design of governance systems for inclusionary participatory democratic practice. Instead, as with the case of the soft infrastructure of the specific instance, what can be offered are 'probing, exploratory questions' for political communities to ask themselves. How and how far, for example, in our governance, do we safeguard the rights of access to influence governance available to all citizens? Is the way these rights are specified sensitive to the capacities and traditions of the different members of a political community? Do some citizens find it particularly hard to articulate their voice and get listened to by government?

Drawing on the previous discussion, the following parameters are suggested as the key questions which political communities should consider when mobilising to change the systemic design of government forms:

1. the nature and distribution of *rights* and *duties;*
2. the control and distribution of *resources;*
3. the specification of *criteria* for redeeming challenges;
4. the distribution of *competencies.*

These four headings are familiar to analysts of legal and political systems. But they need to be considered afresh to help political communities move towards different ways of managing their collective affairs. The core of the argument developed here is that it is not enough merely to use the systems of voting, political party organisation and government officials to bring the state back to serve everyday life, facilitate and contain the business world, and to re-create a public realm. Political parties and government officials quickly develop their own interests and cultures and need systems which force accountability. Further, as discussed in Chapter 7, governance in our contemporary networked world, takes place all around us and not just in formal government agencies. What is needed are ways of calling to account any person or any arenas which claim to be engaging in governance and are acting in some way on matters of collective concern, to answer for their action to all members of a political community. Systemic institutional design thus needs to focus on creating a *structure of challenges*. The next four sections discuss each of these parameters, and develop their implications for managing co-existence in shared spaces.

Rights and duties

The critical principle behind the focus on rights and duties is not to convert our societies into a legal morass of atomistic litigation, but to set up a formalised structure of challenges to which those who engage in governance activity expect to have to respond. Such a structure consists of both the formal specification of rights and duties, and the terms in which challenges based on these may be redeemed. The objective of systemic institutional design would be to create a structure which would encourage practices in which a full range of stakeholders were given respectful consideration, which would foster collaboration and the building of links through which social learning could take place, and which would encourage a public realm of multi-cultural argumentation. The purpose of attention to rights and duties is, then, to encourage people to interact, and to give people the power to demand to be involved.

Rights

The modern discussion of rights dates back to the Enlightenment period. *The Rights of Man* was an influential banner in the struggle for democratic governance focus (Hall and Gieben (ed.), 1992). The critical rights were the right to vote, to share in the control of governance, and the right to freedom from interference by government, as in the enjoyment of private property. In complex contemporary societies, it is clear that such rights are necessary but not sufficient guarantees that governance power is constrained by the interests and values of political communities, as discussed in Chapter 8. Arguments for a raft of further rights have developed, in relation to access to resources and opportunities, such as the right to work, to a minimum wage, to housing, to clean air and water, and to access to urban services. These focus on substantive issues. Another way to consider rights is in relation to processes, of participation in governance, to be consulted and informed. This leads to an interest in rights to 'voice' (to be heard), to 'influence' (to be taken account of), and to 'information' (to enable knowledgeable participation). All these rights give individuals a constitutional basis for holding those who exercise government to account. They could usefully be complemented with a formal right to challenge governance decisions, not just on the grounds of an unwarranted limitation of private interests but for failing to give attention to the diversity of interests and cultures with a stake in an issue, for failing to provide a knowledgeable interpretation of the issues or good reasons and arguments for decisions, or for failing to provide adequate information. Rights, then, help to 'fix a stake', and to strengthen the power of voice.

Land use planning systems in western societies have traditionally been preoccupied with challenges arising from the rights of property owners to the enjoyment of their possessions. This has led to limitations on regulatory power and the power of state preemption of private property (Cullingworth, 1993). In this classic liberal formulation, the state embodies the public interest and must justify the 'taking' away of the privileges of land and property owners. The politics of the exercise of these rights varies with the nature of land and property ownership in different countries. In Scandinavia, the typical property owner tends to be imagined as a small farmer, in a nation where everyone used to be a small farmer. Protecting their rights, and the rights to roam across all lands to hunt and gather fruits, spread power widely (Holt-Jensen, 1994). In contrast, in Britain, land and property ownership is much more concentrated (Massey and Catalano, 1978). Safeguarding property rights therefore protects the interests of big landowners and developers, both in urban and rural areas.

The problem for contemporary planning and environmental systems is that the state can neither know enough, nor stand above its own concerns sufficiently, to act as protagonist for the 'public interest' unaided, even within the discursive transformations sought in Chapter 8. The 'public interest' has to reflect the diversity of our interests and be established discursively. This has led to a complex pressure group politics in many countries, as stakeholder groups organise into political lobbies. In this context, it is easy for some stakeholders to be excluded if they fail to develop lobby organizations. In response to this, spatial planning systems incorporate *rights of challenge* to spatial plans and to regulatory decisions. What varies between systems is the distribution of these rights, their focus, and the ease with which they can be exercised. In British land use planning, rights of challenge are available only to those refused a permit, although all stakeholders have a right to challenge a plan. There is a strong case for strengthening the power of 'third parties' with an 'indirect' interest in a property development, to allow challenges to the granting of permits.

Collaborative inclusionary planning processes might therefore be most effectively promoted by:

- broadly-based rights of voice and influence. Concerned people should be able to call to account governance systems dealing with land use and environmental matters for failing to provide the opportunity to voice their views and to give attention to them;
- provisions to ensure that all parties who can demonstrate a *stake* in an issue have the opportunity to challenge decisions made in governance arenas on the grounds that their stake has not been adequately taken into account;
- a right to good quality information available to all parties, to assist all parties to consider what is at stake;
- a right available to all parties to call any governance agency, formal or informal, to account for failure with respect to the duties and responsibilities which apply to the exercise of governance responsibilities.

Such a broad spreading of rights of voice, of attention, of challenge, and of provision, will have effects not so much in the actual exercise of such rights, although a system would fail if their formal exercise were extraordinarily difficult and costly. In the British planning system, only around 4 per cent of regulatory decisions have been challenged in recent years. (This constituted 30 per cent of total development permit refusals: DoE, 1995.) But the prospect of challenge moulds the decision-making process (Healey *et al.*, 1988). Widely-spread rights among all citizens within a political community and all others with a stake in an issue should foster particular care to their potential concerns.

Duties

The relation between rights and duties, or responsibilities, is a reciprocal one. Citizens have legal rights and culturally-defined entitlement to respect. They also have obligations, to respect laws and to follow culturally-established moral principles as regards behaviour to others and to the natural world. The moral responsibilities of those who take on governance activities in democratic societies are, in principle, particularly heavy. The justification for their activities does not lie in a *divine right* to govern, or some right of conquest. In some way or other, those in governance are at the service of, act for and represent their political communities. In return for the 'right' to exercise governance roles, they have 'duties' – to attend to the concerns of their communities, to undertake programmes which their communities have agreed upon (or that they have agreed upon on behalf of their communities), and to report back to communities on what they have done.

Those in governance positions in democratic societies thus have duties to be democratic (to pay attention), to be effective (to deliver), and to be accountable (to keep within openly agreed principles and to report). Even though governments and governance activities are more noted for their failures in this regard than their successes, it is by these criteria that their performance will be judged. The complement of the specification of rights is the specification of duties, linked to rights to call those involved in governance to account in relation to a duty.

The duty to *pay attention* to the concerns of the members of political communities needs to be interpreted in our diverse and differentiated contemporary societies to include a duty to treat all members not merely with respect, but acknowledging their particular circumstances and values. Within the British planning system, this duty is expressed in consultation requirements and in the legal principle of fair treatment to all parties. This could be linked explicitly to the recognition of the range and diversity of stakeholders. As part of this respectful attitude, those in governance positions should be prepared to be open about their deliberations and promote the availability of good quality, authoritative information. To promote debate and understanding, such information should be provided in ways which recognise the discussions and disputes about how to define and measure things, and about the interpretation of analyses (Innes, 1990; Innes *et al.*, 1994). If the principles of environmental responsibility are taken into account, those in governance positions also have a further duty, beyond the members of their jurisdictional political community, to those beyond their territorial borders (to neighbours, to citizens of other political communities), and to future generations, those who will inherit the legacy of the past and the present.

The duty to carry out agreed policies and programmes *effectively* leads to an agenda of substantive responsibilities for those in governance. The precise form of this agenda will be highly particular to specific times and places. Political communities seeking to promote open collaborative public policy debate will wish to consider not merely what they want governance to perform but how they want performance principles expressed. For example, the British discretionary, judgemental regulatory system for land use permitting may be appropriate in a society with skilled personnel to do the regulating, with many checks and balances on how they do this and with a general tradition of regard for legal process. It could lead to corruption and political manipulation in other circumstances.

The duty to operate within *openly agreed principles and to report back* to members of the political community on what has been done on their behalf complements the duty to pay respectful attention to citizens and the diversity of their values and conditions. In the British planning system, the requirement to base regulatory decisions in the development plan and to review plans regularly reflects this duty. To promote collaborative, inclusionary argumentation requires not merely a duty to report but the specification of the terms of reporting to emphasise the importance of giving good reasons, based on good arguments made legitimate by public discussion and decision-making.

These three duties, if well-performed, would contribute to building up a governance capacity which could regain some public confidence and legitimacy and encourage collaborative strategy-making. The potential to be called to account would encourage good performance. Those in governance positions, however dispersed through their communities, would be encouraged to collaborate in order to avoid challenges of inattentive, ineffective and unaccountable actions. Such challenges would be damaging, in loss of legitimacy and in the costs of both litigation and sanctions. The above three duties could, however, be usefully accompanied by a fourth, the duty to foster the building of *democratic governance capacity*. This could be interpreted as a duty to sustain the conditions for collaboration in consensus-building and participative democratic governance. It would help to maintain a critical dynamic between governance activities and the rest of us.

The impact of such specification of duties would be to create a context within which a discourse of inclusionary accountability and an ethics of inclusionary respect could develop. Such an ethics of governance would emphasise the provision of good and honest information, an inclusionary and respectful attitude among those in governance positions towards the members of political communities and other stakeholders, and a positive view of monitoring and reporting activities. The subtle difference here is between manipulative and persuasive legitimation, and a real sense of a service relation between those in governance positions, whether formal or informal, and the political communities and stakeholders they serve.

Exercising and redeeming challenges

The way rights and duties are formally specified, distributed and redeemed in any legal and administrative system has a significant effect in structuring power relations and governance practices. Their specification reveals much about the political form and culture of a political community. It is, however, not sufficient to specify a right or a duty in general terms. A critical aspect of institutional design is exactly how they are specified. This needs to attend to who has rights; how, when and where they may exercise their rights; the terms in which rights are redeemed; and what responses are required when the neglect of a right or a duty has been successfully challenged. It is through examining the finegrain of these specifications and the way they intermesh with specific social relations in particular places that it will be possible to tell whether the institutional design of a policy system for managing local environmental change has the attributes listed at the start of this chapter. This issue is discussed further in considering criteria.

Resources

The allocation and distribution of public resources has traditionally been the key focus of debate in the politics of welfare states. The level of taxation, government attitudes to spending and the allocation of capital and revenue funds to government departments and levels of government provides a focus of acute attention by all those linked to governance in some way. In the spatial and environmental field, the concern with financial resources has been coupled with consideration of the land resource. To these established considerations have now been added concerns with the development of the capabilities of the labour force, the development of knowledge resources, and, in line with the arguments of this book, building up the institutional capacity of the social relations of places.

Traditionally, the assumption in political debate was that the state should provide the 'resource pot' through taxation measures, and then allocate this to levels and sectors of government activity. This assumption has increasingly been replaced with notions of 'partnership' and 'joint ventures' between private and public resources, and with alternative funding sources, such as the British National Lottery and charitable contributions from business.

This puts increasing pressure on the soft infrastructure of institutional design and the hard infrastructure of rights and duties to shape and monitor how these joint ventures work out.

However, any political community which seeks to promote an inclusionary, collaborative approach to local environmental management is likely to need 'resource pots' of various kinds, which members can draw upon in particular circumstances. These include:

1. Resources to ensure that all members have access to the means to a minimum *quality of life*, as understood in that political community. Without this, it will be hard to

overcome other barriers to stakeholder participation in governance. The result could be to reinforce exclusionary tendencies, the separation of certain groups from access to the 'mainstream' opportunities of the relevant political community.

2. Resources to allow the exercise of *citizenship rights*, to enable participation in governance, to enable rights to be claimed and challenges to be made. This could lead to the provision of resources for travel, to cover work duties or caring responsibilities which would otherwise be neglected. In Britain, for example, allowances are available to those who act as local councillors, and to those who serve on the boards of quangos and other new governance agencies created by central government. But similar resources are not provided to board members of neighbourhood initiat-ives, or other informal governance mechanisms. Some way of redressing this inequality needs to be found, in order to facilitate informal governance activity. Resources are also needed to keep the cost of making challenges and exercising rights low. This has important implications for the format and funding arrangements of formal and semi-formal courts. If cost thresholds are too high, too few will exercise their rights. In the local environmental field, facilities such as the British Planning Aid service could be expanded, with a claim on general taxation or other public funds.
3. Resources for *capital investment*, to fund major infrastructure projects, to deal with those aspects of land reclamation and re-cycling that cannot attract private funds, and to help provide land and property for development needs in local economies without sufficient economic strength to generate interest from the private sector.
4. Resources to *provide redress* to those adversely affected by policy initiatives adopted by majorities. However much agreement has been reached on strategic directions, there will be winners and losers. In some cases, the losers can be compensated by specific actions by the winners. In other cases, such neat equations may be impossible. Everyone benefits from the conservation of energy achieved by better insulation, more efficient central heating boilers and new

technologies for the conversion of fuel to movement in car design. But it is hard for poorer people and smaller companies to afford the capital costs of introducing better products. Environmental groups commonly lobby for a fund to assist poorer people convert to new technologies (Beatley, 1994; Blowers (ed.), 1993).

5. Resources to ensure that a wide range of *good quality information* is available at an accessible cost to members of political communities. In relation to the conditions of local environments, this would include monitoring information on local economic trends and prospects, biospheric conditions, quality of life, and land and property ownership, values and the availability of property. This requires statistics which can be disaggregated to relatively small spatial units, and to categories which both make sense to specific stakeholders and can be compared with conditions in other places. In Britain, there is a considerable amount of local economic data. Environmental data is at last being collected on quite a wide scale, through local efforts at environmental audits, complemented by a few national data surveys (Glasson *et al.*, 1994). However, data on quality of life is limited, and focuses on rather crude league tables (Rogerson, Findlay, Coombes and Morris, 1989), while there is very little comprehensive land and property data available in the public domain due to the lack of an open cadaster, or public register of land transactions and prices. These deficiencies make it difficult to identify stakeholders, to assess the claims stakeholders make, and to develop common understanding. Good quality, public data is a very valuable resource in dispute resolution and in shaping problem definition and policy ideas.

Material resources carry power, as Giddens stresses. There will therefore always be struggles over who controls the collection and distribution of resources. Resolutions to these struggles which promote collaborative consensus-building and multi-cultural inclusionary argumentation may have a different form with respect to each of the above resource pots. Many argue that resources should be controlled as near as possible to the stakeholders in the supply and use of the resources – the *subsidiarity* principle. Yet resource redistribution confined to the local level could produce too small a pot in a situation where people compare their standards of living in a national context. Information systems designed locally could lose the advantages of comparability. One way to approach this variability could be to require as a duty that all levels of formal government, from the European Union to local councils, should seek to ensure that actions are taken on all the above five points, unless another level is adequately dealing with the issue.

Criteria for redeeming challenges

The definition and distribution of rights in relation to the management of local environmental change, the prescription of duties on those with governance roles, and the provision of resources help to frame the power relations of specific governance arenas. But how these rights and duties are interpreted and what are seen to be legitimate purposes are not inherent in the rights and duties. This depends on the political, legal and administrative cultures of governance. These provide the values and the language within which rights are redeemed, duties defined and resources allocated and distributed.

Yet as discussed in Chapter 7, the political communities of formal government systems are likely to contain many systems of valuing and multiple 'languages' for addressing issues. The distribution of rights and duties, and the support provided by resource pots available to promote participation in governance, broadly understood, should bring more of these languages into public debate. Yet it can also happen that powerful languages, for example that of administrative-legal discourse, or that of professionalised planning experts, may come to dominate policy discourse (McAuslan, 1980; Tett and Wolfe, 1991; Grant, 1994; Healey and Hillier, 1995). Further, even if there is a wide-ranging, inclusionary debate, it may come about that issues which were a priority for earlier rounds of collaboration get forgotten later in the process.

This suggests that institutional design efforts could make a difference by targeting specifically the vocabulary of legal and administrative discourse, and specifying the principles which should be satisfied when challenges to rights and duties are redeemed. This would lead to certain explicit requirements to be met in addressing claims for rights, or for redress due to the neglect of duties, or for the allocation of resources. The following might help to encourage an inclusionary argumentative approach:

- All claims for attention by members of political communities and stakeholders should recognise the existence of other claims, to encourage a sharing of concerns, rather than adversarial advocacy.
- All decisions by those in governance roles should be justified in terms of impacts on the various members of political communities and other stakeholders, and the interrelations between them.
- All decisions should be justified by reference to agreed strategies and, specifically, to the argumentation around the strategy (i.e. the plan becomes a store of arguments).
- All those in governance roles should be required to give 'good reasons' for any decision, such reasons relating to all the above.
- In justifying their actions, and in giving 'good reasons', those in governance roles should be required to acknowledge
    - the diverse ways of thinking of the members of a political community and other stakeholders,
    - the diversity of ways in which views and claims may be expressed
    - the diversity of forms of argument, encompassing technical, moral and expressive modes of reasoning and understanding.
    - the agreed strategies of other levels of governance

These could all be qualified by one further requirement, that these discursive requirements with respect to the terms within which claims are redeemed, should themselves be the subject of explicit review. They might even be contained in an agreed strategic planning statement, although there are dangers here as the powerful and knowledgeable might tend to slip changes into the wording of the requirements which other participants did not realise were significant. That such criteria carry significant power can be seen in the present practices of the British planning system, where development plan policies are significantly structured by national government procedural and policy advice and by the precedents of legal judgements (Healey, 1983, 1993). Ultimately, the evolution of governance discourses is a matter of relations within and among political communities, the sets of ideas and concepts available to them, and the choices they make. The principles suggested here would merely serve to foster inclusionary tendencies and impede a regress to administrative or political convenience.

Governance competencies

The question of organisational structure has preoccupied the discussion of planning systems, with debates focusing on the appropriate levels at which planning tasks should be performed and how to achieve territorial co-ordination at the urban region level in contexts structured by functional governance structures. The formal allocation of competencies helps to set up and staff the formal arenas through which many planning issues have to pass before achieving legal status. One reason for the preoccupation with organisational structure is the challenge of interrelating activities of diverse government programmes as these have affected the qualities of local environments. The social, economic and environmental challenges outlined in Part II demand a capability for more horizontal co-ordination at the urban region and local level.

This dimension of institutional design raises five issues:

- the *division* of governance tasks;
- their distribution between *levels* of governance;
- the *boundary* between formal government and the wider society;
- the use of administrative and technical *expertise*;
- the machinery for *dispute resolution.*

With respect to the *division of tasks*, the critical challenge is to encourage organisational forms which can link together the dimensions of the qualities of local environments from the point of view of everyday life, the business world and the biosphere, rather than from the point of view of the producers and deliverers of government services. Some specialisation and division is always necessary. Co-ordination problems are therefore endemic in the organisation of governance activity in complex societies. There is, however, much evidence to suggest that two factors support the capacity to make the links which this book has emphasised. The first is that the primary responsibility for task definition and performance should be as near as possible to where the performance of the task is experienced – the subsidiarity principle mentioned earlier. This emphasises the importance of regional and local levels for many governance tasks related to the management of local environmental change. The second is a duty to pay attention and to consult. This duty has already been emphasised, but it could be specified with particular reference to co-ordination requirements.

Planning systems, especially in Europe, have tended to develop out of strongly hierarchical conceptions of *levels of governance*, even if in practice such hierarchies are moderated by consensus-seeking practices between the levels (Davies *et al.*, 1989; Healey, Khakee, Motte and Needham, 1996). This recognises the reality that the stakeholders in local environmental change are to be found beyond particular urban regions and even beyond national boundaries. The implication of the approach developed in the present book is that a more horizontal, territorial conception of levels is needed. This does not imply the displacement of 'top-down' approaches by 'bottom-up' ones. Planning systems entirely driven by those stakeholders who live in a small local government unit may fail to consider the many stakeholders in what happens in their locale, as the American experience shows (Cullingworth, 1993). Rather than control by small government units, or nesting tiers of competencies, with each tier fitting into the framework provided by a higher tier, all levels need to be given competencies with respect to the qualities of local environments which relate to the justifiable concerns of stakeholders and which are considered appropriate to be addressed at that level. It is quite legitimate for the European Union to establish criteria for air pollution reduction, since one country's pollution is exported to other countries. It is equally justifiable for British central government to seek to ensure that adequate attention is paid to the conservation of national heritage sites. It is less justifiable for it to seek to determine how regions estimate their strategic land needs for housing and industrial development, and what locally valuable landscape resources should be preserved. It is equally inappropriate to leave this to units of government which cover only part of a land market area or a landscape region, such as a British district or a Swiss commune.

The way forward therefore seems to be to allow different government levels to have remits appropriate to the scale of their political communities, but then leave it to each level to develop their response to their task autonomously. The structure of challenges, or rights, duties and criteria governing the terms on which challenges can be redeemed, should ensure that each level can become a stakeholder to be considered by each other level.

These requirements, combined with the other dimensions of institutional design already discussed, should also provide a framework within which informal alliances and intermediary agencies can flourish, but yet remain accountable. It has been argued in this book that governance should spread beyond the *boundaries* of formal government, recognising the governance capabilities spread around the social networks of everyday life and the business world. But it is all too easy for special agencies or informal alliances to develop their own power base and lose their accountability to their political communities or even to the governments which approved their existence. One way to foster such agencies, while ensuring that they continue to operate effectively and accountably when they undertake governance work, is to demand that strict financial and reporting rules are followed, as is being cultivated in the contract culture emerging as a result of the critieria-driven approach to public policy discussed in Chapter 7.

This may be a helpful approach in some circumstances, but it can become bureaucratically cumbersome, and it may pull the governance initiative away from a relevant response to the concerns of stakeholders. Instead, it may come to focus on meeting the criteria set by formal government bodies. The approach of a structure of challenges as developed here is a more effective mechanism for holding diffused power to account. People can appreciate that others have an interest in their area, and what they want to do, and that some way of safeguarding the interests of stakeholders who are not part of their political community may be necessary. But they want to be able to consider the implications and discuss what is involved, rather than following some formal rules constructed in the suspicion that they may be corrupt or incompetent.

Increasing use is being made of *expertise* in addressing local environmental management. In Britain, the discretionary planning system has resulted in the creation of an organised profession of town planners to prepare plans and give regulatory advice. Elsewhere, the increasing complexity of local environmental issues is generating a similar demand for experts, who are being drawn from a range of fields, from architecture, public administration, economic development and environmental science. In the past, planners and other experts have been criticised for their professional arrogance, and/or for too close an identification with a prevailing government regime (Boyer, 1983; Reade, 1987; Healey, 1985; Grant, 1994). The perspective developed in this book is for a more interactive relationship between experts and the stakeholder communities they serve, as well as the development of a knowledge base which combines understanding of both the relational processes reviewed in Part II and the governance processes outlined in this part. This will require a renewal of the expertise of those locked into the ways of thinking and acting of previous government practices, and an enlargement of the fields of attention of the 'new' experts being drawn into the field, to ensure that they are able to relate knowledge about particular areas to the social context of the governance relations within which their expertise is being drawn upon (Albrechts, 1991; Healey, 1991b). This presents a demanding ethical challenge for experts, both in relation to the boundaries of what they know and how their knowledge is being used, and to the way they conduct themselves (Thomas and Healey, 1991). In this context, the traditional spatial planner is in many cases being transformed into a kind of knowledge mediator and broker, using an understanding of the dynamics of the governance situation to draw in knowledge resources and work out how to make them available in a digestible fashion to the dialogical processes of policy development. This role is encapsulated in models of the planner as a 'counsellor' (Bussink, 1995) and a 'critical friend' (Forester, 1996) in collaborative activities in local environmental management.

Finally, the organisation of any planning system needs attention to the design of *courts*. This acknowledges that consensus is never easy to construct or maintain. From time to time, there will be breakdowns in agreement and disputes. As discussed in Chapter 8, exercises in collaborative strategy-making will need to keep under review how to address unresolved disputes. But disputes 'between neighbours', between those co-existing in shared spaces, are common features of life in localities. Some kind of backstop formal arrangement to address these is needed. In the US case, the legal system provides the location not merely for disputes, but for arbitration on a whole range of policy questions in relation to land use planning and policy systems. This ends up being very time-consuming and costly to all parties, and leads to discursive domination by lawyers. The practices of informal consensus-building and environmental mediation have flourished as an alternative in such contexts. But there are all kinds of other possibilities, for informal hearings, or dispute resolution procedures, which could be brought into play.

Building institutional capacity through collaborative planning

The starting point of this book has been the challenge of how to deal with matters of collective concern which arise from the problems and opportunities of the co-existence in shared spaces of relational groups, or cultural communities, often with very different priorities and ways of looking at things. This is the focus of the practices of what is variously called urban and regional planning, spatial planning and local environmental management. Addressing this challenge has taken the discussion into some of the key policy concerns and governance challenges of our age.

I have argued that how political communities which focus on the management of shared spaces in regions, settlements and neighbourhoods come to define and address their policy agendas will have substantial social, economic and environmental effects, which will have significance not merely for that community but for nations, supranational regions and global objectives. A critical capability for such efforts is the capacity to interrelate the concerns of the different cultural communities which co-exist in a place. These may vary enormously in their existing relations with each other, in their systems of meaning and ways of organising and in their spatial reach. The concept of stakeholders helps to capture this diversity. The concept of cultural communities emphasises that people live intersubjectively, embedded in one or more relational worlds, through which we frame our approach to issues and learn new ways of thinking and acting. This concept draws on and develops the insights of an institutionalist approach to social relations and a communicative approach to social learning.

The capacity to interrelate involves the ability to make relational links, across cultural barriers, organisational divisions and fractures in the distribution of power. Building links is an activity of social mobilisation. Social mobilisation can be a force for ideological domination, which would crowd out the ways of thinking and organising of many of the cultural communities of a place. This would be likely in current conditions to reinforce the alienation from mainstream politics and organisation felt by many these days, and prevent the rich social learning which is recognised as helpful to economic development. This book has argued for an inclusionary approach to link-making work, through cultivating the capacity for collaborative, multi-cultural communication and learning, developed through building up relations of understanding and trust. A Habermasian *communicative ethics* provides a valuable conceptual resource for thinking about how to do this.

Collaborative efforts in defining and developing policy agendas and strategic approaches to collective concerns about shared spaces among the members of political communities serve to build up *social, intellectual and political capital* which becomes a new institutional resource. It generates a cultural community of its own, which enables future issues to be discussed more effectively, and provides channels through which all kinds of other issues, such as recognition of the adverse social consequences of new economic tendencies, or knowledge about economic opportunities, or ways to reduce behaviours which are harming biospheric sustainability, may be more rapidly understood and acted upon. In this way, such a collaborative cultural community focused on the governance of local environments should also help to recreate a public realm.

Such relation-making and culture-building work takes place through dialogue, and its qualities and outcomes are the result of the interaction between who gets involved and in what arenas, the communicative routine and styles which build up, and the existing social relational worlds which co-exist in a place. The activity of planning, as a conscious policy-driven effort to insert a strategic, long-term, interrelating viewpoint into governance processes, has the capacity to assist the task of relational capacity-building by its role in informing political communities about the range of stakeholders and about how they like to discuss issues; by its role in helping to shape arenas where stakeholders can meet; and by helping those involved work out what it means to build new collective ways of thinking and acting, to *re-frame* and *re-structure* their ways of proceeding. Those involved as experts in such processes should have an ethical duty to attend to all stakeholders as the interactive process develops. The result is a process of *collaborative planning*.

The effort of collaborative planning is surrounded by powerful pressures, explicit and implicit, from some cultural communities, to produce hegemonic outcomes within which their point of view prevails – the 'I win–you lose' approach. Collaborative planning efforts, however, search for more than the 'win–win' outcome of the conflict management textbooks (Fisher and Ury, 1981). It seeks to re-frame how people think about winning and loosing. It looks for an approach which asks: can we all get on better if we change how we think to accommodate what other people think? If this can be done, then we might think about winning and losing in a different way.

Collaborative planning efforts involve attention to institutional design at two levels. The first focuses on the soft infrastructure of individual efforts in strategic spatial planning and environmental management of some kind. This is the terrain of *planning practices*, through which participants and those they link to through their networks engage in public reasoning about strategies and projects, creating localised frames of reference for future use. I have argued that attention to stakes, arenas, routines and styles, discourses and the nature of agreement could help shape such practices into more fully collaborative and inclusionary forms of collective reasoning and argumentation. But without attention to the hard infrastructure of institutional design, it will be difficult to challenge and change the power of dominant groups as this is embedded in the abstract systems of current governance. This is the terrain of the design of *planning systems.* I argue in this chapter that planning systems need to be critiqued and invented by a careful assessment of the constitution of rights and duties, of resource allocation mechanisms, of performance criteria and of competencies. These generate a *structure of challenges.* The struggle for political mobilisation to change planning systems to encourage more collaborative inclusionary forms of planning practice is to develop a hard infrastructure of institutional design which creates a structure of challenges which requires that challenges are redeemed through public reasoning and argumentation, recognising all stakeholders and their diverse communicative practices.

If the arguments in this book are valid, then a movement in the direction of inclusionary, collaborative planning should help to improve the quality of life for the many cultural communities in a place; to add material value not just to the companies in a place, but to those who share the experience of living there, and to work out how to act to sustain the critical biospheric capacities of a place. These benefits arise through the deliberative work of collaborative capacity-building, not through encouraging individualistic competitive behaviour. Such competitive behaviour is most likely to achieve its beneficial results in liberating creative energies *within* a framework which facilitates diverse activities but which structures these in ways designed to limit the destructive effects of one person's activities on another's. This framing will inhibit and dominate unless it is consciously established and re-established. This cannot be done through competitive processes.

The approach developed in this book may be seen as an idealistic vision. This may in particular be the reaction of British readers. In Britain, the country I know best and which is the place I identify with, we live in a society deeply fractured by the power of class and capital; and recently fragmented by the force of a competitive neo-liberal government philosophy. Yet there is plenty of evidence of collaborative governance, of efforts in re-designing the soft infrastructure of planning practices. These can be found in initiatives in neighbourhood community development, in discussions on Local Agenda 21, and in some recent examples of public consultation in spatial plan-making processes. But the development of these approaches is constrained by the hard infrastructure of the design of our formal policy systems and our overall, and very peculiar, constitution of government.

These formal systems are often seen as immovable constraints, powerful systems which are just 'there'. But the institutionalist approach emphasises that constraints are never fixed. They are socially made and re-made; through dialogue, by re-thinking; by changing perspectives, through social mobilisation. A communicative approach helps to focus on what this task of re-making structures involves. But it is difficult work, requiring recognition of how we come to think what we do and how we come to organise in the ways that we do; and how power can flow unrecognised and embedded through the fine grain of our daily practices. It is power-challenging and ethically-demanding. Yet it is happening around us continuously, in the cultural worlds of the powerful as they create and use what the rest of us see as structures and systems, as we make and re-make our own ways of going on, and in what we all do as we acknowledge, challenge and resist embedded power.

This book is above all a contribution to the effort of re-thinking and changing perspectives. It provides arguments and probing questions to help those struggling to release the constraints of past ways of doing things with respect to addressing our collective concerns with co-existence in shared spaces, and to re-design institutional frameworks to allow a rich, inventive, locally-contingent and inclusionary form of local environmental planning to flourish. This, I believe, will help political communities in western countries release the capacities of their members and re-build a public realm at the service of citizens rather than dominated by the abstract systems of government and economy which, despite the hope of the Enlightenment and the project of modernity, have boxed us into unequal, unrespectful, economically problematic and environmentally unsustainable practices.

Bibliography

Abercrombie, P. (1944) *Town and Country Planning* (Oxford: Oxford University Press (orig. publ. 1933)).

Adams, D. (1994) *Urban Planning and the Development Process* (London: UCL Press).

Albrechts, L. (1991) 'Changing roles and positions of planners', *Urban Studies*, 2810, pp. 123–38.

Allen, J. (1992) *Smoke over the Winter Palace: the politics of resistance and London's community areas*, Occasional Paper Vol. 1, No. 4, School of Construction, Housing and Surveying (London: University of Westminster Press).

Altman, I. and Churchman, A. (eds) (1994) *Women and the Environment* (London: Plenum Press).

Ambrose, P. (1986) *Whatever Happened to Planning?* (London: Methuen).

Amin, A. (ed.) (1994) *Post-Fordism: a Reader* (Oxford: Blackwell).

Amin, A. (1994) 'Post-Fordism: models, fantasies and phantoms of transition', in Idem *Post-Fordism: a reader* (Oxford: Blackwell), pp. 1–40.

Amin, A. and Thrift, N. (1992) 'Neo-Marshallian nodes in global networks', *International Journal of Urban and Regional Research*, Vol. 16(4), pp. 571–87.

Amin, A. and Thrift, N. (1995) 'Globalisation, institutional "thickness" and the local economy' in Healey *et al.* (eds), *Managing Cities: the new urban context* (London: John Wiley) pp. 91–108.

Amin, A. and Thrift, N. (eds) (1995) *Globalisation, Institutions and Regional Development* (Oxford: Oxford University Press).

Argyris, C. and Schon, D. (1978) *Organizational Learning: a theory of action perspective* (San Francisco: Jossey-Bass).

Arnstein, S. (1969) 'The ladder of citizen participation', *Journal of the Institute of American Planners*, Vol. 35(4), pp. 216–24.

Ashworth, G. and Voogd, H. (1990) *Selling the City* (London: Belhaven).

Bacaria, J. (1994) 'Competition and co-operation among jurisdictions: the case of regional co-operation in Science and Technology in Europe', *European Planning Studies*, Vol. 2, pp. 287–302.

Bacharach, P. and Baratz, M. (1970) *Power and Poverty: theory and practice* (New York: Oxford University Press).

Bailey, N., Barker, A. and McDonald, K. (1995) *Partnership Agencies in British Urban Policy* (London: UCL Press).

Ball, M. (1983) *Housing Policy and Economic Power* (London: Methuen).

Ball, M. (1986) 'The built environment and the urban question', *Environment and Planning D: Society and Space*, Vol. 4, pp. 447–64.

Banister, D. and Button, K. (eds) (1993) *Transport, the Environment and Sustainable Development* (London: E. and F.N. Spon).
Barlow, J. (1995) *Public Participation in Urban Development: the European experience* (London: Policy Studies Institute).
Barnes, B. (1982) *T.S. Kuhn and the Social Sciences* (London: Macmillan).
Barras, R. (1987) 'Technical change and the urban development cycle', *Urban Studies*, Vol. 24(1), pp. 5–30.
Barras, R. (1994) 'Property and the economic cycle: building cycles revisited', *Journal of Property Research*, Vol. 113, pp. 183–97.
Barrett, S. and Fudge, C. (1981a) 'Examining the policy–action relationship' in idem, *Policy and Action* (London: Methuen) pp. 3–32.
Barrett, S. and Fudge, C. (1981b) 'Reconstructing the field of analysis', in idem, *Policy and Action* (London: Methuen) pp. 249–79.
Batley, R. and Stoker, G. (eds) (1991) *Local Government in Europe* (London: Macmillan).
Beatley, T. (1994) *Ethical Land Use* (Baltimore: Johns Hopkins University Press).
Beauregard, R. (1991) 'Without a net: modernist planning and the postmodern abyss', *Journal of Planning Education and Research*, Vol. 10(3), pp. 189–94.
Beck, U. (1992) *The Risk Society* (London: Sage).
Beer, S. (1982) *Britain Against Itself: the political contradictions of collectivism* (London: Faber).
Beevers. R. (1988) *The Garden City Utopia: a critical biography of Ebenezer Howard* (London: Macmillan).
Bell, D. (1960) *The End of Ideology: on the exhaustion of political ideas in the fifties* (New York: Free Press).
Bell, G. (1996) 'Stake and chips added to the menu for sustainable delivery', *Planning*, 1153, pp. 9–10.
Benfield, M. (1994) *Planning regulation: who benefits?*, paper for AESOP Congress, Istanbul, August.
Berger, P. and Luckman, T. (1967) *The Social Construction of Reality* (Harmondsworth: Penguin).
Berry, M. and Huxley, M. (1992) 'Big World: Property capital, the state and urban change in Australia', *International Journal of Urban and Regional Research*, Vol. 16(1), pp. 35–59.
Bianchini, F. (1990) 'The crisis of urban public social life in Britain: the origins of the problems and possible responses', *Planning Practice and Research*, Vol. 5(3), pp. 4–8.
Bicanic, R. (1967) *Problems of Planning: East and West* (The Hague: Mouton Press).
Bishop, M., Kay, J. and Mayer, C. (1995) *The Regulatory Challenge* (Oxford: Oxford University Press).
Black, A. (1990) 'The Chicago Area Transportation Study', *Journal of Planning Education and Research*, Vol. 101, pp. 27–38.
Blackman, T. (1995) *Urban Policy in Practice* (London: Routledge).
Blakeley, E. (1989) *Planning Local Economic Development* (London: Sage).
Blowers, A. (ed.) (1993) *Planning for a Sustainable Environment* (London: Earthscan).

Boden, D. (1994) *The Business of Talk* (Cambridge: Polity Press).

Bolan, R. (1969) 'Community decision behaviour: the culture of planning', *Journal of the American Institute of Planners*, Vol. XXXV, pp. 301–10.

Bondi, L. and Domosh, M. (1992) 'Other figures in other places: on feminism, postmodernism and geography', *Environment and Planning D: Society and Space*, Vol. 10, pp. 119–240.

Bonneville, M. (1995) 'Le renouvellement du schèma directeur par le project d'agglomeration: reflexions a propos de Lyon', in A. Motte (ed.), *Schèma Directeur et projet d'agglomeration* (Paris: Editions Juris Service) pp. 47–63.

Boorah, V.K. and Hart, M. (1995) 'Labour market outcomes and economic exclusion', *Regional Studies*, Vol. 29(5), pp. 433–8.

Bourdieu, P. (1990) *In Other Words: essays towards a reflexive sociology* (Oxford: Polity Press).

Boyer, C. (1983) *Dreaming the Rational City* (Boston, Mass.: MIT Press).

Boyer, R. (1991) 'The eighties: the search for alternatives to Fordism', in *The Politics of Flexibility*, ed. Jessop, B. Kastendiek, H and Nielsen, K., Petersen, I.K. Aldershot, Hants: Edward Elgar.

Bramley, G., Bartlett, W. and Lambert, C. (1995) *Planning, the Market, and Private House- Building* (London: UCL Press).

Braybrooke, D. and Lindblom, C.E. (1963) *A Strategy for Decision* (New York: Free Press).

Breheny, M. (1992) 'The Compact City: an introduction', *Built Environment*, 18(4), pp. 241–6.

Breheny, M. and Hooper, A. (eds) (1985) *Rationality in Planning* (London: Pion).

Brindley, T., Rydin, Y. and Stoker, G. (1989) *Remaking Planning: the politics of urban change in the Thatcher years* (London: Unwin Hyman).

Bruton, H. and Nicholson, D. (1987) *Local Planning in Practice* (London, Hutchinson University Press).

Bryson, J. and Crosby, B. (1992) *Leadership for the Common Good: Tackling public problems in a shared-power world* (San Francisco: Jossey-Bass).

Bryson, J. and Crosby, B. (1993) 'Policy planning and the design of forums, arenas and courts', *Environment and Planning B*, 20(2), pp. 123–252.

Bryson, J.M., Crosby, B. and Carroll, A.R. (1991) 'Fighting the Not-in-My-Back-Yard syndrome', *Journal of Planning Education and Research*, pp. 66–74.

Burke, E. (1987) *A Philosophical Enquiry into Our Ideas of the Sublime and Beautiful*, edited by J.T. Boulton (Oxford: Blackwell).

Bussink, B. (1995) 'Advocacy and counsel in Dutch Regional Planning: an inescapable tension', paper to AESOP Congress, Glasgow, August

Camagni, R. (ed.) (1991) *Innovation networks: spatial perspectives* (London: Belhaven Press).

Camagni R and Salone, C. (1993) 'Network urban structures in Northern Italy: elements for a theoretical framework', *Urban Studies*, Vol. 30(6), pp. 1053–64.

Campbell, B. (1993) *Goliath* (London: Methuen).

Campbell, M. (1990) *Local Economic Policy* (London: Cassell).
Carson, R. (1960) *Silent Spring* (Boston: Houghton Mifflin).
Castells, M. (1977) *The Urban Question* (London: Edward Amold).
Chadwick, G. (1971) *A Systems View of planning* (Oxford: Pergamon).
Champion, A. (1992) 'Urban and regional demographic trends in the developed world', *Urban Studies*, 29, 461–482.
Champion, A. (ed.) (1993) *Population Matters: the local dimension* (London: Paul Chapman Publishing).
Chapin, F.S. (1965) *Urban Land Use Planning* (Urbana: University of Illinois Press).
Christensen, K. (1985) 'Coping with uncertainty in planning', *Journal of the American Planning Association*, Vol. 51(1), pp. 63–73.
Clapham, C. (1985) *Third World Politics: an introduction* (London: Croom Helm).
Clegg, S. (1990) *Modern Organizations* (London: Sage).
Cochrane, A. (ed.) (1987) *Developing Local Economic Strategies* (Milton Keynes, Bucks: Open University Press).
Cockburn, C. (1977) *The Local State* (London: Pluto Press).
Commission of the European Communities (CEC) (1990) *Green Paper on the Urban Environment* (Luxembourg: Office for Official Publications of the European Communities).
Commission of the European Union (CEC) (1991) *Europe 2000* (Luxembourg: Office for Official Publications of the European Communities).
Commission of the European Union (CEC) (1994) *Europe 2000+ Cooperation for European Territorial Development* (Luxembourg: Official Publications of the European Communities).
Cowell, R. 1993 '*Take and Give': managing the impact of development with environmental compensation,* UK CEED Discussion paper No 10 (Cambridge, UK: CEED).
Cowling, T. and Steeley, G. (1973) *Sub-Regional Planning Studies: an evaluation* (Oxford: Pergamon).
Cox, K. and Johnston, R.J. (1982) *Conflict, Politics and the Urban Scene* (London: Longmans).
Crawley, I. (1991) 'Some reflections on planning and politics in inner London', in H. Thomas and P. Healey, *Dilemmas of Planning Practice* (Aldershot, Hants: Avebury).
Cullingworth, J.B. (1993) *The Political Culture of Planning: American land use planning in contemporary perspectives* (London: Routledge).
Cullingworth, J.B. (1994) 'Alternate planning systems: is there anything to learn from abroad?' *Journal of the American Planning Association* Vol. 60(2), pp. 162–72.
Darin-Drabkin, H. (1977) *Land Policy and Urban Growth* (Oxford: Pergamon).
Davidoff, P. (1965) 'Advocacy and pluralism in planning', *Journal of the American Institute of Planning,* Vol. 31(Nov), pp. 331–8.
Davidoff, P. and Reiner, T. (1962) 'A choice theory of planning', *Journal of the American Institute of Planners,* Vol. 28(May), pp. 103–15.

Davies, H.W.E, Edwards, D., Hooper, A and Punter, J. (1989) *Planning Control in Western Europe* (London: HMSO).

Davies, J.G. (1972) *The Evangelistic Bureaucrat* (London: Tavistock Press).

Davoudi, S. (1995) 'City challenge: the three-way partnership', *Planning Practice and Research,* Vol. 10, pp. 333–44.

Davoudi, S. and Healey, P. (1995) 'City Challenge: Sustainable process or temporary gesture?', *Environment and Planning C: Government and Policy,* Vol. 13, pp. 79–95.

Davoudi, S., Healey, P. and Hull, A. (1996) 'Rhetoric and reality in British structure planning in Lancashire 1993–1995, in P. Healey, A. Khakee, A. Motte and B. Needham (eds), *Making Strategic Spatial Plans: Innovation in Europe* (London: UCL Press).

Dear, M. (1995) 'Prolegomena to a postmodern urbanism', in P. Healey, S. Cameron, S. Davoudi, S. Graham and A. Madani Pour (eds), *Managing Cities: the New Urban Context* (London: John Wiley).

DeGrove, J. (1984) *Land, Growth and Politics* (Washington, DC: Planners Press).

Department of the Environment (DoE) (1991) *Circular 16/91 Planning Obligations* (London: HMSO).

Department of the Environment (DoE) (1995) *Development Control Strategies: England 1993/94* (Ruislip, Middlesex: DoE Sales Unit).

Douglas, M. (1987) *How Institutions Think* (London: Routledge & Kegan Paul).

Douglas, M. (1992) *Risk and Blame: Essays in Cultural Theory* (London: Routledge).

Dryzek, J.S. (1990) *Discursive democracy: politics, policy and political science* (Cambridge: Cambridge University Press).

Dunleavy, P. and O'Leary, B. (1987) *Theories of the State: the politics of liberal democracy* (London: Macmillan).

Dyckman, J. (1961) 'Planning and decision theory', *Journal of the American Institute of Planners,* Vol. XXVII, pp. 335–45.

Eagleton, T. (1991) *Ideology: an introduction* (London: Verso).

Eisenstadt, S.N. and Lamarchand R. (eds) (1981) *Political Clientelism: patronage and development* (London: Sage).

Ekins, P. (1986) *The Living Economy: a new economics in the making* (London: Routledge and Kegan Paul).

Elson, M.J. (1986) *Green Belts* (London: Heinemann).

Emery, R.E. and Trist, E.L. (1969) 'The causal texture of organizational environments, in ed Emery, R.E. *Systems Thinking* (Harmondsworth: Penguin).

Esping-Anderson, G. (1990) *The Three Worlds of Welfare Capitalism* (Cambridge: Polity Press).

Etzioni, A. 1968 *The Active Society: A Theory for Societal and Political Processes* (New York: Free Press).

Evans, A. (1985) *Urban Economics: an introduction* (Oxford: Blackwell).

Fainstein, S. (1994) *The City Builders: property, politics and planning in London and New York* (Oxford: Blackwell).

Fainstein, S. and Hirst, C. (1995) 'Urban Social Movements' in D. Judge, G. Stoker and H. Wolman (eds), *Theories of Urban Politics* (London: Sage).

Faludi, A. (1973) *Planning Theory* (Oxford: Pergamon).

Faludi, A. (1987) *A Decision-Centred View on Environmental Planning* (Oxford: Pergamon).

Faludi, A. (1996) 'Framing with images', *Environment and Planning B: Planning and Design*, Vol. 23, pp. 93–108.

Faludi, A. and Van der Valk, A. (1994) *Rule and Order: Dutch Local Planning Doctrine in the Twentieth Century* (Dordrecht: Dluwer Academic Publishers).

Farthing, S., Coombes, T. and Winter, J. (1993) 'Large development sites and affordable housing', *Housing and Planning Review*, Feb./March, pp. 11–13.

Findlay A. and Rogerson R. (1993) 'Migration, places and quality of life', in A. Champion (ed.), *Population Matters* (London: Paul Chapman Publishing).

Fischer, F. (1990) *Technocracy and the Politics of Expertise* (London: Sage).

Fischer, F. and Forester, J. (1993) *The Argumentative turn in policy analysis and planning* (London: UCL Press).

Fischer, R. and Ury, W. (1981) *Getting to Yes: Negotiating Agreement without giving in* (Harmondsworth: Penguin).

Flyvberg, B. (1996) *Rationality and Power* (Aldershot: Avebury).

Foley, D. (1960) 'British Town Planning: One Ideology or Three', *British Journal of Sociology*, Vol. 11, pp. 211–31.

Forester, J. (1989) *Planning in the Face of Power* (Berkeley, California: University of California Press).

Forester, J. (1992a) 'Critical enthnography: fieldwork in a Habermasian way', in M. Alvesson and H. Willmott (eds), *Critical Management Studies* (Los Angeles: Sage).

Forester, J. (1992b) 'Envisioning the politics of public sector Dispute Resolution', in S. Silbey, and A. Sarat, (eds), *Studies in Law, Politics and Society*, Vol. 12 (JAI Press), pp. 83–122.

Forester, J. (1993) *Critical Theory, Public Policy and Planning Practice* (Albany: State University of New York Press).

Forester, J. (1994) 'Perception, political judgement and learning about value in transportation planning: Bridging Habermas and Aristotle', in H. Thomas (ed.) *Values in Planning* (Aldershot, Hants: Avebury).

Forester, J. (1996) 'Beyond dialogue to transformative learning: how deliberative rituals encourage political judgement in community planning processes', in S. Esquith (ed.), *Democratic Dialogues: Theories and Practices* (Poznan: University of Poznan).

Francis, J. (1993) *The Politics of Regulation* (Oxford: Blackwell).

Frankenberg, R. (1966) *Communities in Britain: Social Life in Town and Country* (Harmondsworth: Penguin).

Friberg, T. (1993) *Everyday Life: Women's Adaptive Strategies in Time and Space* (Stockholm: Swedish Council of Building Research).

Friedmann, J. (1973) *Retracking America* (New York: Anchor Press).
Friedmann, J. (1987) *Planning in the Public Domain* (New Jersey: Princeton University Press).
Friedmann, J. (1992) *Empowerment: the politics of alternative development* (Oxford: Blackwell).
Friedmann, J. and Weaver, C. (1979) *Territory and Function: the evolution of reginal planning* (London: Edward Arnold).
Friend, J. and Hickling, A. (1987) *Planning under Pressure: the strategic choice approach* (Oxford: Pergamon).
Friend, J. and Jessop, N. (1969) *Local Government and Strategic Choice* (London: Tavistock).
Friend, J., Power, J. and Yewlett, C. (1974) *Public Planning: the intercorporate dimension* (London: Tavistock).
Galtung, J. (1986) 'The green movement: a sociological explanation', *International Sociology*, Vol. 1(1), pp. 75–90.
Gamble, A. (1988) *The Free Economy and the Strong State* (London: Macmillan).
Gans, H. (1969) 'Planning for people, not buildings', *Environment and Planning A*, Vol. 1, pp. 33–46.
Gans, H. (1990) 'Deconstructing the underclass: the term's dangers as a planning concept', *Journal of the American Planning Association*, Vol. 56(3), pp. 271–7.
Geddes, P. (1949) *Cities in Evolution* (London: Williams & Norgate).
Geertz, C. (1983) *Local Knowledge: further essays in interpretive anthropology* (New York: Basic Books).
Geertz, C. (1988) *Works and Lives: the anthropologist as author* (Stanford, California: Stanford University Press).
Giddens, A. (1984) *The Constitution of Society* (Cambridge: Polity Press).
Giddens, A. (1987) *Social Theory and Modern Sociology* (Cambridge: Polity Press).
Giddens, A. (1990) *Consequences of Modernity* (Cambridge: Polity Press).
Gilroy, R. (1993) *Equal Opportunities in Planning and Housing* (Aldershot: Avebury).
Gilroy, R. and Woods, R. (1994) *Housing Women* (London: Routledge).
Glasson, J., Therivel, R. and Chadwick, A. (1994) *Introduction to Environmental Impact Assessment* (London: UCL Press).
Goldsmith, M. (1993) 'The Europeanisation of local government', *Urban Studies*, Vol. 30, pp. 683–700.
Goodchild, B. (1990) 'Planning and the modern/postmodern debate', *Town Planning Review*, 61.20, pp. 119–37.
Goodin, R. (1992) *Green Political Theory* (Cambridge: Polity Press).
Goodman, R. (1972) *After the Planners* (Harmondsworth: Penguin).
Goodwin, M., Duncan, S. and Halford, S. (1993) 'Regulation Theory, the local state and the transition to urban politics', *Environment and Planning D. Society and Space*, Vol. 11, pp. 67–88.
Granovetter, M.N. (1985) 'Economic action and social structure: the problem of embeddedness', *American Journal of Sociology*, Vol. 91, pp. 481–510.

Grant, J. (1994) *The Drama of Democracy* (Toronto: University of Toronto Press).
Grant, W. (1989) *Pressure Groups, Politics and Democracy in Britain* (Hemel Hempstead: Philip Allan).
Grove-White, R. (1991) 'Land, the Law and Environment', *Journal of Law and Society*, Vol. 181, pp. 32–47.
Habermas, J. (1984) *The Theory of Communicative Action: Vol 1: Reason and the Rationalisation of Society* (London: Polity Press).
Habermas, J. (1987) *The Philosophical Discourse of Modernity* (Cambridge; Polity Press).
Habermas, J. (1993) *Justification and Application: Remarks on Discourse Ethics* (Cambridge: Polity Press).
Hajer, M. (1995) *The Politics of Environment Discourse: a study of the acid rain controversy in Great Britain and the Netherlands* (Oxford: Oxford University Press).
Hajer, M. (1993) 'Discourse Coalitions and the Politics of Washington Think Tanks', in F. Fischer and J. Forester (eds), *The Argumentative Turn in Policy Analysis and Planning* (London: UCL Press) pp. 43–76.
Hall, P. (1988) *Cities of Tomorrow* (Oxford: Blackwell).
Hall, P. (1995) 'Bringing Abercrombie back from the shades', *Town Planning Review*, 663, pp. 227–42.
Hall, P., Thomas, R., Gracey, H. and Drewett, R. (1973) *The Containment of Urban England* (London: George Allen and Unwin).
Hall, S. and Gieben, B. (1992) *Formations of Modernity* (Milton Keynes: Open University Press).
Handy, C. (1990) *The Age of Unreason* (London: Arrow Books).
Hanson, S., Pratt, G., Mattingly, D. and Gilbert, M. (1994) 'Women, work and metropolitan environments', in I. Altman and A. Chuchman (eds), *Women and the Environment* (New York: Plenum Press) pp. 227–54.
Harding, A. (1995) 'Elite theory and growth machines' in D. Judge, G. Stoker and H. Wolman (eds), *Theories of Urban Politics* (London: Sage) pp. 35–53.
Harrison, B. (1994a) 'The Italian industrial disticts and the crisis of co-operative form: Part I', *European Planning Studies*, Vol. 21, pp. 3–22.
Harrison, B. (1994b) 'The Italian industrial districts and the crisis of co-operative form: Part II', *European Planning Studies*, Vol. 24, pp. 159–74.
Harrison, A. (1977) *The Economics of Land Use Planning* (London: Croom Helm).
Harvey, J. (1987) *Urban Land Economics* (London: Macmillan).
Harvey, D. (1982) *The Limits of Capital* (Oxford: Blackwell).
Harvey, D. (1973) *Social Justice and the City* (London: Edward Arnold).
Harvey, D. (1985) *The Urbanization of Capital* (Oxford: Blackwell).
Harvey, D. (1989a) 'From managerialism to entrepreneurialism: the formation of urban governance in late capitalism', *Geografisker Annaler*, 71B, pp. 3–17.
Harvey D. (1989b) *The Condition of Modernity* (Oxford: Blackwell).
Hayden, D. (1981) *The Grand Domestic Revolution* (Cambridge, Mass: MIT Press).

Healey, P. (1979) 'Networking as a normative principle', *Local Government Studies*, Vol. 5(1), pp. 55–68.
Healey, P. (1983) *Local Plans in British Land Use Planning* (Oxford: Pergamon).
Healey, P. (1985) 'The professionalisation of planning', *Town Planning Review*, Vol. 56(4), pp. 492–507.
Healey, P. (1988) 'The British planning system and managing the urban environment', *Town Planning Review*, Vol. 59(4), pp. 397–417.
Healey, P. (1991a) 'Urban regeneration and the development industry' *Regional Studies*, Vol. 25(2), pp. 97–110.
Healey, P. (1991b) 'The content of planning education programmes: some comments from the British experience', *Environment and Planning B: Planning and Design*, Vol. 18(2), pp. 177–89.
Healey, P. (1992a) 'Planning through debate: the communicative turn in planning theory', *Town Planning Review*, 632, pp. 143–62.
Healey, P. (1992b) 'A planner's day: knowledge and action in communicative perspective', *Journal of the American Planning Association*, Vol. 58(1), pp. 9–20.
Healey, P. (1993) 'The communicative work of development plans', *Environment and Planning B: Planning and Design*, 20.10, pp. 183–94.
Healey, P. (1994a) 'Urban policy and property development: the institutional relations of real-estate development in an old industrial region', *Environment and Planning A*, 26, pp. 177–98.
Healey, P. (1994b) 'Development plans: new approaches to making frameworks for land use regulation', *European Planning Studies*, Vol. 21, pp. 38–58.
Healey, P. (1994c) 'Regulating property development' in P. Burton and M. O'Toole (eds), *21 years of urban Policy* (London: Chapman & Hall).
Healey, P. (1995) 'The institutional challenge for sustainable urban regeneration', *Cities*, Vol. 12(4), pp. 221--30.
Healey, P. (1996a) 'The communicative turn in planning theory and its implication for spatial strategy-making', *Environment and Planning B: Planning and Design*, Vol. 23, pp. 217–34.
Healey, P. (1996b) 'City fathers, mandarins and neighbours: crossing old divides with new partnerships' in Kallthorp and I. Elander (eds), *Cities in Transformation; Transformations in Cities* (Aldershot, Hants: Avebury).
Healey, P. and Barrett, S. (1990) 'Structure and agency in land and property development processes', *Urban Studies*, Vol. 27(1), pp. 89–104.
Healey, P., Ennis, F. and Purdue, M. (1992) 'Planning gain and the "new" local plans', *Town and Country Planning*, Vol. 61(2), pp. 39–43.
Healey, P. and Gilbert, A. (1985) *The Political Economy of Land: urban development in Venezuela* (Aldershot: Gower).
Healey, P. and Hillier, J. (1995) *Community Mobilization in Swan Valley: Claims, Discourses and Rituals in Local Planning*, Working Paper No. 49, Department of Town and Country Planning (Newcastle: University of Newcastle).
Healey, P., Khakee, A., Motte, A. and Needham, B. (1996) *Making Strategic Spatial Plans: Innovation in Europe* (London: UCL Press).

Healey, P., McNamara, P., Elson, M. and Doak, J. (1988) *Land Use Planning and the Mediation of Urban Change* (Cambridge: Cambridge University Press).

Healey, P., Purdue, M. and Ennis, F. (1995) *Negotiating Development* (London: E. And F.N. Spon).

Healey, P. and Shaw, T. (1994) 'Changing meanings of "environment" in the British planning system', *Transactions of the Institute of British Geographers*, Vol. 19(4), pp. 425–38.

Healey, P. and Barrett, S. (eds) (1985) *Land Policy: problems and alternatives* (Aldershot, Hants: Gower).

Healey, P., Cameron, S.J., Davoudi, S., Graham, S., Madani Pour, A. (eds) (1995) *Managing Cities: the new urban context* (London: John Wiley).

Healey, P., S. Davoudi, M. O'Toole, S. Tavsanoglu and D. Usher (eds) (1993) *Rebuilding the City: Property-led urban regeneration* (London: E. and F.N. Spon).

Healey, P., Thomas, M.J. and McDougall, G. (eds) (1982) *Planning Theory: Prospects for the 1980s* (Oxford: Pergamon).

Held, D. (1987) *Models of Democracy* (Cambridge: Polity Press).

Hillier, J. (1993) 'To boldly go where no planners have ever ...', *Environment and Planning D: Society and Space*, 11, pp. 89–113.

Hoch, C. (1992) 'The paradox of power in planning practice', *Journal of Planning Education and Research, Vol. 11(3), pp. 206–15.*

Hodgson G. (1993) *The Economics of Institutions* (Aldershot, Hants: Edward Elgar).

Hoggett, P. (1995) 'Does local government want local democracy', *Town and Country Planning*, Vol. 64(4), pp. 107–09.

Holt-Jensen, A. (1994) Tendencies in Development Plan Making in Norway', in Healey, P. (ed) *Tendencies in Development Plan-Making in Europe*, Working Paper No. 42, Department of Town and Country Planning, University of Newcastle.

Holt-Jensen, A. (1996) 'Strategic Planning: between economic forces and democractic prossures in Hordaland county and the city of Bergen', in P. Healey, A. Khakee, A. Motte and B. Needham (eds), *Making Strategic Spatial Plans* (London: UCL Press).

Horelli, L. and Vepsa, K. (1994) 'In search of supportive structures for everyday life' in I. Altman and A. Chushman (eds), *Women and the Environment* (New York: Plenum Press).

Hudson, B. (1979) 'Comparison of current planning theories: counterparts and contradictions', *Journal of the American Planning Association*, Vol. 45(4), pp. 387–98.

Hull, A. (1995) 'New models for implementation theory: striking a consensus on windfarms', *Journal of Environmental Planning and Management*, Vol. 38(3), pp. 285–306.

Huxley, M. (1994) 'Planning as a framework of power: Utilitarian reform, Enlightenment logic and the control of space', in S. Ferber, C. Healey and C. McAuliffe (eds), *Beasts of Suburbs: Reinterpreting culture in Australian Suburb* (Melbourne: Melbourne University Press).

Innes, J. (1990) *Knowledge and Public Policy: the search for meaningful indicators* (New Brunswick: Transaction Press).

Innes, J. (1992) 'Group processes and the social construction of growth management: the cases of Florida, Vermont and New Jersey', *Journal of the American Planning Association*, Vol. 58, pp. 440–453.

Innes, J. (1994) *Planning Through Consensus-Building: a new view of the comprehensive planning ideal* (Berkeley: University of California IURD).

Innes, J. (1995) 'Planning theory's emerging paradigm: communicative action and interactive practice', *Journal of Planning Education and Research*, Vol. 14(3), pp. 183–90.

Innes, J., Gruber, J., Thompson, R. and Neuman, M. (1994) *Coordinating Growth and Environmental Management through consensus-building*, Report to the California Policy seminar (Berkeley: University of California).

Jacobs, J. (1961) *The Death and Life of Great American Cities* (New York: Vintage Books).

Jacobs, M. (1991) *The Green Economy* (London: Pluto Press).

Jencks, C. (1987) *Le Corbusier: the tragic view of architecture* (Harmondsworth, Herts: Penguin Cambridge).

Jencks, C. and Peterson, P.E. (eds) (1991) *The Urban Underclass* (Washington, DC: Brookings Institutions).

Jessop, B. (1991) 'The Welfare State in the transition from Fordism to Post-Fordism', in B. Jessop, H. Kastendiek, K. Nielsen and I.K. Petersen (eds), *The Politics of Flexibility* (Aldershot, Hants: Edward Elgar).

Jessop, B., Kastendiek H., Nielsen, K., Petersen, I.K. (eds), *The Politics of Flexibility* (Aldershot, Hants: Edward Elgar).

Jowell, J. and Oliver, D. (eds) (1985) *The Changing Constitution Restructuring State and Industry in Britain, Germany and Scandinavia* (Oxford: Clarendon Press).

Judge, D., Stoker, G. and Wolman, H. (eds) (1995) *Theories of urban politics* (London: Sage).

Kaiser, E. and Godschalk, D. (1993) 'Twentieth Century Land Use Planning: a stalwart tree', paper to ACSP Congress, Philadelphia, October.

Kearns G. (ed.) (1993) *Selling places: the city as cultural capital, past and present*, (Oxford: Butterworth).

Keeble, L. (1952) *Principles and Practice of Town and Country Planning* (London: Estates Gazette).

Kennedy-Skipton, H. (1994) 'Property development and urban regeneration: policy-led office development in Glasgow/Clydebank and Manchester/Salford', University of Strathclyde, Glasgow, unpublished PhD Thesis.

Keogh, G. and D'Arcy, E. (1994) 'Market maturity and property market behaviour: a European comparison of mature and emergent markets', *Journal of Property Research*, Vol. 113, pp. 215–35.

Khakee, A., Elander, I. and Sunnesson, S. (1995) *Remaking the Welfare State* (Aldershot, Hants: Avebury).

Khakee, A. (1996) 'Working in a democratic culture: structure planning in Marks Kommun', in P. Healey, A. Khakee, A. Motte and B. Needham (eds), *Making Strategic Spatial Plans* (London: UCL Press).

Kirk, G. (1980) *Urban Planning in a Capitalist Society* (London: Croom Helm).

Kitchen, J.E (1991) 'A client-based view of the planning service in H. Thomas and P. Healey (eds), *Dilemmas in Planning Practice* (Aldershot, Hants: Avebury).
Kitching G. (1988) *Karl Marx and the Philosophy of Praxis* (London: Routledge).
Korfer, H.R. and Latniak, E. (1993) 'Approaches to technology policy and regional milieux – experiences of programmes and projects in North Rhine-Westphalia', *European Planning Studies,* Vol. 2(3), pp. 303–20.
Krabben, E. and Lambooy, J.G. (1993) 'A theoretical framework for the functioning of the Dutch property market', *Urban Studies,* 30(8), pp. 1382–97.
Krumholz, N. and Forester, J. (1992) *Making Equity Planning Work* (Philadelphia: Temple University Press).
Kuhn, T. (1962) *The Structure of Scientific Revolutions* (Chicago: University of Chicago Press).
Laffin, M. (1986) *Professionalization and Policy: the role of the professions in central–local relationships* (Aldershot, Hants: Gower).
Latour, B. (1987) *Science in Action* (Cambridge: Mass.: Harvard University Press).
Lauria, M. and Whelan, R. (1995) 'Planning theory and political economy: the need for reintegration', *Planning Theory,* Vol. 14.
Lee, D. (1973) 'Requiem for large-scale models', *Journal of the American Planning Association,* Vol. 39, pp. 153–79.
Lefebvre, H. (1991) *The Production of Space* (London: Blackwell).
Lichfield, N. and Darin-Drabkin, H. (1980) *Land Policy and Urban Growth* (London: George Allen & Unwin).
Lichfield, N. (1992) 'From planning obligations to community impact analysis', *Journal of Planning and Environmental Law,* pp. 1103–18.
Liggett, H. and Perry, D. (ed.) (1995) *Spatial Practices* (Thousand Oaks, California: Sage).
Lindblom, C.E. (1959) 'The science of "muddling through"', *Public Administration Review,* Vol. 19, pp. 79–99.
Lindblom, C.E. (1965) *The Intelligence of democracy* (New York: Free Press).
Little, J. (1994a) *Gender, Planning and the Policy Process* (Oxford: Pergamon).
Little, J. (1994b) 'Women's initiatives in town planning in England: a critical review', *Town Planning Review,* 653, 261–76.
Lizieri, C. and Venmore-Rowland, P. (1991) 'Valuation accuracy: a contribution to debate', *Journal of Property Research,* Vol. 8, pp. 115–22.
Logan, J.R. and Molotch, H. (1987) *Urban Fortunes: the political economy of place* (Berkeley, California: University of California Press).
Lovelock, J. (1979) *Gaia – A New Look at Life on Earth* (Oxford: Oxford University Press).
Lovering, J. (1995) 'Creating discourses rather than jobs: the crisis in the cities and the transition fantasies of intellectuals and policy-makers', in P. Healey *et al.* (eds), *Managing Cities: the New Urban Context* (London: John Wiley).

Low, N. (1991) *Planning, Politics and the State: political foundations of planning thought* (London: Unwin Hyman).

Lowe, P. and Goyder, J. (1983) *Environmental Groups in Politics* (London: George Allen and Unwin).

Lowe, P., Murdoch, J. and Cox, G. (1995) 'A civilised retreat? Anti-urbanism, rurality and the making of an anglo-centric culture', in Healey *et al.* (eds) *Managing Cities, the new urban context* (London: John Wiley).

Lukes, S. (1974) *Power: a radical view* (London: Macmillan).

Macnaghten, P., Grove-White, R., Jacobs, M. and Wynne, B. (1995) *Public Perceptions and Sustainability in Lancashire: indicators, institutions and participation* (Preston, Lancashire: Lancashire Country Council).

Madani Pour, A. (1990) 'A study of urban form', unpublished PhD Thesis, University of Newcastle.

Mannheim, K. (1940) *Man and Society in an Age of Reason: Studies in modern social structure* (London: K. Paul, Trench, Trusner & Co. Ltd).

Marriott, O. (1967) *The Property Boom* (London: Pan).

Marsden, T., Murdoch, J., Lowe, P., Munton, R. and Flynn, A. (1993) *Constructing the Countryside* (London: UCL Press).

Marshall, T. (1992) *Environmental sustainability: London's UDPs and strategic planning*, Occasional Paper No. 4, School of Land Management and Urban Policy (London: South Bank University).

Massey, D. and Catalano, A. (1978) *Capital and Land* (London: Edward Arnold).

Massey, D. and Meegan, R. (1982) *The Anatomy of Job Loss* (London: Methuen).

Mayo, M. (1994) *Communities and Caring: the mixed economy of welfare* (London: Macmillan).

McArthur, A.A. (1993) 'Community business and urban regeneration', *Urban Studies*, 30(4/5), 849–73.

McAuslan, P. (1980) *The Ideologies of Planning Law* (Oxford: Pergamon).

McDowell, L. (1992) 'Doing gender: feminism, feminists and research methods in human geography', *Transactions of the Institute of British Geographers*, 174, pp. 399–416.

McLoughlin, B. (1969) *Urban and Regional Planning: a systems approach* (London: Faber).

McLoughlin, B. (1992) *Shaping Melbourne's Future? Town planning, the state and civic society* (Cambridge: Cambridge University Press).

Mier, R. (1995) Economic development and infrastructure: planning in the context of progressive politics in D. Perry, (ed.), *Building the Public City: the politics, governance and finance of public infrastructure* (Thousand Oaks, California: Sage).

Meyerson, M. and Banfield, E. (1955) *Politics, Planning and the Public Interest* (New York: Free Press).

Mingione, E. (1991) *Fragmented Societies: A sociology of economic life beyond the market paradigm* (Oxford: Blackwell).

Mishra, R. (1990) *The Welfare State in Capitalist Society* (London: Harvester-Wheatsheaf).

Montgomery, J. (ed.) (1995) 'Urban vitality and the culture of cities: special issue', *Planning Practice and Research*, Vol. 10.

Moore Milroy, B. (1991) 'Into postmodern weightlessness', *Journal of Planning Education and Research*, 10(3), pp. 181–7.

Morphet, J. (1995) 'Planning research and the policy process', *Town Planning Review*, 66(2), pp. 199–206.

Moser, C. (1989) 'Community Participation in urban development programmes in Third World Cities', *Progress in Planning*, Vol. 32, pp. 71–133.

Motte, A. (1996) 'Building strategic urban planning in France: The Lyons urban area experiments 1981–1993', in P. Healey, A. Khakee, and B. Needham (eds), *Making Strategic Spatial Plans* (London: UCL Press).

Motte, A. (ed.) (1995) *Schèma Directeur et projet d'agglomeration: l'experimentation de nouvelles politiques urbaines spatialisees 1981–1993* (Paris: Les editions Juris Service).

Moulaert, F. and Todtling, F. (1995) 'The geography of advanced producer services in Europe', *Progress in Planning*, Vol. 43, parts 2/3.

Mumford, L. (1961) *The City in History* (Harmondsworth: Penguin).

Myerson, G. and Rydin, Y. (1994) '"Environment" and planning: a tale of the mundane and the sublime', *Environment and Planning D: Society and Space*, Vol. 12 (4), pp. 437–52.

Needham, B. and Lie, R. (1994) 'The public regulation of property supply and its effects on private prices, risks and returns', *Journal of Property Research*, Vol. 11, pp. 199–213.

Needham, B., Koenders, P. and Kruijt, B. (1993) *Urban Land and Property Markets in The Netherlands* (London: UCL Press).

Newby, H. (1979) *Green and Pleasant Land* (Harmondsworth: Penguin).

Nijkamp, P. (1993) 'Towards a network of regions: the United States of Europe', *European Planning Studies*, Vol. 12, pp. 149–68.

Nijkamp, P. and Perrels, A. (1994) *Sustainable Cities in Europe* (London: Earthscan).

Nijkamp, P., Vleugel, J.M. and Kreutzberger, E. (1993) 'Assessment of capacity in infrastructure networks: a multidimensional view', *Transportation Planning and Technology*, Vol. 17, pp. 301–10.

Nord, 1991 *The New Everyday Life* (Stockholm, The Nordic Council).

Nussbaum, M. (1990) *Love's Knowledge* (New York: Oxford University Press).

O'Callaghan, J. (1995) 'The NELUP programme', in special issue of the *Journal of Environmental Planning and Management*, 38(1).

O'Riordan, T. (1981) *Environmentalism* (London: Pion).

O'Riodan, T., Kramme, L. and Weale, A. (1992) *The New Politics of Pollution* (Manchester: Manchester University Press).

Oatley, N. (1995) 'Competitive urban policy and the regeneration game', *Town Planning Review*, 661, pp. 1–14.

Offe, C. (1977) 'The theory of the capitalist state and the problem of policy formation', in L.N. Lindberg and A. Alford (eds), *Stress and*

Contradiction in Modern Capitalism (Lexington, Massachusetts: D.C. Heath) pp. 125–44.

Oregon Progress Board (1994) *Oregon Benchmarks: Standard for Measuring Statewide Progress and Institutional Performance,* Report to the 1995 Legislature (December) (Oregon: State of Oregon).

Ottes, L., Poventud, E., van Schendslen, M, Segard von Banchet, G. (eds) (1995) *Gender and the Built Environment* (Assen, Netherlands: van Goram).

Ostrom, E. (1990) *Governing the Commons: the political economy of institutions and decisions* (Cambridge: Cambridge University Press).

Owens, S. (1994) 'Land, limits and sustainability: a conceptual framework and some dilemmas for the planning system', *Transactions of the Institute of British Geographers,* Vol. 19(4), pp. 439–56.

Owens, S. (1995) 'From "predict and promote" to "predict and prevent"? Pricing and planning in transport policy', *Transport Policy,* Vol. 2(1), pp. 45–9.

Pahl, R. (1984) *Divisions of Labour* (Oxford: Blackwell).

Painter, J. (1995) 'Regulation Theory, Post-Fordism and Urban Politics' in D. Judge, G. Stoker and H. Wolman, (eds), *Theories of Urban Politics* (London: Sage).

Patterson, A. and Theobald, K. (1995) 'Sustainable development, Agenda 21 and the new local governance in Britain', *Regional Studies,* Vol. 29(8), pp. 773–8.

Pearce, D., Markandya, A., and Barber, D. (1989) *Blueprint for a Green Economy* (London: Earthscan).

Peck, J. (1993) 'The trouble with TECs ... a critique of the Training and Enterprise Councils initiative', *Policy and Politics,* Vol. 21(4), pp. 289–306.

Peck, J. and Emmerich, M. (1994) 'Training and Enterprise Councils: Time for Change' Local Economy, Vol. 8(1), pp. 4–21.

Perroux, F. (1955) 'Note sur la notion de pôle de oroissance', *Economie Appliqueé,* Vol. 7, pp. 307–20.

Perry, D. (1995) 'Making space: planning as a mode of thought', in H. Liggett and D. Perry, *Spatial Practices* (Thousand Oaks, California: Sage).

Petts, J. (1995) 'Waste management strategy development: a case study of community involvement and consensus-building in Hampshire', *Journal of Environmental Planning and Management,* Vol. 38 (4), pp. 519–36.

Pickvance, C. (1995) 'Marxist theories of urban politics' in D. Judge, G. Stoker and H. Wolman (eds), *Theories of Urban Politics* (London: Sage).

Pinch, S. (1993) 'Social polarisation: a comparison of evidence from Britain and the US', *Environment and Planning A,* Vol. 25, pp. 779–815.

Piore, M.J. and Sabel, C.F. (1984) *The Second Industrial Divide* (New York: Basic Books).

Powell, W.W. and Dimaggio, P.J. (1991) *The New Institutionalism in Organizational Analysis* (Chicago: University of Chicago Press).

Pressman, J. and Wildavsky, A. (1984) *Implementation,* 3rd edition (Berkeley, California: University of California Press).

Preteceille, E. (1993) *Mutations urbaines et politques locales, Volume 2: Segregation sociale et budgets locaux en île-de-France* (Paris: Centre de Sociologie Urbaine).

Pryke, M. (1994) 'Looking back on the space of a boom: (re)developing spatial matrices in the City of London', *Environment and Planning A*, Vol. 26 (2), pp. 235–64.

Rabinow, P. (ed.) (1984) *The Foucault Reader* (London: Penguin).

Ravetz, A. (1980) *Remaking Cities* (London: Croom Helm).

Reade, E. (1987) *British Town and Country Planning* (Milton Keynes, Bucks: Open University Press).

Rein, M. and Schon, D. (1993) 'Reframing policy discourse', in F. Fischer and J. Forester (eds), *The Argumentative Turn in Policy Analysis and Planning* (London: UCL Press).

Rhodes, R. (1988) *Beyond Westminster and Whitehall: the sub-central governments of Britain* (London: Unwin Hyman).

Rhodes, R. (1992) 'Policy networks', *Journal of Theoretical Politics*, Vol. 2, pp. 293–317.

Richardson, H. (1969) *Elements of Regional Economics* (Harmondsworth: Penguin).

Ringli, H. (1996) 'Strengthening the urban core in a polycentric context: plan-making for Zurich cantons', in P. Healey, A. Khakee, A. Motte and B. Needham (eds), *Making Strategic Spatial Plans* (London: UCL Press).

Rittel, H. and Webber, M. (1973) 'Dilemmas in a general theory of planning', *Policy Sciences*, Vol. 4, pp. 155–69.

Ritzdorf, M. (1986) 'Women and land use zoning', *Urban Resources*, Vol. 3(2), pp. 23–7.

Rodriguez-Bachiller, A. (1988) *Town Planning Education* (Aldershot, Hants: Gower).

Rogerson, R.J., Findlay, A.M., Paddison, R. and Morris, A.S. (1996) 'Class, consumption and quality of life', in B. Diamond and B. Massam (eds), *Progress in Planning*, Vol. 45(1), pp. 1–66.

Rydin, Y. (1986) *Housing Land Policy* (Aldershot, Hants: Gower).

Rydin, Y. (1992) 'Environmental Impacts and the Property Market', in M.J. Breheny (ed.), *Sustainable Development and Urban Form* (London: Pion) pp. 217–41.

Rydin, Y. (1993) *The British Planning System* (London: Macmillan).

Sager, T. (1994) *Communicative Planning Theory* (Aldershot, Hants: Avebury).

Sagoff, M. (1988) *The Economy of the Earth* (Cambridge: Cambridge University Press).

Sandbach, F. (1980) *Environment, Ideology and Public Policy*. (Oxford: Blackwell).

Saunders, P. (1981) *Social Theory and the Urban Question* (London: Hutchinson).

Savage, M., Dickens, P. and Fielding T. (1988) 'Some social and political implications of the contemporary fragmentation of the "service class" in Britain', *Journal of Urban and Rural Research*, Vol. 12(3), pp. 455–76.

Saxenian, A. (1994) *Regional Advantage* (Cambridge, Mass.: Harvard University Press).

Schmitter, P. (1974) 'Still the century of corporatism', *Review of Politics*, Vol. 36, pp. 85–131.

Schneecloth, L. and Sibley, R. (1995) *Place-Making: the art and practice of building communities* (New York: John Wiley).

Schon, D. (1983) *The Reflective Practitioner* (New York: Basic Books).

Scott, A.J. and Roweis, S.T. (1977) 'Urban planning in Theory and Practice', *Environment and Planning A*, Vol. 9, pp. 1097–1119.

Sennet, R. (1991) *The Conscience of the Eye: the design and social life of cities* (London: Faber).

Shotter, J. (1993) *Conversational Realities: constructing life through language* (London: Sage).

Silverman, D. (1970) *The Theory of Organizations* (London: Heinemann).

Silverman, D. (1993) *Interpreting Qualitative data* (London: Sage).

Simmons, I.G. (1993) *Interpreting Nature: cultural constructions of the environment* (London: Routledge).

Stein, J. (1993) *Growth Management: the planning challenge of the 1990s* (Newbury Park, California: Sage).

Stoker, G. (1995) 'Regime theory and urban politics', in D. Judge, G. Stoker, G. and H. Wolman (eds), *Theories of Urban Politics* (London: Sage).

Stoker, G. and Young, S. (1993) *Cities in the 1990s* (London: Longman).

Stone, C. (1989) *Regime Politics: Governing Atlanta 1946–1988* (Kansas: University of Kansas Press).

Stretton, H. (1978) *Capitalism, Socialism and the Environment* (Cambridge: Cambridge University Press).

Susskind, L. and Cruikshank, J. (1987) *Breaking the Impasse: Consensual approaches to resolving public disputes* (New York: Basic Books).

Sutcliffe, A. (1981) *Towards the Planned City* (Oxford: Blackwell).

Tett, A. and Wolfe, J.M. (1991) 'Discourse analysis and city plans', *Journal of Planning Education and Research*, Vol. 10(3), pp. 195–200.

Thomas, H. (1995) '"Race" and public policy in planning', *Planning Perspectives*, Vol. 10, pp. 123–48.

Thomas, H. and Healey, P. (1991) *Dilemmas of Planning Practice* (Aldershot, Hants: Avebury).

Thomas, H. and Krishnarayan, V. (1993) 'Race equality and planning', *The Planner*, 79.30, pp. 17–19

Thompson, G., Frances, J., Levacic, R. and Mitchell, J. (1991) *Markets, Hierarchies and Networks* (Milton Keynes: Open University Press).

Thornley, A. (1991) *Urban Planning under Thatcherism* (London: Routledge).

Throgmorton, J. (1992) 'Planning as persuasive story-telling about the future: negotiating an electric power settlement in Illinois', *Journal of Planning Education and Research*, Vol. 12(1), pp. 17–31.

Tickell, A. and Dicken, P. (1993) 'The role of inward investment strategies: the case of Northern England', *Local Economy*, Vol. 8(3), pp. 197–208.

Tickell, A. and Peck, J.A. (1992) 'Accumulation, regulation and the geographies of post-fordism: missing links in regulationist research', *Progress in Human Geography*, Vol. 16(2), pp. 190–218.

Townsend, P. (1975) *Sociology and Social Policy* (London: Allen Lane).

Turner R. (ed.) (1993) *Sustainable environmental economics and management: principles and practice* (London: Belhaven).

Turok, I. (1992) 'Property-led urban regeneration: panacea or placebo?', *Environment and Planning A*, Vol. 24, pp. 361–79.

Urry, J. (1980) *The Anatomy of Capitalist Societies* (London: Macmillan).

Vanderplatt, M. (1995) 'Beyond technique: Issues in evaluating for empowerment', *Evaluation*, Vol. 11, pp. 81–96.

Vasconcelos, L. and Reis, A. (1996) 'Building new institutions for strategic planning: transforming Lisbon into the Atlantic Capital of Europe', in P. Healey, A. Khakee, A. Motte and B. Needham (eds), *Making Strategic Spatial Plans* (London: UCL Press).

Vickers, J. (1991) 'New directions for industrial policy in the area of regulatory reform', in G. Thompson, J. Francis, R. Levacic and J. Mitchell (eds), *Markets, Hierarchies and Networks* (London: Sage) pp. 163–70.

Wannop, U. (1985) 'The practice of rationality: the case of Coventry–Solihull–Warwickshire Subregional Planning Study' in M.J. Breheny and A.J. Hooper (eds), *Rationality in Planning* (London: Pion) pp. 196–208.

Wannop, U. (1995) *The Regional Imperative* (Cambridge: Cambridge University Press).

Ward, S. (1994) *Planning and Urban Change* (London: Paul Chapman Publishing).

Ward, S. (1984) 'List Q: a missing link in interwar public investment', *Public Administration*, Vol. 62, pp. 348–58.

Webber, M. (1978) 'A difference paradigm for planning' in R.W. Burchell and G. Sternleib (eds), *Planning Theory in the 1980s* (Rutgers, New Jersey: Centre for Urban Policy Research).

Weber, M. (1970) *Essays in Sociology*, edited by H.H. Gerth and C. Wright Mills (London: Routledge & Kegan Paul).

Weiss, M.A. (1987) *The Rise of the Community Builders* (New Brunswick: Columbia University Press).

Wekerle, G. (1984) 'A women's place is in the city', *Antipode*, Vol. 16(5), pp. 11–19.

Whatmore, S. and Boucher, S. (1993) 'Bargaining with nature: the discourse and practice of "environmental planning gain"', *Transactions of the Institute of British Geographers*, 182, pp. 166–78.

Wheelock, J. (1990) *Husbands at Home: The Domestic Economy in a post-industrial society* (London: Routledge).

Wheelan, R., Young, A., and Lauria, M. (1994) 'Urban regimes and racial politics in New Orleans', *Journal of Urban Affairs*, Vol. 16(1), pp. 1–21.

Whitelegg, J. (1993) *Transport for a Sustainable Future* (Lada: John Wiley).

Wiener, M.J. (1981) *English Culture and the Decline of the Industrial Spirit 1850–1980* (London: Penguin).

Williams, C. (1993) 'Planners carry capacity for unsustainable development', *Planning*, 1022, pp. 18–19.

Williams, C.C. (1995) 'Trading Flavours in Calderdale', *Town and Country Planning', Vol. 64(80), pp. 214–15.*

Williams, C.C. and Windebanck, J. (1994) 'Spatial variations in the informal sector: a review of evidence from the European Union', *Regional Studies*, Vol. 28(8), pp. 819–25.

Williams, R. (1975) *The Country and the City* (Harmondsworth: Penguin).

Williams, R. (1976) *Keywords* (Glasgow: Fontana).

Williams, R.H.W. (1992) 'Internationalizing planning education and the European ERASMUS Programme', *Journal of Planning Education and Research*, Vol. 10(1), pp. 75–8.

Wilmott, P. and Young, M. (1960) *Family and Class in a London Suburb* (London: Routledge & Kegan Paul).

Wittgenstein, L. (1968) *Philosophical Investigations*, tr. G.E. Anscombe (New York: Macmillan).

Wolman, H.L., Coit Cook 111F, and Hill, E. (1994) 'Evaluating the Success of Urban Success Stories', *Urban Studies*, 31(6), pp. 835–50.

Wolsink, M. (1994) 'Entanglement of interests and motives: assumptions behind the NIMBY-theory on facility siting', *Urban Studies*, 31(6), pp. 851–66.

Wood, B. and Williams, R.H. (eds) (1992) *Industrial development in Western Europe* (London: E. & F.N. Spon).

Wood J. Gilroy, R., Healey, P. and Speak, S. (1995) *Changing the way we do things here*, Research Report, Department of Town and Country Planning (Newcastle: University of Newcastle).

World Commission on Environment and Development (1987) *Our Common Future* (The Brundtland Report) (Oxford: Oxford University Press).

Worster, D. (1977) *Nature's Economy: a history of ecological ideas* (Cambridge: Cambridge University Press).

Young, I.M. (1990) *Justice and the Politics of Difference* (Princeton: Princeton University Press).

Index